Cases in Production and Operations Management

Joe C. Iverstine

Jerry Kinard

Southeastern Louisiana University

Charles E. Merrill Publishing Company
A Bell & Howell Company
Columbus, Ohio

Published by
Charles E. Merrill Publishing Company
A Bell & Howell Company
Columbus, Ohio 43216

This book was set in Melior.

The Production Editor was Michael Robbins.

The cover was designed by Will Chenoweth.

International Standard Book Number: 0–675–08521–7

Library of Congress Catalog Card Number: 76–25933

3 4 5 6 7 8 9 10 — 80 79

Printed in the United States of America

Preface

This casebook is written primarily as a supplement to basic texts used in introductory courses in production and operations management. However, because of the applied approach taken to illustrate production/operations concepts, instructors of business policy and other integrated courses will find it useful. It is particularly applicable for schools of business which satisfy the production requirement, as stipulated by the American Assembly of Collegiate Schools of Business, by covering production/operations techniques and concepts in courses other than production management.

The cases included in this book incorporate the most widely used analytical techniques and production concepts employed in industry today. They cover a wide spectrum of business operations and illustrate both traditional and contemporary problems facing production managers. Chapter 8, "New Factors in Production/Operations Management," is a significant departure from material typically presented in a production management textbook. Included in this section are issues of critical importance to production management today — for example, environmental protection, energy conservation, occupational safety and health, and economic crises. Cases which illustrate the operations of public organizations (municipal and state agencies) are also included.

Specific production concepts are illustrated in chapters 1 through 8. Chapter 9 contains integrated cases that show the interrelationships among these concepts and the relationships between production and the other functional areas of business.

Since this book is intended primarily as a supplement to basic introductory texts, mathematical requirements are minimal. Emphasis is placed on applied decision making rather than on the manipulation of theoretical models. The models used in the book support general inventories of business concepts by incorporating the models in situations that demand a multifaceted, applied approach to decision making. Consequently, a strong background in quantitative methods is not essential for the mastery of techniques and tools in this book.

The authors are indebted to the people who willingly gave of their time and energies throughout the writing of this manuscript. Special thanks are extended to the following: Leon Poirier, Noel Poirier, Sidney Ross, T. H. Burt, Jr., Arnie Blankers, Dan Klug, Thomas Brandon, III, James Moore, Jr., William Slaughter, John LaRock, John Ross, Anil Patel, Vaughn Seale, Jerry Correjolles, Louis Ridgel, Sharon Macaluso, Gail Richards, Mary Frances Barker, Georgine Burt, and Steve Brown.

The authors would like to thank and acknowledge the following people who read part of the manuscript: Alfred Edge, Howard Plotkin, and Robert Smith. The authors would especially like to acknowledge and thank John S. Fryer, John Hebert, and Will Henderson, who read the entire manuscript.

Contents

1 Analytical Methods   **1**

  1. Coastal States Chemicals and Fertilizers   2
  2. Union Industrial Chemical Corporation   8
  3. Sure-Sweet Sugar Mill   13
  4. Blue Lake Boat Company   16
  5. Redwood Industrial Detergents, Inc.   19
  6. Pierce and Pierce Public Warehouse   21
  7. Haygood Bros. Construction Company   23

2 Product/Process Planning and Control   **27**

  8. Cunningham Water Well Service   28
  9. Buffalo Aire-Tool   31
  10. Great Lakes Tire and Rubber Company   35
  11. Amalgamated Machine Works, Incorporated   39
  12. Bayfield Mud Company   42
  13. The Morristown Daily Tribune   46
  14. Gulfside Terminal (Part A)   48

3 Plant Location and Capital Budgeting   **51**

  15. Kellwood Company   52
  16. Southern Recreational Vehicle Company   56
  17. Jack's Cookie Corporation   58
  18. Trident Valve & Manufacturing Corporation   65
  19. Acadian Airlines, Inc.   73
  20. Circle Chemical Corporation   83

4 Maintenance   88

21. Wayland Refinery   89
22. Alutex Aluminum Company   93
23. National Garment Factory (Part A)   97
24. Midwestern Tractor and Combine   101
25. Prescott Plastics, Inc. (Part A)   105

5 Production Planning   107

26. Cumberland Ford Company   108
27. Merriwell Bag Company (Part A)   110
28. Merriwell Bag Company (Part B)   113
29. Gulfside Terminal (Part B)   117
30. T. H. Burton and Sons, Wholesalers   122
31. Brunswick Business Machines   124
32. Sturdivant Sound Systems   126

6 Job Analysis   127

33. Pasadena Toys, Inc.   128
34. National Garment Factory (Part B)   131
35. Prescott Plastics, Inc. (Part B)   135
36. Allstate Automotive Analyzers, Inc.   140

7 Management of Human Resources   143

37. Precision Tool Company   144
38. McKinley Oil Company   147
39. National Chemical Corporation:
     East Texas Plant (Part A)   149
40. National Chemical Corporation:
     East Texas Plant (Part B)   158
41. National Chemical Corporation:
     East Texas Plant (Part C)   165

8 New Factors in Production/Operations Management   168

42. North American Pipeline Company   169
43. National Chlor-Alkali: Geismar, Louisiana, Plant   175
44. East Texas Oil Company   194

45. The Saga of Chrysler's "Clean" Foundry   196
46. National Chlor-Alkali: East St. Louis, Illinois, Plant   204
47. U. S. Plywood (Part A)   216
48. LaCrosse Furniture Company   218
49. Dibert, Bancroft, and Ross Foundry   220

9 Integrated Cases in Production/Operations Management   232

50. Michigan Alkali Corporation   233
51. Morrison Distributing Company   240
52. H. T. Rosenbloom Company   245
53. Oliver Treated Products Company   249
54. U. S. Plywood (Part B)   256
55. First Central Bank   259
56. Hammond Water Works   266
57. Louisiana Department of Highways   269

Description of Cases

Firm Name   Description of Case

Chapter 1: Analytical Methods

1. Coastal States Chemicals and
    Fertilizers

    Allocation of limited natural gas
    supply to multiplant, multiproduct
    complex; uses linear programming
    model.

2. Union Industrial Chemical
    Corporation

    Labor problems caused by compulsory
    overtime for railroad switching crew;
    uses simulation with poisson arrival
    patterns to predict overtime
    requirements.

3. Sure-Sweet Sugar Mill

    Renovation of sugar mill bagging
    system; uses Markov Analysis to aid
    in selection of new bagging machine.

4. Blue Lake Boat Company

    Proposed construction of a new boat
    plant; uses general optimization model
    to determine optimal output and
    pricing for new boats.

5. Redwood Industrial
    Detergents, Inc.

    Determination of optimal component
    blend to meet customer specifications
    for an industrial detergent; uses
    linear programming model.

6. Pierce and Pierce Public
    Warehouse

    Forecasting of the number of loading
    docks for a new warehouse; uses
    simulation with poisson arrival
    patterns.

7. Haygood Bros. Construction
    Company

    Planning and control of a construction
    project; uses PERT model.

Firm Name   Description of Case

Chapter 2: Product/Process Planning and Control

8. Cunningham Water Well   Development of a new check valve for
    Service   water wells.

9. Buffalo Aire-Tool   Development of a specialized impact
                                    wrench to meet a customer's
                                    requirement.

10. Great Lakes Tire and Rubber   Decision to introduce a new radial tire
    Company   given existing production facilities.

11. Amalgamated Machine Works,   Quality control of diameter of balls for
    Incorporated   high pressure ball valves.

12. Bayfield Mud Company   Quality control of bag weights for oil
                                    well mud chemicals.

13. The Morristown Daily Tribune   Quality control of printing errors in a
                                    newspaper.

14. Gulfside Terminal (Part A)   Determination of a control point to
                                    meet product specifications for liquid
                                    caustic soda shipped to Jamaica;
                                    preparation of control charts to
                                    monitor product while loading into
                                    tankers.

Chapter 3: Plant Location and Capital Budgeting

15. Kellwood Company   Plant site selection for a garment
                                    factory.

16. Southern Recreational Vehicle   Relocation of an existing plant to a
    Company   new site.

17. Jack's Cookie Corporation   Utilization of facilities after plant
                                    relocation.

18. Trident Valve and   Capital budgeting decision for
    Manufacturing Corporation   computerized lathe purchase.

19. Acadian Airlines, Inc.   Capital budgeting decision for
                                    selection of type of aircraft.

20. Circle Chemical Corporation   Decision to renovate production
                                    facilities or to discontinue operations.

Chapter 4: Maintenance

21. Wayland Refinery   Conflict between production and
                                    maintenance departments on
                                    philosophy of maintenance.

Firm Name   Description of Case

22. Alutex Aluminum Company   Institution of a total planning and
                                         scheduling system for maintenance.

23. National Garment Factory   Determination of the feasibility of a
     (Part A)   preventive maintenance program.

24. Midwestern Tractor and   Validity of the use of certain standards
     Combine   to control maintenance costs.

25. Prescott Plastics, Inc. (Part A)   Impact of stand-by equipment on the
                                         level of maintenance.

Chapter 5: Production Planning

26. Cumberland Ford Company   Scheduling problems of an automotive
                                         body shop; uses the Johnson method
                                         of scheduling.

27. Merriwell Bag Company   Forecasting problem of a product
     (Part A)   highly affected by seasonal demand.

28. Merriwell Bag Company   Inventory control for a stock bag
     (Part B)   manufacturer.

29. Gulfside Terminal (Part B)   Scheduling problems of a terminal-
                                         tank farm with variable production
                                         rates and arrival patterns of vessels.

30. T. H. Burton and Sons,   Decision to implement a computer-
     Wholesalers   based MIS system of inventory control
                                         for a small wholesaler.

31. Brunswick Business Machines   Inventory control for a distributor of
                                         business machines and office
                                         equipment.

32. Sturdivant Sound Systems   Inventory control for a manufacturer
                                         of stereo components.

Chapter 6: Job Analysis

33. Pasadena Toys, Incorporated   Time and motion study of a drill press
                                         operation in the manufacture of
                                         wooden toys.

34. National Garment Factory   Establishment of an incentive wage
     (Part B)   plan for garment workers.

35. Prescott Plastics, Inc.   Productivity-on-the-job measurement
     (Part B)   for employees of a plastic bag
                                         manufacturer.

36. Allstate Automotive   Establishment of production standards
     Analyzers, Inc.   for an automotive test equipment
                                         manufacturer.

Firm Name   Description of Case

Chapter 7: Management of Human Resources

37. Precision Tool Company   Problem of job classification of
                                          skilled employees.

38. McKinley Oil Company   Creation of an indispensable
                                          employee; he was the only person who
                                          knew where underground pipelines
                                          and valves were located.

39. National Chemical   Problems with low pay and lack of
     Corporation: East Texas Plant   discipline at a manufacturing plant.
     (Part A)

40. National Chemical   Wage and salary administration under
     Corporation: East Texas Plant   wage-price controls.
     (Part B)

41. National Chemical   Wage and salary administration during
     Corporation: East Texas Plant   a period of chronic inflation.
     (Part C)

Chapter 8: New Factors in Production/Operations Management

42. North American Pipeline   Problems of payoffs and their impact
     Company   on quality control during pipeline
                                          construction.

43. National Chlor-Alkali: Crisis created by a plant fatality;
     Geismar, Louisiana, Plant   impact of OSHA.

44. East Texas Oil Company   Environmental protection issue;
                                          saltwater disposal problem.

45. The Saga of Chrysler's "Clean"   Problems of air and noise pollution
     Foundry   because of the location of a foundry in
                                          a residential area.

46. National Chlor-Alkali: East   Installation of a totally captive waste
     St. Louis, Illinois, Plant   recovery system.

47. U. S. Plywood (Part A)   Utilization of wood scraps as boiler
                                          fuel at a plywood plant.

48. LaCrosse Furniture Company   Problems of noise pollution at a
                                          furniture manufacturing plant.

49. Dibert, Bancroft, and Ross   Problems of air pollution at a steel
     Foundry   foundry.

Chapter 9: Integrated Cases in Production/Operations Management

50. Michigan Alkali Corporation   Management of a production facility
                                          with maintenance problems and a
                                          declining technology.

Firm Name   Description of Case

51.   Morrison Distributing   Direction and control of a beer
      Company   distributorship.

52.   H. T. Rosenbloom Company   Operations control of a large
                                           department store.

53.   Oliver Treated Products   Management of a wood treating plant
      Company   with rising costs and declining
                                           demand.

54.   U. S. Plywood (Part B)   Direction and control of a large
                                           plywood plant.

55.   First Central Bank   Control of banking operations.

56.   Hammond Water Works   Direction and control of a municipal
                                           water system.

57.   Louisiana Department of   Control of maintenance and
      Highways   construction activities of a state
                                           highway department.

chapter 1

Analytical Methods

case 1

Coastal States
Chemicals and Fertilizers

In December, 1975, Bill Stock, General Manager for the Louisiana Division of Coastal States Chemicals and Fertilizers, received a letter from Fred McNair of Cajan Pipeline Company which notified Coastal States that priorities had been established for the allocation of natural gas.[1] The letter stated that Cajan Pipeline, the primary supplier of natural gas to Coastal States, might be instructed to curtail natural gas supplies to its industrial and commercial customers by as much as 40 percent during the ensuing winter months. Moreover, Cajan Pipeline had the approval of the Federal Power Commission (FPC) to curtail such supplies.

Possible curtailment was attributed to the priorities established for the use of natural gas:

First Priority: Residential and commercial heating

Second Priority: Commercial and industrial users whereby natural gas is used as a source of raw material

Third Priority: Commercial and industrial users whereby natural gas is used as boiler fuel

Almost all of Coastal States' use of natural gas was in the "second" and "third" priorities. Hence, its plants were certainly subject to brown-outs, or natural gas curtailments. The occurrence and severity of the brown-outs depended on a number of complex factors. First of all, Cajan Pipeline was part of an interstate transmission network which delivered natural gas to residential and commercial buildings on the Atlantic Coast and in northeastern regions of the United States. Hence, the severity of the forthcoming winter in these regions would have a direct impact on the use of natural gas.

Secondly, the demand for natural gas was soaring because it was the cleanest and most efficient fuel. There were almost no environmental problems in burning natural gas. Moreover, maintenance problems due to fuel-

---

[1]See appendix A to this case.

fouling in fireboxes and boilers were negligible with natural gas systems. Also, burners were much easier to operate with natural gas as compared to the use of oil or the stoking operation when coal was used as fuel.

Finally, the supply of natural gas was dwindling. The traditionally depressed price of natural gas had discouraged new exploration for gas wells; hence, shortages appeared imminent.

Stock and his staff at Coastal States had been aware of the possibility of shortages of natural gas and had been investigating ways of converting to fuel oil or coal as a substitute for natural gas. Their plans, however, were still in the developmental stages. Coastal States required an immediate contingency plan to minimize the effect of a natural gas curtailment on its multiplant operations. The obvious question was, what operations should be curtailed and to what extent to minimize the adverse effect upon profits? Coastal States had the approval from the FPC and Cajan Pipeline to specify which of its plants would bear the burden of the curtailment if such cutbacks were necessary. McNair, of Cajan Pipeline, replied, "It's your 'pie': we don't care how you divide it if we make it smaller."

The Model

Six plants of Coastal States Louisiana Division were to share in the "pie". They were all located in the massive Baton Rouge-Geismar-Gramercy industrial complex along the Mississippi River between Baton Rouge and New Orleans. Products produced at those plants which required significant amounts of natural gas were phosphoric acid, urea, ammonium phosphate, ammonium nitrate, chlorine, caustic soda, vinyl chloride monomer, and hydrofluoric acid.

Stock called a meeting of members of his technical staff to discuss a contingency plan for allocation of natural gas among the products if a curtailment developed. The objective was to minimize the impact on profits. After detailed discussion, the meeting was adjourned. Two weeks later, the meeting reconvened. At this session, the following data were presented:

Table 1–1   *Contribution to Profit and Overhead*

Product	$/ton
phosphoric acid	60
urea	80
ammonium phosphate	90
ammonium nitrate	100
chlorine	50
caustic soda	50
vinyl chloride monomer	65
hydrofluoric acid	70

Table 1–2   *Operating Data*

Product	Capacity (tons/day)	Production Rate (Percent of Capacity)	Natural Gas Consumption (1000 cu ft /ton)
phosphoric acid	400	80	5.5
urea	250	80	7.0
ammonium phosphate	300	90	8.0
ammonium nitrate	300	100	10.0
chlorine	800	60	15.0
caustic soda	1000	60	16.0
vinyl chloride monomer	500	60	12.0
hydrofluoric acid	400	80	11.0

Coastal States' contract with Cajan Pipeline specified a maximum natural gas consumption of 36,000 cu ft X 10^3 per day for all of the six member plants. With these data, the technical staff proceeded to develop a model that would specify changes in production rates in response to a natural gas curtailment. (Curtailments are based on contracted consumption and not current consumption.)

Discussion Questions

1. Develop a contingency model and specify the production rates for each product for: a) a 20 percent natural gas curtailment and b) a 40 percent natural gas curtailment.

2. Explain which of the products in Table 1-2 should require the most emphasis with regard to energy conservation.

3. What problems do you foresee if production rates are not reduced in a planned and orderly manner?

4. What impact will the natural gas shortage have on company profits?

appendix A
Natural Gas Developments[1]

As the producer of 36 percent of the nation's natural gas, Louisiana is vitally affected both in industry and in state revenues by developments in the natural gas market. As the winter of 1975–76 approached, the sixth in which there were marked natural gas shortages in the nation, belated attention was once again

---

[1]Louisiana Energy Report, State of Louisiana, Department of Conservation, Public Information Office, No. 28, November 15, 1975.

focused on the problems involved with natural gas supply. Following is a sampling of developments.

I. **Cajan Pipeline Company,** the supplier of about two-thirds of Louisiana's interstate gas and about 14 percent of Louisiana's total gas consumption, on November 5, 1975, received approval from the Federal Power Commission for a 12-month plan for determining reduced amounts of natural gas to be delivered to its customers.

Under this curtailment plan, no residential or small commercial customers should be cut back in supply. According to Cajan's projections of available supply, industrial customers using 1,500,000 cu ft of gas or less per day should not be curtailed at all on most days in the winter. Therefore, the plan was primarily for determining reduced amounts of natural gas to be supplied during the winter to larger industrial and commercial firms in Cajan's service area of Louisiana, Texas, Mississippi, Alabama, and Florida.

The increased cutback in the amount of natural gas available for larger users became necessary because of a continuing drop in production from the southern fields that support the Cajan system. The newly approved plan was actually a settlement proposal which had been in some form of litigation for several years. The settlement was supported by Cajan, by most of its direct industrial and city-rate customers, and by its seven pipeline customers.

As the plan went into effect, checks were made to determine its impact. The FPC ordered a conference on or before November 15, 1975, so that Cajan customers could make known any unusual problems encountered under the new curtailment program. R. T. Sutton, Louisiana Commissioner of Conservation, furnished the services of his office to help Cajan's customers as they reviewed special problems or dealt with greater curtailments in their gas supply.

The settlement contained provisions that shielded the smaller industrials from reduction of supply, that allowed for a feature called "grouping," that dealt with extraordinary peak-day problems, that granted emergency relief where necessary to forestall irreparable injury to life or property, and that entitled Cajan's customers category II priority treatment for their feedstock requirements. (Feedstock gas is natural gas used as raw material for its chemical properties in creating such end products as fertilizers or plastics.)

The "grouping" feature allowed a greater flexibility in shifting gas to where the greatest need was. Large individual customers (such as an industry, a town, or a city) served by the same distribution company were to be curtailed collectively, instead of individually, as in the past. Large distributors (primarily those which serve more than one city) would have more flexibility in allocating their industrial gas to those industrial users which had the greatest need because of lack of either alternate fuel supplies or capabilities. Previous regulations prohibited shifting surplus gas from one customer to another, even if the same distribution company served both.

Cajan estimated that it would curtail gas supplies to industrial firms which used in excess of 1,500,000 cu ft per day during November through February. During March, supplies would be curtailed to industrial firms which used in excess of 3,000,000 cu ft per day.

You may acquire a more detailed explanation of the provisions of Cajan's curtailment settlement by contacting the Louisiana Department of Conservation.

II. **The Fifth U. S. Circuit Court of Appeals** on November 14, 1975, issued an order to the FPC which had a direct bearing on the Cajan Pipeline situation. In fact, the suit out of which the order came was filed by Cajan's customers, the Mississippi Public Service Commission and Mississippi Power and Light.

Under the federal court order, the FPC was to look into a plan that would equalize the financial burdens of those firms receiving a mandatory cut in natural gas supply. High-priority industries receiving larger amounts of natural gas would subsidize other, low-priority industries that were forced by curtailment to use more expensive energy, such as fuel oil in this case.

While the court was careful not to comment on the merits of the utility company proposals, it did rule that the FPC had authority in the matter. Instead of passing on the three-to-five times greater cost of fuel oil to their customers by way of a fuel adjustment clause, the utility companies would have the pipeline add a surcharge to the gas prices for high-priority users and refund money to low-priority users.

In the highest, human-needs category were private homeowners, who depended solely upon natural gas. Utility companies were in the lowest priority because they employ natural gas in one of its least efficient uses, as boiler fuel, and because they can conceivably burn oil as an alternate fuel.

III. **The Louisiana State Mineral Board,** meanwhile, was working on a program intended to keep as much as possible of the state's gas (and oil) production within the state where it is needed to fuel Louisiana industries and heat Louisiana homes.

The basis of the program was a plan whereby applicants could obtain oil and gas from the state's "in-kind" royalties. Most of the first 30 applications were requests for an additional supply of natural gas.

Another aspect of the program was the provision added to all state leases that requires the producers "to make an honest effort to market all of the oil or gas in Louisiana."

The major difficulties encountered in keeping the supplies in the state, according to Mineral Board Secretary C. J. Bonnecarrere, have been in the practical area of shipping the state's in-kind gas and oil from the wellhead to the user. A producer is usually able to bring about this kind of delivery through a "swap-out" with another producer of the oil or gas volume that each delivers to separate pipelines.

IV. **The Federal Energy Administration,** which reflects the administration's view in favor of natural gas decontrol, has been before the U. S. Congress urging immediate action on pending natural gas legislation. FEA's Deputy Administrator and Natural Gas Task Force Chairman, John Hill, testifying November 6, 1975, before a House Government Operations Subcommittee, urged that "winter is now upon us and it is clearly time to stop testifying to get legislation and begin implementing it." Hill outlined the actions the FEA has taken under existing authorities to deal with the natural gas problem, including the following:

— Publication of "The Natural Gas Shortage: A Preliminary Report," which identified key states with interstate gas pipeline problems.
— Establishment of a Natural Gas Task Force to collect natural gas information and distribute it to programs (legislative, educational, conservation, etc.)
— Completion of a comprehensive natural gas end-use data base.
— Publication of "Natural Gas Curtailments, 1975–76 Heating Season," which provided detailed data on deliveries, curtailments, and requirements at the end-user level, as well as information on the availability of alternative fuels in 21 key states.
— Development of an index of all federal assistance programs which might be used by states and local communities facing natural gas shortages.

— Assignment of regional natural gas representatives to channel information on local situations back to Washington and to coordinate with Federal Regional Councils in assistance activities.

V. **Conservation-of-natural-gas programs** were established by a number of private and public organizations to make the public aware that the nation's 40 million residential gas customers could make a significant contribution to easing shortages during the winter. "Save natural gas and you'll help save a job" was the theme of FEA's campaign for natural gas conservation.

During phase one of the campaign, two spot announcements were to be sent to states most likely to feel the impact of the gas shortage, especially those states in which the conservation of natural gas could make the difference between open factories and closed factories, between jobs and unemployment. Phase two of the campaign would include newspaper ads and TV announcements to the same states.

The FEA estimates that the average gas-consuming residence uses about 125,000 cu ft of gas each year. Turning down the home thermostat from 72 to 68 degrees can cut natural gas use for heating by 20 percent. Dialing down to 60 degrees at night can save an additional 10 percent. Lowering the temperature setting on a gas-fired hot water heater from 140 to 110 degrees can cut natural gas use by 15 percent and still provide ample hot water.

case 2

Union Industrial
Chemical Corporation

The decision confronting the management of the Baker Plant of Union Industrial Chemical Corporation was whether or not to reinstate plant railroad conductor, Larry Phillips, who had been suspended for a week without pay. The suspension was a result of Phillips' failure to obey a direct order regarding compulsory overtime. The plant rank-and-file harshly challenged the disciplinary action because they believed the company imposed unreasonable demands upon Phillips as well as upon other members of the plant railroad crew. They threatened a wildcat strike. Following is information about this issue.

The Baker Plant

Union Industrial Chemical is a large, diversified, multinational corporation with plants located throughout the United States and in 12 foreign countries. Union's second largest plant is located in Baker, Louisiana, a small community ten miles north of Baton Rouge. The plant produces a wide variety of industrial chemicals as well as several consumer products, such as all-purpose detergents and drain cleaners.

The plant is bordered on the west by the Mississippi River and on the east by a main line of the Illinois Central Railroad (ICRR). The river dock facility is used for bulk shipment of products and also for receipt of certain raw materials. A large majority of the plant's shipments, however, are by railroad. There is a multitrack spur connecting the plant to the ICRR's main line.

The ICRR normally services the plant once a day between 7:00 a.m. and noon. The service consists of switching empty boxcars and tank cars into the plant for loading. Also, any loaded cars that have been released by the laboratory, weighed, and sealed are removed during this switch by ICRR for shipment to customers. Approximately 90 percent of the loaded cars, however, are removed each afternoon between 4:00 and 6.00.

After the morning switch, the plant railroad crew "breaks down" the lineup of cars placed into the plant by the ICRR. This procedure consists of separating the boxcars from the tank cars and switching the empty cars that have been requested by respective loading supervisors into their loading terminals. (There are five loading terminals at the Baker Plant.) The loading supervisors normally are present for the morning switch by the ICRR. They note delivery of empty tank cars that are used exclusively for shipment of their products. (Tank cars tend to be used for only one product because of special linings, safety valves, steam jacketing, unloading valves, etc.) They also inspect boxcars to determine if they are suitable for shipment of bulk or containerized products. The boxcars are "common carriers" which carry a wide variety of products and are used by different plants and railroad lines. For example, a Missouri Pacific boxcar may be loaded in Tallahassee, Florida, and used on the Seaboard Coast Line Railroad. A boxcar is returned to its parent line upon request.

The boxcars are switched into the respective loading terminals on a first-request basis. Disputes between loading terminals over priorities for empty boxcars are resolved by the traffic manager, who has the final authority over movement of all rail traffic within the plant. The unused boxcars are retained up to the demurrage limit and then released back to the ICRR for removal from the plant. The nationwide scarcity of boxcars invariably causes delays in shipments. Hence, the traffic manager has an open order with the ICRR for as many empty boxcars as possible. Only boxcars that are in very poor condition are released unloaded back to the ICRR.

The plant railroad crew switches the cars in and out of the respective loading terminals. The crew is comprised of the conductor, brakeman, and engineer. The conductor is the "boss" of the crew. He receives switching instructions from the loading supervisors and the traffic department. He directs the switching activities from the lead car of a lineup and is responsible for throwing switches, receiving permission to enter terminals, and observing flags/de-rails.[1]

The brakeman acts as liaison between the conductor and the engineer. He relays hand signals which supplement the walkie-talkies that the conductor and engineer use. Also, he couples and uncouples cars as required.

The engineer operates the plant switch engine. He receives all instructions from the conductor. The engineer, conductor, and brakeman are all union employees.

The Issue

Due to many variables, the work load of the switching crew is erratic. Loading rates may drop because of production problems. High inventory

---

[1]De-rails are fail-safes which prevent moving a car at a terminal that is connected to loading lines or is being entered by loading personnel. The de-rail will actually "de-rail" the train from the track if it is not heeded.

levels may dictate accelerated loading to use railroad cars as "moving storage." The receipt of empty boxcars and tank cars may be irregular, causing periods of inactivity followed by a very busy and hectic loading schedule.

The primary reason that work requirements of the switching crew vary so widely is the time of the morning switch by the ICRR. The ICRR itself faces so many variables in receipt and disbursal of cars to the respective plants that it cannot precisely determine when Union's Baker Plant will receive its morning switch. Some switches are made as early as 6:30 a.m. and as late as 2:00 p.m.

The plant railroad crew report for work at 6:00 a.m. and clock out at 2:00 p.m. They eat and take breaks around their switching schedule. When they first report for work, they normally have approximately three hours of work switching cars that have been loaded during the previous evening and night shifts and switching in any available empty cars. By approximately 9:00 each morning, they are available to break down the morning switch from the ICRR. If the ICRR switch occurs before 10:30 a.m., they can normally break down the cars received, line up the loaded cars to be picked up in the afternoon by the ICRR, and clock out by 2:00 p.m. without having to work overtime. This situation, of course, depends on the size of the lineup received from the ICRR and the complexity of the switching requests from the respective loading terminals.

Larry Phillips thought the frequency of overtime required to complete the plant railroad duties was excessive. Phillips was a young conductor with four years of plant seniority. He believed that "constantly" being forced to work overtime was unreasonable. The union contract provided for compulsory overtime when requested by the company. Phillips was a member of a car pool that consisted of a mechanic, two carpenters, and a welder — all living approximately 30 miles from the plant and working the 6:00 a.m. to 2:00 p.m. shift.

Because of several incidents in which Phillips was forced to work overtime, the entire car pool was delayed approximately an hour because they were using Phillips' car on those occasions. Hence, Phillips ceased to drive and paid other members a transportation fee. Whenever Phillips was required to work overtime, he was left at the plant. The company had a policy (not written into the union contract) of providing transportation home via taxi if a worker was unexpectedly detained for overtime and missed his car pool. There were delays, however, in securing the taxi and inconveniences often resulted that were not fully compensated by the minimum two hour overtime pay.

Phillips' dislike of overtime was aggravated by the fact that he and his brother had just opened a convenience store near his home. Phillips was expected to be at the store at 3:00 p.m. His brother was a deputy sheriff who worked the 3:00 p.m. to 11:00 p.m. shift at the sheriff's station. The brother was on duty at the store in the mornings. Phillips' wife and sister-in-law relieved him and his brother as required. Both Phillips and his brother thought that one of them should be on duty at the store as much as possible.

The company did not endorse such "moonlighting" by its workers, but did not take an official position against it as long as it clearly did not interfere with work at the plant. Phillips complained bitterly, however, when forced to work overtime. His supervisor, Frank Greenway, told him on several occasions that his first obligation was to his job at the plant and that he would get into trouble if he continued to complain and "stir up trouble." Phillips replied that his first obligation was to his family, that he owed the plant only eight hours, and that he was entitled to his opinion about company policy.

Phillips had many supporters among the plant rank-and-file. His fellow crew members also began complaining about the "nuisance overtime." The relief railroad workers were also vocal in their opposition to the high overtime frequency. The issue of compulsory overtime severely agitated the majority of the 1,000 union employees at the plant. A grievance was filed to force the company to add a second railroad crew that would work from 9:00 a.m. to 5:00 p.m. From 9:00 a.m. to 2:00 p.m., they would be assigned duties such as driving trucks, cranes, cherry pickers, and other vehicles. At 2:00 p.m. (when Phillips' crew clocked out), they would then operate the plant switch engine and complete any switching duties until 5:00 p.m. The company opposed the grievance, claiming that the staffing of the work force was an inherent management right.

The Incident

Before the grievance was fully processed, Phillip was given a one-week suspension without pay. This suspension stemmed from the following incident. Phillips received a call from his wife at 1:00 p.m., who told him that the ice cream freezer at their store was not operating and that the ice cream had begun to melt. Phillips was very anxious to get to the store to assist with the problem. Just prior to 2:00 p.m., Greenway put Phillips on notice that he would be required to work overtime for a couple of hours to do some late switching. Phillips informed Greenway of his problem at the store. Greenway indicated that he sympathized with Phillips but that his excuse was not valid. Greenway repeated his earlier warning that moonlighting could not interfere with the plant job. Phillips retorted, "The hell with you; I'm going home." Phillips proceeded to clock out at 2:00 p.m. At 6:00 the following morning, a disciplinary hearing was held. Phillips was given the one-week suspension without pay for insubordination and failure to follow a valid, direct order. Phillips had no prior record of disciplinary action.

The Reaction

Plant reaction to Phillips' suspension was harsh. Milt Stonebreaker, the local union president, warned the company that a wildcat strike was a certainty if Phillips was not reinstated with full pay by 6:00 the next morning.

The plant notified the international union office in Washington, D.C., of Stonebreaker's warning. An international representative, Harry Carter, flew in from Washington and met with the company that afternoon. Carter stated that he would do everything possible to avoid a wildcat strike, but the issue was very important to the rank-and-file.

Carter said that the real issue was not so much the current level of compulsory overtime but the expected level in the future. He stated that if the company could give him some evidence that the current level was unusual and that it could be expected to decrease in the future, he might be able to avert a strike. This plea was to be coupled with a reduction in the suspension to two days and immediate arbitration of the suspension as well as of the grievance to add a second railroad switching crew.

Management pondered Carter's offer. They, too, wished to avert a wildcat strike. It would severely delay shipping schedules that were already behind due to a surge in demand. But they absolutely did not want to compromise their compulsory overtime rights guaranteed in the contract as well as the right of their supervisors, such as Greenway, to issue orders.

The production manager, Charles Blackwell, believed that he could provide valuable information that would bear upon the decision. He knew that data were available that would allow the company to predict overtime requirements of the rairoad crew. From past log records, he noted that the ICRR averaged five switches between noon and 2:00 p.m. each month (20 working days). These were the late switches that would most likely cause the compulsory overtime. Blackwell also knew from studies of railroad crew productivity that the time required by the plant railroad to service these switches averaged two hours with a standard deviation of one-half hour. He believed that this information could assist management in this difficult decision.

Discussion Questions

1. Develop a model to predict overtime requirements for the plant railroad crew.

2. What problems does the implementation of compulsory overtime cause?

3. What are the alternatives to compulsory overtime?

4. What additional data could be gathered to refine the overtime prediction model?

5. What should company policy be with respect to moonlighting? Coverage of expenses incurred as a result of compulsory, unplanned overtime?

Sure-Sweet
Sugar Mill

Sure-Sweet Sugar's largest mill is located in Livonia, Louisiana, a small town approximately 25 miles west of Baton Rouge in the heart of the sugar cane belt. In April, 1975, initial plans were formulated to modernize the mill as a result of the enormous profits the sugar industry enjoyed in 1974. By November, specific details were being worked out by Pierre LeBlanc, manager of the Livonia mill, and by representatives of North American Foods, the parent corporation.

A large percentage of sugar profits was directly attributable to soaring sugar prices in 1974. Although sugar prices declined during the first half of 1975, they remained substantially higher than in the pre-1974 period. Certain factors supported the higher prices. First, the possible lifting of trade embargoes with Cuba was not expected to have a significant influence on price. Cuba had established alternative markets for her sugar during the embargo, and a removal of the embargo was not expected to substantially affect the supply of sugar in the United States.

A second reason for the higher price was the failure of consumers to endorse artificial sweeteners as a sugar substitute. The unfavorable publicity surrounding the alleged carcinogenic properties of cyclamates tended to cause certain consumers to doubt the safety of all artificial sweeteners. Consequently, consumers were willing to pay higher prices to retailers who were passing along higher costs.

The increased profits had a profound effect on sugar cane growers and sugar processors alike. The sugar cane growers of south Louisiana were planning to cultivate and plant sugar cane on farmland that had been dormant for decades. Sugar processors were discovering financial incentives for the modernization of old mills to gain additional processing capacities and efficiencies.

The incentive to modernize mills was particularly strong for Sure-Sweet Sugar because the parent company, North American Foods, needed a reliable supplier of sugar, which was a basic raw material used by many of its food processing subsidiaries. In fact, approximately 40 percent of Sure-Sweet

Sugar's output was captive (sold to the parent corporation). As North American expected to enjoy substantial growth in the years ahead, its own demand for sugar would grow at a commensurate rate.

The Livonia Mill

Because it was the largest supplier of sugar to the parent corporation, there was particular interest in modernizing the Livonia mill. A prominent local sugar cane plantation owner built the mill in 1921. In 1957, Sure-Sweet Sugar purchased it. Over the years, capital improvements to the mill were negligible. In fact, a few pieces of the original equipment were still being used in the process. As a result, the Livonia mill's maintenance department had to manufacture many spare parts for the old equipment because vendors had stopped supplying parts for the old, somewhat obsolete machines.

A thorough modernization of the mill was planned, however. Antiquated equipment was to be replaced, and the mill's capacity was to be increased by 50 percent. The representatives from North American Foods stated clearly to Pierre LeBlanc and other representatives from Sure-Sweet Sugar that policies of efficiency and process reliability should guide the modernization program.

One segment of the mill that was to be modernized was the bagging operation. The existing operation consisted of an old single-line bagging system. The single-line bagging system was comprised of a hopper which fed a single, stationary weight-feeder that deposited the appropriate weight of sugar into a bag. The loaded bag was then dumped onto a V-belt conveyor which carried the bag through a sealing machine and finally to a packing station. At the packing station, the bags were palletized (100-pound bags) or placed into cardboard cases (less than 100-pound bags) for shipment.

The single-line system was to be replaced by a carrousel bagging system. The proposed system consisted of a carrousel weight-feeder which loads eight bags as the carrousel completes a revolution. The carrousel bagging machine would also seal the bag and deposit it on one of several V-belt conveyors for multi-distribution in the warehouses.

Two vendors, Mechanized Transit and Amalgamated Container Co., submitted bids to supply the carrousel bagging machine. The machines from each of these companies were almost identical in loading rates, price, and installment cost. Pierre LeBlanc and sugar engineers from the Livonia mill visited plants (arranged by the vendors) and observed the operation of each bagging machine. They decided that the factor that determined selection would be process reliability, because the reliability of the bagging system was critical to the entire operation of the mill. The hoppers that fed the bagging system had a normal inventory capacity to store mill output for 12 hours if the bagging system was not in operation. Because of the planned increases in mill capacity, this inventory time had been reduced to 8 hours. (The bagging machine for both the old and the planned system had excess capacity; therefore, the inventory of sugar in the feed hoppers would be reduced quickly to create the normal inventory space of 12 and 8 hours respectively.) If the bagging system was down for more than 8 hours, the mill would have to sharply reduce rates of production or shut down. This caused severe process upsets and costly inefficiencies. Because of the problems encountered in storing large volumes of sugar in hoppers, the mill engineers decided not to expand the size of the feed hopper.

Mechanized Transit indicated that its bagging machine had a demonstrated stream factor[1] of 0.92. Amalgamated Container Co. stated that the stream factor for its bagging machine was 0.88, but due to local service engineers and a spare parts distribution center located in Baton Rouge (25 miles away), the probability that its machine would be in operation within 8 hours following a major breakdown was 0.80. In contrast, the closest service center for Mechanized Transit was in Atlanta, Georgia. Hence, Mechanized Transit could commit only to a 0.30 probability that its machine would be in operation within 8 hours following a major breakdown. The duration of very unusual breakdowns (those that would halt operations of both machines for periods in excess of 8 hours) was determined to be equal for both machines. LeBlanc pondered his purchasing decision.

Discussion Questions

1. Considering process reliability as a major objective, which machine would you recommend?

2. What problems are encountered in most operations when there is either a sharp curtailment in production rates or a shutdown?

3. What additional information would be of value to LeBlanc in his purchasing decision?

---

[1]Stream factor is the percentage of time that a given piece of equipment is operable.

case 4

Blue Lake
Boat Company

The strategic planning committee of Blue Lake Boat Company was discussing specifications for a new boat factory to be located in Grand Rapids, Minnesota. The boats were to be constructed of fiber glass at a standardized length of 16 feet. The standardization of length was expected to create numerous production efficiencies over competitor factories that produced multi-length boats. Grand Rapids was selected as an ideal site for the new factory because of its location in the heart of Minnesota's lake country. Economies in distribution were expected to be gained by locating a plant close to the boat-popular states of Minnesota, Wisconsin, and Michigan. Also, the community of Grand Rapids welcomed a "clean," nonpolluting industry, such as a boat factory. The boats were to be marketed under the firm's "Blue-Hydro" brand name.

Major items facing the planning committee were factory capacity and projected unit cost of new boats. With the standardization of length (16 feet), the committee expected to enjoy a substantial cost advantage over competitors. This cost advantage could be readily reflected in a pricing strategy that was expected to increase Blue Lake's market share from 15 to 25 percent of the domestic pleasure-boat market.

In capacity planning, the committee desired to compute break-even and optimum production rates. Also, given a demand forecast and the previously mentioned cost structure, they wished to determine break-even and optimum prices. The comprehensive promotion and distribution strategy was contingent upon the preceding determinants. If a favorable cost-price structure developed, Blue Lake might seek additional outlets through the country's large catalog sales firms.

Projected Cost

The committee, in consultation with the factory project manager, projected the cost structure for the new facility. First of all, the capital cost for the factory was expected to be $18,000,000. Annual maintenance expenses were

16

projected to total 5 percent of capital. Fuel and utility costs were expected to be $500,000 per year plus $20 per boat. An analysis of the area's labor market indicated that a wage rate of $6 per hour could be expected. The new facility was estimated to require 500,000 man-hours of operating labor. Fringe benefits paid to the operating labor were expected to equal 20 percent of direct labor costs. Supervisory, clerical, technical, and managerial salaries were forecast to total $1,000,000 per year. Taxes and insurance would cost $700,000 per year. Miscellaneous contract services were estimated at $50,000 per year. Demurrage, security, and other miscellaneous expenses were expected to total $250,000 per year. Depreciation would be $70 per boat per year. Fiber glass, solvent, and catalyst costs were projected to be $0.80 per pound. The yield[1] on these materials was estimated to be 83.2 percent. A boat without any metal attachments and accessories was projected to weigh 500 pounds. Paints, metal attachments, and accessories were estimated to total $20 per boat. The crating and shipping supplies were expected to cost $10 per boat.

Demand Forecast

While the project manager and other members of the planning committee were developing these cost estimates, Blue Lake's marketing manager was attempting to forecast demand for the distribution area of the new plant facility. Through analysis of industry sales and interviews with area distributors, the marketing manager and her staff derived the following table.

Table 1-3

Year	Avg. Sales Price ($/boat)	Area Sales (in units)
1969	$600	28,000
1970	650	27,000
1971	700	26,000
1972	680	26,400
1973	800	24,000
1974	950	21,000
1975	1040	19,200
1976	1090	18,200

As the table indicates, sales were expected to be highly sensitive to price for the new facility.

---

[1]Yield is the ratio of output to raw material input.

Discussion Questions

1. Develop demand and cost functions for the new facility.

2. Determine optimum price per boat and production rate for the new factory.

3. Compute optimum profit.

4. Given optimum price, determine the break-even production rate.

5. Given the optimum production rate, determine break-even price per boat.

6. What factors are irrelevant in optimization analysis?

Redwood
Industrial Detergents, Inc.

Redwood Industrial Detergents, Inc., located in Bethlehem, Pennsylvania, is a compounding firm which blends solid and liquid components according to precise specifications to produce special products, including industrial detergents and degreasers. The wide variations in specifications for these products (due to the many different cleaning applications) require production to be on a job-order basis. The large manufacturers of component chemicals produce primarily for inventory; consequently, they cannot profitably serve the special detergent market, which is cultivated by compounding firms.

The primary components mixed by compounding manufacturers to produce industrial detergents are wetting and emulsifying agents. (Dirt and other impurities which adhere to surfaces by means of films of oil are removed through detergent action which is largely the result of wetting and emulsification.[1]) The wetting action is produced by the introduction of a detergent which will readily adhere to the surface being cleaned. The wetting agent has a great attraction for water. Hence, the wetting agent will decrease surface tension of the water to a level whereby water will adhere to the surface of the object being cleaned. Thus, wetting removes and displaces the impurities which previously adhered to the object.

Before wetting can effectively occur, the oil film (which provides the medium for adherence of impurities to the surface) must be removed. This removal is the primary function of the emulsifying agent. Oil and water do not mix because there is a greater attraction of water molecules for each other (and of oil molecules for each other) than of water molecules for oil molecules.[2] The emulsifying agent forms a colloidal suspension in water that attracts the oil molecules. If shaken or agitated, the emulsifying agent will disperse the oil in tiny droplets which form an oil-in-water emulsion. The removal of the oil film allows displacement of the impurities by the wetting agents, resulting in a cleaning process.

---

[1]Carl R. Noller, *Textbook of Organic Chemistry* (Philadelphia: W. B. Saunders Company, 1962), p. 146.

[2]Noller, *Organic Chemistry*, p. 146.

Redwood Industrial Detergents typically uses four compounds in making detergent blends. These compounds are Red-Detergent 10 (RD-10). Red-Detergent 20 (RD-20), Red-Detergent 30 (RD-30), and Red-Detergent 40 (RD-40).[3] Redwood's sales engineers work closely with industrial customers to prescribe blends of the four compounds that will best satisfy the particular cleaning requirements. Recently, they have been working with representatives of Hanover Boiler Tube and Heat Exchanger Company to develop a cleaner and degreaser for heat exchanger tubes. One of Hanover's customers requires thorough cleaning and degreasing of heat exchanger tubes before shipment. Hanover's customer's product will react violently with any oil film or impurities present in the tubes.

After lengthy experimentation, Hanover placed an order with the following specifications:

1. The detergent would be shipped in 50-pound polyethylene bags.
2. RD-10 and RD-20 would constitute no more than 40 percent of the mixture.
3. RD-30 and RD-40 would constitute at least 50 percent of the mixture.
4. RD-40 would constitute at least 10 percent of the mixture.

Redwood's cost schedules were as follows:

Compound	Cost (per lb.)
RD-10	$0.40
RD-20	0.50
RD-30	0.60
RD-40	0.80

Redwood then began to determine the amounts of each compound to be used to fill the order.

Discussion Question

1. With the objective to minimize the cost of the order, how much of each compound would you specify?

---

[3]Red-Detergent is a brand name for different types of alkali metal salts (such as sodium or potassium) of fat acids.

Pierce and Pierce
Public Warehouse

Jerry and John Pierce are making plans for their new public warehouse in Memphis, Tennessee. Presently, the Pierce brothers own and operate a public warehouse in Tulsa, Oklahoma. Their father, Sinclair Pierce, built it in 1948 and financed it by an inheritance received in 1946. Prior to the inheritance, Sinclair Pierce managed a supply depot for one of the major oil drilling companies in Tulsa. The idea for a public warehouse originated because the drilling company received numerous requests from area industrial firms to store equipment and supplies in its large, well-secured depot warehouses. The oil drilling company issued storage permits as a favor to area firms, but permits were always temporary and were quickly rescinded if the storage space was required by the drilling company. Hence, Sinclair Pierce had a "ready-made" market for his warehouse in 1948.

Pierce's sons, Jerry and John, took over the management of the warehouse in 1967 when Sinclair retired after a minor heart attack. Jerry directs the operations of the warehouse, and John is primarily responsible for customer relations. Although each owns 50 percent of the company, their father appointed the elder son, Jerry, to the position of president and as the ultimate decision-maker in the company's operations. Under this arrangement, the warehouse has enjoyed a great deal of success. The Tulsa warehouse was expanded by 50 percent in 1970. Clients are both private firms and public organizations, including the Tulsa County School Board and the City of Tulsa Streets and Parks Commission.

Because of the success of the Tulsa warehouse, the Pierce brothers have decided to build another facility in Memphis. The site was selected because Memphis is located at the intersection of Interstate Highways 55 and 40 and is located on the Mississippi River. Also, Memphis is one of the main hubs of the Illinois Central Railroad. Hence, in 1973, land was purchased to build the new facility on a spur of the ICRR in southeast Memphis.

A major factor in planning the new warehouse is the determination of the number of docking platforms to service the incoming and outgoing trucks. The Pierce brothers do not own any trucks, so the warehouse schedule is to be almost totally dependent upon the arrival of customer trucks and common carriers for receipt and shipment of equipment and supplies. (The warehouse will also receive and ship materials by rail, but this activity can be accurately scheduled by working closely with the Illinois Central Railroad yard in Memphis.)

The frequency of arrival of customer trucks and common carriers, together with the time required to service these trucks, will determine the number of docking platforms and the number of docking crews that will be required. The number of docking platforms will determine the warehouse configuration and roadway design. The number of docking crews will dictate staffing requirements and the number of fork-lift trucks. (Typically, a fork-lift truck is used by each docking crew, and one or more is used for general warehouse operations.)

From market forecasts in the Memphis area and data from the Tulsa warehouse, four trucks per hour are expected to arrive for loading or unloading during the planned warehouse hours of 7:00 a.m. to 5:00 p.m. (Moday through Friday). The time required for servicing the trucks is expected to average 50 minutes, with a standard deviation of 15 minutes. With this information, the Pierce brothers believe that they can make docking and servicing plans.

Discussion Questions

1. How many docking platforms and servicing crews would you recommend for the new warehouse?

2. What nonquantitative factors would you include in this analysis?

3. What additional information would be helpful? How might you obtain this information?

Haygood Bros.
Construction Company

George and Harry Haygood are building contractors who specialize in the construction of private home dwellings, storage warehouses, and small businesses (less than 20,000 sq ft of floor space). Both George and Harry entered a carpenter union's apprenticeship program in the early 1960s and, upon completion of the apprenticeship, became skilled craftsmen in 1966. Prior to going into business for themselves, they worked for several local building contractors in the Detroit area.

Typically, the Haygood Brothers submit competitive bids for the construction of proposed dwellings. Whenever their bids are accepted, various aspects of the construction (electrical wiring, plumbing, brick laying, painting, etc.) are subcontracted. George and Harry, however, perform all carpentry work. In addition, they plan and schedule all construction operations, frequently arrange interim financing, and supervise all construction activities.

The philosophy under which the Haygood Brothers have always operated can be simply stated — "Time is Money". Delays in construction increase the costs of interim financing and postpone the initiation of other building projects. Consequently, they deal with all bottlenecks promptly and avoid all delays whenever possible. To minimize the time consumed in a construction project, the Haygood Brothers use PERT (Program Evaluation and Review Technique), a planning and control technique developed in 1958 through the combined efforts of the U. S. Navy Special Projects Office and Booz-Allen and Hamilton, a management consulting firm.

First, all construction activities and events are itemized and properly arranged (in parallel and sequential combinations) in a network. Then, time estimates for each activity are made; the expected time for completing each activity is determined; and the critical (longest) path is calculated. Finally, earliest time (T_E), latest time (T_L), and slack values are computed. (See appendix A.) Having made these calculations, George and Harry can place their resources in the critical areas in order to minimize the time of completing the project.

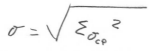

$$\sigma = \sqrt{\Sigma \sigma_{ce}^{2}}$$

Following are the activities which constitute an upcoming project (home dwelling) of the Haygood Brothers:

- arrange financing (AB)
- let subcontracts (BC)
- set and pour foundations (CD)
- plumbing (CE)
- framing (DF)
- roofing (FG)
- electrical wiring (FH)
- installation of windows and doors (FI)
- duct work and insulation (including heating and cooling units) (FJ)
- sheet rock, paneling, and paper hanging (JK)
- installation of cabinets (KL)
- bricking (KM)
- outside trim (MN)
- inside trim (including fixtures) (LO)
- painting (OP)
- flooring (PQ)

The PERT diagram, together with the optimistic (a), most likely (m), and pessimistic (b) time estimates, are as follows:

Activity	a	m	b
AB	4	5	6
BC	2	5	8
CD	5	7	9
CE	4	5	6
DF	2	4	6
FG	3	5	9
FH	4	5	6
FI	3	4	7
FJ	5	7	9
JK	10	11	12
KL	4	6	8
KM	7	8	9
MN	4	5	10
LO	5	7	9
OP	5	6	7
PQ	2	3	4

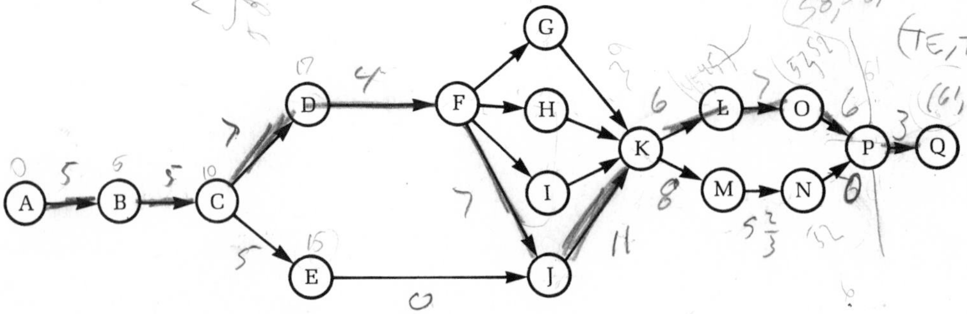

(handwritten annotations:)

$C.P. = 61\ DAYS$

$.52 = z$

START WITH T_e
COPY
FIND T_L

ADD FROM A - 0 TAKE LARGEST

SUBTRACT FROM Q - P (TAKE SMALLEST AT INTERCEPT)

9 TAKE LARGEST 7 AT INTERSECTION (T_e)

(T_c)

(58,58)

(T_e, T_c)

(61,61)

$S = T_c - T_e$

Discussion Questions

1. What is the time length of the critical path? What is the significance of the critical path?

2. Compute the amount of time that the completion of each event can be delayed without affecting the overall project.

3. The project was begun August 1. What is the probability that this project can be completed by September 30? (Note: Scheduled Completion Time (T_S) = 60 days)

appendix A
Glossary of Terms and Symbols for PERT

Activity: A work effort of a program. It is represented by an arrow on a network. An activity may represent a process, task, procurement cycle, waiting time, or simply a connection or interdependency between two events on the network. An activity cannot be started until the event preceding it has occurred.

Critical Path: The most time-consuming path through the network. It is that sequence of events and activities on the network that has the greatest negative, or least positive, algebraic slack.

Earliest Time (T_E): The earliest calendar date on which an event can be expected to occur. The T_E value for a given event is equal to the sum of the expected elapsed times (t_e) for the activities on the longest path from the start of the project to the given event.

Event: A specific definable accomplishment in a program which is recognizable at a particular instant in time. Events do not consume time or resources.

Expected Elapsed Time (t_e): The time which an activity is estimated to require. It is derived from the calculation of a statistically weighted average time estimate, incorporating the optimistic (a), most likely (m), and pessimistic (b) estimates for the work to be accomplished: $t_e = \dfrac{(a + 4m + b)}{6}$

Latest Time (T_L): The latest calendar date on which an event can occur without delaying the completion of the project. The T_L value for a given event is calculated by subtracting the sum of the expected elapsed times (t_e) for the activities on the longest path between the given event and the end event of the project from the latest date allowable for completing the program. (If a directed date is not specified, $T_L = T_E$ for the event.)

Most Likely Time: The most realistic estimate of the time an activity will consume.

Network: A flow diagram consisting of activities and events which must be accomplished to reach the program objectives, showing their logical and planned sequences of accomplishment, interdependencies, and interrelationships.

Optimistic Time Estimate: The time in which an activity can be completed if everything goes exceptionally well.

Pessimistic Time Estimate: An estimate of the longest time an activity will require under the most adverse operating conditions.

Probability: A statistical measure of the chance of an event occurring by a scheduled completion date (T_S). This probability is determined through the following equation:

$$z = \frac{T_S - T_E}{\sigma T_E}$$

To compute σT_E, the variance of each activity time on the critical path is calculated. The variances are then totaled and the square root of the sum is determined. The z value and corresponding probability value can be found on a normal probability distribution table.

Scheduled Completion Time (T_S): A date assigned for the accomplishment of an event for purposes of planning and control.

Slack: The difference between the latest time (T_L) and the earliest time (T_E). It represents the amount of time that the completion of an event can be delayed without affecting the overall project.

Standard Deviation of Activity Time: A measure of the expected variation about the expected elapsed time for an activity. It is computed through the following formula:

$$\sigma = \frac{b - a}{6}$$

Variance of Activity Time: The square of the standard deviation of an activity time:

$$\sigma^2 = \left(\frac{b - a}{6}\right)^2$$

chapter 2

Product/Process Planning and Control

case 8

Cunningham
Water Well Service

Paul Cunningham, sole proprietor of Cunningham Water Well Service, began operations in Oklahoma City, Oklahoma, in 1967. Initial water well drilling operations were started with a used drilling rig mounted on a 1960 Chevrolet two-ton truck. The drilling rig and the truck were purchased at a total cost of $3,500 from a local firm which had gone bankrupt.

During the early years of operation, Cunningham drilled shallow wells for home owners within a 75-mile radius of Oklahoma City. Occasionally, he was employed to drill wells for oil exploration companies and other firms which required large amounts of water in their industrial operations. Although wells drilled for oil-producing firms were more profitable, they constituted only a small percentage of the total business transacted by Cunningham. Since industrial wells do not require the same degree of purity as those for human consumption, they can be bored in less time and at lower costs.

Prior to 1972, Cunningham supplemented his income from drilling and servicing water wells by performing other varied contractural work, including the hauling of dirt, sand, and gravel and the disking, bush-hogging, and grading of plots of land with his tractor and equipment. By 1972, the water well service had expanded to occupy all his available time and energy.

In September, 1972, Cunningham purchased new equipment that allowed him to drill deeper wells in less time. Water filters, pipe, valves, and pumps installed by Cunningham were usually purchased from Sooner Industrials, Inc. and Mid-City Industrial Supply Company. Both companies handled many different valves and filters, and each sold the Ruth Berry brand of water pump.

Throughout his years of servicing water wells, Cunningham learned that simple, inexpensive check valves caused as many problems for homeowners as all other well parts combined. Metal valves rusted and corroded, preventing the plunger from seating properly. (The plunger apparatus of a check valve is lifted from its seat by the force of water being pumped upward. Whenever the pumping ceases, the plunger returns to its seat, thereby preventing the water above it from returning to the water level in the well.

Seepage of water back through the valve as a result of improper seating causes a well to lose its prime.)

Improper seating can be caused by a particle between the plunger and its seat or by wear to the sealing elements (Water, with its impurities, can cause wear to metal over a long period of time.).

In July, 1975, Cunningham decided to invest his savings in the manufacture of a valve which, in his opinion, encompassed all the advantages and none of the shortcomings of existing valves. Figure 2–1 shows Cunningham's Chaparral Valve.

Plastic will not deteriorate, and it resists corrosion more readily than metal when exposed to water. More importantly, the rubber ball, which acts as a sealing device, has an infinite number of "sides." Consequently, it can never wear out. Furthermore, the Chaparral Valve contains no springs, lifts, or other devices which can malfunction. Finally, the rubber ball is soft enough to absorb small sand particles, thereby providing a secure seal when it settles against its base.

Figure 2–1

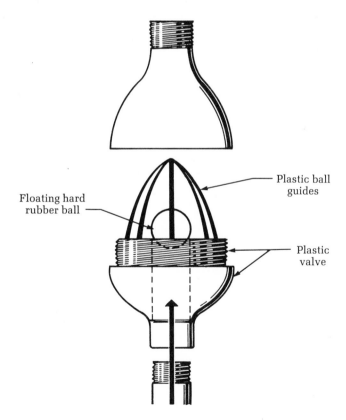

At the suggestion of Les Morrall, manager of Mid-City Industrial Supply Company, Cunningham contacted T. R. Marks, chief engineer of Lone Star

Plastic Products, Inc. of Fort Worth, Texas. After thoroughly discussing the idea, Marks informed Cunningham that the valve could be molded in different sizes. Although the initial investment to design the required molds would be quite high, the cost of producing each additional unit would vary between $4 and $5, depending upon the size of valve produced. (The valves would vary in size from 3/4 in. to 2 in.) The total initial investment, including blueprints, molds, plastic, and balls, amounted to slightly more than $6,500.

In November, 1977, Cunningham received his first shipment of valves from Lone Star Plastic Products. Upon receipt of the goods, he realized that he had given little attention to the problems of marketing his product.

Discussion Questions

1. Analyze the approach Paul Cunningham took in developing a product based on an idea developed through experience.

2. Develop a marketing plan for Paul Cunningham. Include in your plan promotional, pricing, and distribution activities. Are there other markets for the valve? If so, include them in your overall plan.

3. What problems might be encountered in selling the Chaparral Valve? How should these problems be overcome?

Buffalo
Aire-Tool

Diana Whitaker, manager of New Product Development for Buffalo Aire-Tool, received a call from Greg Barlow, chief of Research and Development for Northeast Chemical Corporation, to arrange a meeting between Buffalo's product development team and Northeast's Research and Development staff at Northeast's Technical Services Center in Syracuse, New York. The purpose of the meeting was to discuss the design of a special pneumatic impact wrench to service a new electrolytic chlorine cell that Northeast Chemical was developing. The wrench would be used on $1^1/_2$ in. bolts that fasten 50-pound copper connectors to the anode and cathode of adjacent cells in a circuit.

Buffalo Aire-Tool designs and manufactures a wide variety of general and special purpose pneumatic tools used in industry. Its principal research and manufacturing center is located in Buffalo, New York, and its primary products include an assortment of impact wrenches with direct and angular drives. The firm also manufactures pneumatic chipping hammers, pavement breakers, caulking guns, sanders, grinders, etc. A great deal of Buffalo's success has been attributed to its ability to fulfill special needs of its industrial customers. Hence, the New Product Development Department plays a vital role in the company's growth and ongoing success.

Diana Whitaker had been particularly successful in capturing profitable new business for Buffalo Aire-Tool. The formula for her success lies in her ability to aggressively develop new products that Buffalo's plants can efficiently produce. Her department constantly seeks to employ standardization and simplification in the design of a new tool and yet reliably perform the function required by the customer. On numerous occasions, she has declined a customer's invitation to design and produce a particular tool because the tool required wide deviations from Buffalo's product standards. Whitaker reasoned that the set-up and production costs would be so high that the necessary selling price would be prohibitive to the customer. Rather than quote such a high price, Whitaker preferred to assist the customer in investigating how the required application could be modified so that it would be effectively served by a tool which could be produced within existing product standards. The result would be an acceptable profit margin for Buffalo Aire-Tool and a reasonable price charged to the customer. This result promoted repeat business and greatly enhanced Buffalo's reputation.

The Meeting With Northeast Chemical Corporation

Buffalo's product development team carried this strategy into the meeting with Greg Barlow and his Research and Development staff. The Northeast Research and Development staff was developing a new chlorine cell and needed an impact wrench that would develop 750 foot-pounds of torque to connect and disconnect $1^1/_2$ in. bolts that fasten eight 50-pound copper connectors to the anode and cathode of adjacent cells in a circuit. (See Figure 2–2.) A total of 16 bolts, or 2 bolts per connector, is to be used for each intercell connection.

Figure 2–2

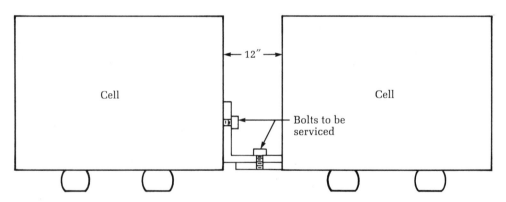

Because of the very high cost of copper intercell connectors, the cells are to be placed as close to one another as possible and still allow for cooling through air circulation and access to the connectors for servicing the cell. (Cell servicing includes removal of the connectors to attach a jumper switch that allows by-passing of the electric current around the cell to be serviced; removal of the old cell from the circuit; replacement of the old cell with one that has been restored; disconnecting the jumper switch; and re-connecting the intercell connectors.) Northeast specified that the distance between the cell is to be 12 in. (Again, see Figure 2–2.) Twelve in. was the minimum distance calculated by Northeast that would still allow for proper cell ventilation (cooling). Now, Northeast wanted to determine if 12 in. would allow access to the connectors for servicing the call.

Hence, Buffalo Aire-Tool's assignment was to design an impact wrench that could develop 750 foot-pounds of torque (required to ensure proper electrical contact between the anode/cathode and the intercell connectors) and be operated by maintenance personnel within the 12 in. space limitation. Moreover, Northeast preferred that the wrench be constructed of nonmagnetic metal, if possible, because of the high level of magnetism created by the passage of 70,000 amps of electrical current through the new cells. Using nonmagnetic tools would greatly facilitate cell servicing. This provision was not, however, an absolute specification.

The Design of The Tool

A torque rating of 750 foot-pounds was no problem for Buffalo Aire-Tool. It had numerous standard impact wrenches that would develop at least that torque rating. None of these standard direct drive models, however, could be operated within that 12 in. space. Angular drive models could be operated within that space limitation, but these wrenches that had a 750 foot-pound torque rating all weighed in excess of 45 pounds. This high weight coupled with the high level of magnetism prevented use of this wrench by all but the exceptionally strong maintenance man. Even then, the fatigue factor would be very high.

Upon consultation with the company metallurgist, Whitaker concluded that nonmagnetic impact wrenches for this service were not practical. Metals such as aluminum, brass, or magnesium could not stand the required stress. More sophisticated nonmagnetic alloys that could withstand the stress were found to be extremely costly, difficult to obtain, and almost impossible to process with Buffalo's existing manufacturing system. Consequently, Whitaker immediately notified Barlow that a nonmagnetic tool was being eliminated from consideration. Barlow agreed and asked that Buffalo continue to work on the design and construct the wrench out of the steel normally used to manufacture impact wrenches.

At this stage, the product development team reached the following conclusions:

1. The impact wrench must be direct drive (angular drive wrenches were too heavy).
2. The impact wrench must use their standard 9-in. housing. (The team experimented with 9-, 10-, and 11-in. housings between two plywood sheets with a spacing of 12 in. to simulate the spacing between the cells. They found that the 9-in. housing provided the required flexibility in operation. Also, the weight was 15 pounds, which could be readily used in the magnetic environment.)

The maximum torque rating on their most powerful 9-in. impact wrench, however, was 350 foot-pounds. This standard wrench typically costs $200 to manufacture and sells for approximately $350. The engineers on Whitaker's team calculated that a 9-in. wrench with a 750 foot-pound torque rating was possible if the following modifications were made:

1. Use oversized pistons and cams.
2. Increase supply air minimum pressure from 80 pounds to 105 pounds.
3. Change tolerance level for drive mechanism parts from 0.007 in. to 0.003 in.

Through consultation with a cost accountant, the purchasing agents, and the production supervisor, Whitaker estimated the cost of the new wrench as follows:

1. Oversized pistons and cams would add $50 to the cost of the 350 foot-pound wrench.
2. Set-up for the new wrench would cost $1,000, and a normal production run would be 50 wrenches.
3. To estimate the additional machining costs required to improve the tolerance level from 0.007 in. to 0.003 in. for drive mechanism parts, the production supervisor with assistance from engineers from the product development department derived the following cost estimation formula:

$$AMC = \text{TC of Reference Wrench} \times 1.05 \text{ (old tolerance } - \text{ new tolerance) } 1,000$$

(Note: formula applies only if new tolerance is less than old tolerance.)

After developing a 9-in. test wrench with the preceding design changes, the product development team verified the 750 foot-pound torque rating. Whitaker then contacted Barlow to set up a demonstration of the new wrench. Barlow was pleased with the demonstration. He believed that the 105 pound minimum air pressure supply to the wrench would not present much of a problem because most plant air systems operate at a minimum of 110 pounds. Moreover, Barlow did not object to the relatively expensive lubricating oil used in the in-line oiler to the wrench. (The oiler or lubricator is placed in the air line to the wrench.) Buffalo recommended the expensive lubricating oil to help maintain the tight tolerance level specified. Wear and improper lubrication would result in a significant loss of torque for the wrench. Hence, Barlow asked Whitaker for a formal quote on the new wrench.

Discussion Questions

1. Name and discuss product design principles illustrated by the case.

2. What price would you have quoted Northeast Chemical on the new wrench?

3. What benefits do you believe are forthcoming for Buffalo Aire-Tool if it successfully markets the new wrench to Northeast Chemical?

4. What are possible risks involved in new product design?

Great Lakes
Tire and Rubber Company

In 1977, the Executive Committee[1] of Great Lakes Tire and Rubber Company faced a highly crucial decision regarding its product line. For the first time in its 35-year history, the company's automobile tire division was expected to suffer a net loss on sales of $5 million. Revenues of the auto tire division reached an all-time high of $23.5 million in 1970 and thereafter declined steadily. Table 2–1 shows the divisional sales, profit, and percent of total revenues attributed to the auto tire division from 1966 to 1976.

The decline in revenues of the auto tire division was more than offset by increases in sales in the tractor, airplane, truck, and heavy equipment tire divisions. Primarily, the decline in auto tire sales was attributed to the failure

Table 2–1   *Revenue and Profit Data — Automobile Tire Division*
   (in millions of dollars)

Year	Sales	Percent of Total Corporate Sales	Profit
1966	$11.7	59	$0.8
1967	13.0	50	0.9
1968	18.8	49	1.1
1969	19.2	49	1.8
1970	23.5	38	2.4
1971	22.1	28	1.9
1972	17.3	24	1.7
1973	15.5	20	1.4
1974	14.2	20	0.8
1975	11.0	10	0.3
1976	9.9	6	0.2
1977	5.0*	5*	(2.8)*

*Projected

[1]Great Lakes Tire and Rubber Company's Executive Committee was composed of divisional managers, corporate vice-presidents of all functional areas, and the president and chief executive officer of the corporation.

of the company to add a steel-belted radial to its product line. In 1970, management decided not to manufacture a steel-belted radial passenger car tire because it did not believe that consumers would be willing to pay the additional cost for steel-belted tires. Consequently, Great Lakes Tire and Rubber Company continued to offer only nylon-, rayon-, polyester-, and glass-belted tires. In 1975, when management learned that approximately 30 percent of all replacement tires purchased were steel-belted radials, it realized that a serious error in judgment had been made. Not only had the company suffered a loss of revenue and profit as a result of its decision, but it had allowed its competitors to capture a larger share of the automobile tire market virtually uncontested. Since loyalty to brand names in the auto tire market is reasonably strong, recapturing lost customers is always difficult and often impossible.

Two members of the corporate Executive Committee felt that the company should seriously contemplate discontinuing the auto tire division and concentrate its efforts in the other divisions, all of which had shown uninterrupted growth since their introduction. Others felt that the company would ultimately suffer a decline in overall sales and profit if it did not offer a complete line of tires. Mark Bowman, Executive Vice-President of Marketing, contended that the future of the auto tire division looked dim unless a steel-belted radial was manufactured and sold. Even with a steel radial, he asserted, the division could be expected to show only moderate success in the immediate years ahead because of the difficulties of making inroads into a new market that was dominated by other manufacturers. In addition, Bowman indicated that a reduction in the variety of tires produced would cut costs of operations and allow the marketing division to focus its efforts in the areas in which the company was recognized as a national leader.

John Barrett, manager of the auto tire division, was adamant about the need for the company to introduce a steel-belted radial tire. Prior to top management's decision not to manufacture a steel-belted radial tire in 1970, Barrett had worked closely with the R&D department which, at that time, experimented with various designs. Because much of the preliminary developmental work associated with the development of a new tire had been completed, Barrett believed that the production of a high-quality steel-belted radial tire could begin within three months. The future of the company, he asserted, depended on its decision to manufacture the tire. Furthermore, he accused the other divisional managers of being irresponsible by suggesting the deletion of his division, since it accounted for a significant share of total corporate revenues.

Michael Ritter, president of the company and chairman of the Executive Committee, asked the vice-presidents of the Production and Marketing divisions to prepare ten-year cost and revenue projections associated with the manufacture and distribution of a new steel-belted tire. Both divisional vice-presidents were assured of complete cooperation and assistance from the Accounting and R&D departments.

On October 1, the revenue and cost projections were submitted to the president. The data contained in these reports appear in Tables 2–2 and 2–3.

Table 2–2   *Projected Revenues and Costs for Steel-Belted Radial Tire*

Year	Estimated Sales (in thousands of units)	Estimated Revenue (in millions of dollars)
1978	10	0.75
1979	20	1.50
1980	40	3.00
1981	85	6.38
1982	120	9.00
1983	160	12.00
1984	200	15.00
1985	250	18.75
1986	340	25.50
1987	350	33.75

-2.65
-2.56
-2.446
-2.

Fixed Costs: $2.8 million (annually)
Incremental Costs per unit: $60 in 1977; expected to increase 5 percent per year thereafter

Table 2–3   *Revenue and Cost Projections of Auto Tire Division with Steel-Belted Radial Tire (in millions of dollars)*

Year	Projected Revenue*	Projected Costs	Profit
1978	8	14.0	(6.0)
1979	13	18.0	(5.0)
1980	19	23.3	(4.3)
1981	25	28.4	(3.4)
1982	29	31.0	(2.0)
1983	34	34.0	—
1984	36	35.5	0.5
1985	38	36.2	1.8
1986	39	37.0	2.0
1987	40	37.5	2.5

*Sales of nylon-, rayon-, polyester-, and glass-belted tires were not expected to be affected by the introduction of the steel-belted radial tire. Increases in revenue attributed to the steel-belted radial are due to a greater share of the automobile tire market.

After reviewing the data submitted to him, Mr. Ritter, the corporate president, concluded that the company would be forced to follow one of the following courses of action:

1. Discontinue the passenger-car tire division (estimated net cost: $16.5 million).

2. Produce a steel-belted radial tire along with the nylon-, rayon-, poly-
   ester-, and glass-belted tires.
3. Produce only the steel-belted radial tire.
4. Continue operating with the present line of tires.

When he announced his recommendation to the Executive Committee,
Mr. Ritter wanted to be able to justify his position.

Discussion Questions

1. Compute profit or loss for the automobile tire division if the steel-belted radial
   is not introduced. Explain the effect of the steel-belted radial on profit (loss).

2. Explain "contribution margin." *AMOUNT OF PRICE TO "PAY" FOR PROFIT AND
   FIXED COSTS*

3. What course of action should Mr. Ritter recommend to the Executive Committee?

4. Rank order the alternatives from best to worst. On what basis did you make your
   decision?

Amalgamated
Machine Works, Incorporated

Amalgamated Machine Works, one of the country's oldest manufacturers of steel balls and bearings, produces on a job-order basis a wide range of balls, seats, and bearings used in industrial pumps and pressure valves. Customers of Amalgamated Machine Works typically purchase the balls to be used in the final assembly of high-pressure valves which, in turn, are sold to companies engaged in the production and transmission of oil, gas, and chemicals.

The largest single customer of Amalgamated Machine Works is Trident Valve & Manufacturing Company of Cleveland, Ohio. Trident, like most of Amalgamated's other customers, manufactures all parts of its valves except the balls which, when installed, regulate the flow of liquids and gases through the valves. (See Figure 2–3.)

Figure 2–3

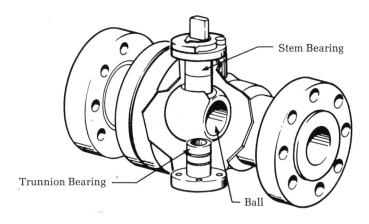

Stem Bearing

Trunnion Bearing

Ball

As an integral part of its quality control program, Amalgamated Machine Works has established rigid tolerance limits for all metal balls produced, regardless of size or type of metal used. All steel balls used in high-pressure valves, for example, are produced under a tolerance range of ± 0.004 in.

from the predetermined standard.[1] To assure uniform quality (including size), the quality control engineers of Amalgamated randomly sample the physical output of all lathes and drill presses used in manufacturing operations. Whenever variations in output are found to be significant, corrective control techniques are immediately introduced in an effort to minimize costs, waste, and risk of error.

Amalgamated recently purchased and installed two new steel lathes on which balls are turned from castings. During the first two weeks of their use, every ball and bearing turned out was inspected. Thereafter, the output was randomly sampled to assure that the quality of the total output was of the desired level. Deviations from standards and the range of variations were recorded and analyzed daily.

On June 5, four weeks after the lathes were installed, John Reeves, a recently employed technician, measured and recorded the inside dimensions of ten steel balls chosen at random from each of the two new lathes. The following table shows the recorded data:

Table 2–4   *Inside Diameter Dimensions (in inches)*

Sample Item No.	Lathe 1	Lathe 2
1	6.000	5.997
2	6.001	5.998
3	6.003	6.000
4	6.003	6.001
5	6.004	6.000
6	6.003	5.998
7	6.003	5.997
8	6.002	5.996
9	6.001	5.996
10	6.000	5.996

A brief glance at the recorded data revealed that the inside dimensions of the sample balls turned out on Lathe 1 equalled or exceeded the standard of six in. Even so, all sample items fell within the tolerance limits of $\pm$ 0.004 in. Also, he noted that the sample items from Lathe 2 appeared to be somewhat smaller in actual diameter measurements. The differences, he knew, might be due to chance or might be significant.

After contemplating the variations, Reeves decided to compare sample means to determine if the variations were significant. To make this comparison, Reeves chose to use the t-test statistic[2] where:

---

[1] Amalgamated Machine Works, Inc. produces balls ranging in size from one in. to thirty-six in. With a tolerance of $\pm$ 0.004 in., a standard four-inch ball woud be acceptable if its actual inside diameter measured between 3.996 and 4.004 in.

[2] If the population is normally distributed, while the standard deviation is unknown but can be determined from the two sample estimates, the t-test can be used.

$$t^* = \frac{\overline{X}_1 - \overline{X}_2}{s\sqrt{\dfrac{1}{n_1} + \dfrac{1}{n_2}}}$$

and s is the estimate of the population standard deviation:

$$s = \sqrt{\frac{\Sigma(x_1 - \overline{X}_1)^2 + \Sigma(x_2 - \overline{X}_2)^2}{n_1 + n_2 - 2}}$$

Discussion Questions

1. Are the variations in sample means significant at the 0.01 level?

2. Explain the nature of the variations. Since all sample items fell within the established tolerance limits, was there a need to test the variances for significance?

3. What elements should be included in a complete quality control program? Design such a program for Amalgamated Machine Works, Inc.

---

*The value of t at the 0.01 level of significance for 18 degrees of freedom $(n_1 + n_2 - 2)$ can be found in a t distribution table.

case 12

Bayfield
Mud Company

In November, 1976, John Wells, a customer service representative of Bayfield Mud Company, was summoned to the Houston, Texas, warehouse of Wet-Land Drilling, Inc. to inspect three boxcars of mud treating agents which Bayfield Mud Company had shipped to the Houston firm. (Bayfield's corporate offices and its largest plant are located in Orange, Texas, which is just west of the Louisiana-Texas border.) Wet-Land Drilling had filed a complaint that the 50-pound bags of treating agents that it had just received from Bayfield were short-weight by approximately 5 percent.

The light-weight bags were initially detected by one of Wet-Land's receiving clerks who noticed that the railroad scale tickets indicated that the net weights were significantly less on all three of the boxcars than those of identical shipments received on October 25, 1976. Bayfield's traffic department was called to determine if lighter weight dunnage or pallets were used on the shipments. (This might explain the lighter net weights.) Bayfield indicated, however, that no changes had been made in the loading or palletizing procedures. Hence, Wet-Land randomly checked 50 of the bags and discovered that the average net weight was 47.51 pounds. They noted from past shipments that the bag net weights averaged exactly 50.0 pounds, with an acceptable standard deviation of 1.2 pounds. Consequently, they concluded that the sample indicated a significant short-weight. (The reader may wish to verify the above conclusion.) Bayfield was then contacted, and Wells was sent to investigate the complaint. Upon arrival, Wells verified the complaint and issued a 5 percent credit to Wet-Land.

Wet-Land's management, however, was not completely satisfied with only the issuance of credit for the short shipment. The charts followed by their mud engineers on the drilling platforms were based on 50-pound bags of treating agents. Lighter weight bags might result in poor chemical control during the drilling operation and might adversely affect drilling efficiency. (Mud treating agents are used to control the pH and other chemical properties of the cone during drilling operation.) This could cause severe economic consequences because of the extremely high cost of oil and natural gas well drilling operations. Consequently, special use instructions had to accompany the delivery of these shipments to the drilling platforms. Moreover, the light-weight shipments had to be isolated in Wet-Land's warehouse, causing extra handling and poor space utilization. Hence, Wells was informed that Wet-Land's Drilling might seek a new supplier of mud treating agents if, in the future, it received bags that deviated significantly from 50 pounds.

The quality control department at Bayfield suspected that the light-weight bags may have resulted from "growing pains" at the Orange plant. Because of the 1973 energy crisis, oil and natural gas exploration activity had greatly increased. This increased activity, in turn, created increased demand for products produced by related industries, including drilling muds. Consequently, Bayfield had to expand from a one-shift (6:00 A.M. to 2:00 P.M.) to a two-shift (6:00 A.M. to 10:00 P.M.) operation in mid-1974 and finally to a three-shift operation (24 hours per day) in the fall of 1976.

The additional night-shift bagging crew was staffed entirely by new employees. The most experienced foremen were temporarily assigned to supervise the night-shift employees. Most emphasis was placed on increasing the output of bags to meet the ever-increasing demand. It was suspected that only occasional reminders were made to double-check the bag weight-feeder. (A double-check is performed by systematically weighing a bag on a scale to determine if the proper weight is being loaded by the weight-feeder. If there is a significant deviation from 50 pounds, corrective adjustments are made to the weight-release mechanism.)

To verify this expectation, the quality control staff randomly sampled the bag output and prepared the following chart. Thirty-six bags were sampled and weighed each hour.

Table 2–5

Time	Avg. Weight (pounds)	Range	
		Smallest	Largest
6:00 AM	49.6	48.7	50.7
7:00	50.2	49.1	51.2
8:00	50.6	49.6	51.4
9:00	50.8	50.2	51.8
10:00	49.9	49.2	52.3
11:00	50.3	48.6	51.7
12:00 Noon	48.6	46.2	50.4
1:00 P.M.	49.0	46.4	50.0
2:00	49.0	46.0	50.6
3:00	49.8	48.2	50.8
4:00	50.3	49.2	52.7
5:00	51.4	50.0	55.3
6:00	51.6	49.2	54.7
7:00	51.8	50.0	55.6
8:00	51.0	48.6	53.2
9:00	50.5	49.4	52.4

Time	Avg. Weight (pounds)	Range	
		Smallest	Largest
10:00	49.2	46.1	50.7
11:00	49.0	46.3	50.8
12:00 Midnight	48.4	45.4	50.2
1:00 A.M.	47.6	44.3	49.7
2:00	47.4	44.1	49.6
3:00	48.2	45.2	49.0
4:00	48.0	45.5	49.1
5:00	48.4	47.1	49.6
6:00	48.6	47.4	52.0
7:00	50.0	49.2	52.2
8:00	49.8	49.0	52.4
9:00	50.3	49.4	51.7
10:00	50.2	49.6	51.8
11:00	50.0	49.0	52.3
12:00 Noon	50.0	48.8	52.4
1:00 P.M.	50.1	49.4	53.6
2:00	49.7	48.6	51.0
3:00	48.4	47.2	51.7
4:00	47.2	45.3	50.9
5:00	46.8	44.1	49.0
6:00	46.8	41.0	51.2
7:00	50.0	46.2	51.7
8:00	47.4	44.0	48.7
9:00	47.0	44.2	48.9
10:00	47.2	46.6	50.2
11:00	48.6	47.0	50.0
12:00 Midnight	49.8	48.2	50.4
1:00 A.M.	49.6	48.4	51.7
2:00	50.0	49.0	52.2
3:00	50.0	49.2	50.0
4:00	47.2	46.3	50.5
5:00	47.0	44.1	49.7
6:00	48.4	45.0	49.0
7:00	48.8	44.8	49.7
8:00	49.6	48.0	51.8
9:00	50.0	48.1	52.7
10:00	51.0	48.1	55.2
11:00	50.4	49.5	54.1
12:00 Noon	50.0	48.7	50.9
1:00 P.M.	48.9	47.6	51.2
2:00	49.8	48.4	51.0
3:00	49.8	48.8	50.8
4:00	50.0	49.1	50.6
5:00	47.8	45.2	51.2
6:00	46.4	44.0	49.7
7:00	46.4	44.4	50.0
8:00	47.2	46.6	48.9

Time	Avg. Weight (pounds)	Range	
		Smallest	Largest
9:00	48.4	47.2	49.5
10:00	49.2	48.1	50.7
11:00	48.4	47.0	50.8
12:00 Midnight	47.2	46.4	49.2
1:00 A.M.	47.4	46.8	49.0
2:00	48.8	47.2	51.4
3:00	49.6	49.0	50.6
4:00	51.0	50.5	51.5
5:00	50.5	50.0	51.9

Discussion Questions

1. What is your analysis of the bag weight problem?

2. What procedures would you recommend to maintain proper quality control?

case 13

The Morristown
Daily Tribune

In July, 1977, the Morristown *Daily Tribune* published its first newspaper in direct competition with two other newspapers — the Morristown *Daily Ledger* and the *Clarion Herald*, a weekly publication. Presently, the *Ledger* is the most widely read newspaper in the area, with a total circulation of 38,500. The *Tribune*, however, has made significant inroads into the readership market since its inception. Total circulation of the *Tribune* now exceeds 27,000.

Wilbur Sykes, editor of the *Tribune*, attributes the success of the newspaper to the accuracy of its contents, a strong editorial section, and the proper blending of local, regional, national, and international news items. In addition, the paper has been successful in getting the accounts of several major retailers who advertise extensively in the display section. Finally, experienced reporters, photographers, copy writers, typesetters, editors, and other personnel have formed a "team" dedicated to providing the most timely and accurate reporting of news in the area.

Of critical importance to quality newspaper printing is accurate typesetting. To assure quality in the final print, Mr. Sykes has decided to develop a procedure for monitoring the performance of typesetters over a period of time. Such a procedure involves sampling output, establishing control limits, comparing the *Tribune's* accuracy with that of the industry, and occasionally up-dating the information.

First, Mr. Sykes randomly selected 30 newspapers published during the preceding 12 months. From each paper, 100 paragraphs were randomly chosen and were read for accuracy. The number of errors in each paper was recorded, and the fraction of errors in each sample was determined. Table 2–6 shows the results of the sampling.

Table 2–6

Sample	Errors in Sample	Fraction of Errors (No./100)	Sample	Errors in Sample	Fraction of Errors (No./100)
1	2	0.02	16	2	0.02
2	4	0.04	17	3	0.03
3	10	0.10	18	7	0.07
4	4	0.04	19	3	0.03
5	1	0.01	20	2	0.02
6	1	0.01	21	3	0.03
7	13	0.13	22	7	0.07
8	9	0.09	23	4	0.04
9	11	0.11	24	3	0.03
10	0	0.00	25	2	0.02
11	3	0.03	26	2	0.02
12	4	0.04	27	0	0.00
13	2	0.02	28	1	0.01
14	2	0.02	29	3	0.03
15	8	0.08	30	4	0.04

The overall fraction of errors $(\bar{f})$ and the standard deviation (s) were then calculated by using the following formulae:

$$\bar{f} = \frac{\text{No. of errors in all samples}}{\text{No. of samples} \times \text{Sample size}}$$

$$s = \sqrt{\frac{\bar{f}\,(1 - \bar{f})}{\text{Sample size}}}$$

Upper and lower control limits were then calculated under a confidence level of 95.0 percent. Thus,

$$\text{UCL} = \bar{f} + 1.96(s)$$
$$\text{LCL} = \bar{f} - 1.96(s)$$

Discussion Questions

1. Plot the overall fraction of errors $(\bar{f})$ and the upper and lower control limits on a control chart.

2. Assume the industry upper and lower control limits are 0.1000 and 0.0400 respectively. Plot them on the control chart.

3. Plot the fraction of errors in each sample. Do all fall within the firm's control limits? When one falls outside the control limits, what should be done?

case 14

Gulfside
Terminal
(Part A)

A major operation at Gulfside Terminal is the loading of 20,000 tons of 50 percent caustic soda in tankers for shipment to aluminum plants in Jamaica, West Indies.[1] (Caustic soda is sodium hydroxide (NaOH); 50 percent is the particular grade of caustic soda. Actual concentration may vary slightly from producer to producer.) The caustic soda is produced by electrolysis of brine to form chlorine gas, hydrogen gas, and caustic soda. After electrolysis, caustic soda exists in a 10 percent solution that also contains 17 percent salt (sodium chloride or NaCl). This solution is called *cell liquor.* The cell liquor is evaporated in a triple-effect evaporator to increase the concentration of caustic soda from 10 percent to approximately 50 percent. (Triple-effect evaporation is the result of pressure or vacuum differences among three evaporation vessels, so that the vapor discharged from the first vessel will boil or evaporate the liquid in the second vessel, which in turn boils or evaporates the liquid in the third vessel. Liquid in the first vessel is evaporated by steam which is under 125 pounds of pressure and has a temperature of approximately 400° F. This steam heating initiates the triple-effect evaporation. Vapor from the third vessel is condensed in a barometric condenser to create a vacuum. This vacuum and the differences in caustic soda concentration among the vessels permit the vapor from one vessel to boil the liquid in another vessel. The cell liquor is fed continuously into the third vessel, which feeds the second vessel. The second vessel continuously feeds the first, or steam-heated, vessel. The 50 percent product is discharged from the first vessel.)

The salt in the cell liquor precipitates as a solid during the evaporation process. It is removed from the 50 percent product by cooling and filtration. The salt content in the product is lowered to approximately 1 percent.

The finished product specification for minimum caustic concentration is 49.0 percent. If the concentration drops below 49.0 percent, the product is down-graded and sold at a distressed price. The distressed price is typically

---

[1]For a complete description of the terminal operation, see case 29, "Gulfside Terminal, Part B."

$8 to $12 per ton lower than the market price. Heretofore, to ensure that the concentration did not drop below 49.0 percent, the evaporation plant maintained the concentration at approximately 51.0 percent. (The evaporator operators check this control point by using a hydrometer to take specific gravity measurements termed *degrees Baumé*. For example, a 52.0 degree Baumé, after temperature correction, will yield a 51.0 percent caustic concentration. Specific gravity, which is expressed as degrees Baumé, is directly proportional to caustic concentration.) The 51.0 percent control point would allow dilution of the product that might lower the concentration. Dilution could result from water washing of pipelines and vessels or from excessive leakage of water through pump seals into the finished product. The finished product concentration, however, rarely dropped below the specification of 49.0 percent.

Because of spiraling costs of natural gas to generate steam, management contemplated lowering the concentration control point from 51.0 percent to 50.0 percent. They realized that the risk of producing below minimum concentration product would increase. The savings in steam (and natural gas), however, would be substantial with this drop in product concentration. (Another benefit is increased evaporation capacity because of a drop in the concentration control point.) Management believed that the fuel savings could be gained without a significant risk of producing below minimum concentration product. The belief was based on a preliminary examination of the analyses of daily composite or average samples of the finished product. The analyses were run on samples taken over the last quarter of 1976, when the control point concentration was 51.0 percent. These analyses were as follows:

Table 2-7

Date	Analysis[2]	Date	Analysis	Date	Analysis
10/1/76	49.8	11/1/76	49.0	12/1/76	50.2
2	50.4	2	49.6	2	50.0
3	50.2	3	49.8	3	49.9
4	50.6	4	50.3	4	50.8
5	49.8	5	50.2	5	50.5
6	50.0	6	50.0	6	49.2
7	49.2	7	49.7	7	49.9
8	50.4	8	49.8	8	50.0
9	49.4	9	49.2	9	50.0
10	49.2	10	49.2	10	50.0
11	50.1	11	50.0	11	50.0
12	49.7	12	49.9	12	50.1
13	49.8	13	49.7	13	49.9
14	50.5	14	50.2	14	49.6

[2]Analysis is percent concentration of sodium hydroxide.

Date	Analysis	Date	Analysis	Date	Analysis
15	50.1	15	49.6	15	49.8
16	50.0	16	50.0	16	49.7
17	50.0	17	49.8	17	50.0
18	49.2	18	50.2	18	51.2
19	49.9	19	50.3	19	50.0
20	49.8	20	49.6	20	50.2
21	50.2	21	49.8	21	50.0
22	50.6	22	49.9	22	49.5
23	50.0	23	49.7	23	49.7
24	49.8	24	50.1	24	49.8
25	50.6	25	48.6	25	50.0
26	49.4	26	49.2	26	49.6
27	50.3	27	50.0	27	50.0
28	50.0	28	49.8	28	49.7
29	49.7	29	50.4	29	50.0
30	49.4	30	50.2	30	50.2
31	49.9			31	50.2

Discussion Questions

1. Do you agree that the concentration control point can be lowered from 51.0 percent to 50.0 percent and yet meet minimum concentration specification?

2. What concentration control point would you recommend? Justify your recommendation.

3. Prepare quality control charts for the product.

chapter 3

Plant Location and Capital Budgeting

case 15

Kellwood
Company

In September, 1972, the management of Kellwood Company, a primary apparel manufacturer for Sears, faced the problem of selecting a site for the construction of a new 40,000 sq. ft. manufacturing facility. Most of the company's manufacturing plants are located in the Southeast and South Central regions of the United States, and it was to this geographic area that management had given most of its attention. Of primary importance to Kellwood were four factors which play a significant role in the success or failure of a branch plant — labor, politics, the tax structure of the state, and the desire of a community to attract new industry into it.

Background of the Company

Kellwood Company is one of the nation's leading manufacturers of apparel, home fashions, and recreation equipment. The company's apparel division is composed of five subgroups which constitute Sears' largest apparel source. Kellwood provides product lines for several apparel programs of Sears, including Toughskins jeans, Ban-Lon shirts, Clingalon hosiery, and Winnie-the-Pooh children's wear.

Kellwood's home fashion division produces tailored bedspreads, mattress pads, curtains, slumber bags, quilts, sheets, and so forth. Its recreation products division manufactures a multitude of dissimilar goods including tents, canoes and fiberglass boats, electrical components, backpacks, and tarpaulins.

In addition to its three major product divisions, Kellwood owns Perry Manufacturing Company, a subsidiary which produces fashion-coordinated sportswear in misses' and women's size ranges. Perry's customers include most major national retailers, leading retail chains, and department stores. Also, Kellwood owns Stahl-Urban Company, another subsidiary which produces men's and boys' leisure suits, coordinates, slacks, jackets, jeans, and franchised professional sports apparel. Stahl-Urban sells to department and specialty stores.

Kellwood operates 62 plants in 17 states and Mexico. Apparel produced for men, women, and children totals more than 100 million units a year.

Factors Influencing Site Location

Kellwood's proposed plant would employ 275 workers who would produce work clothing identical to that produced in two other plants in the Kingswell Group (one of five subgroups of the apparel division). One of these existing facilities is located in Wesson, Mississippi, and the other is located in Monticello, Mississippi. Because of the success of these operations, Kellwood wanted to build another facility in the same geographic region. An original list of 50 prospective site locations was narrowed to 20, with special consideration being given to Amite, Louisiana, the parish seat of Tangipahoa Parish, because of its location, labor supply, and the efforts to attract industry into the state by the Louisiana Power and Light Company and by Governor Edwin Edwards, Senator Russell Long, and other state administrative officials.

Representatives of Kellwood completed a labor survey of Amite, Louisiana, and the surrounding area. Although the survey indicated that labor was available, Kellwood officials were reluctant to commit themselves to the city officials. The mayor of the city owned the proposed site; other firms in town appeared to be somewhat hesitant to welcome a Kellwood plant into the area because it would compete for labor in a limited market; and the proposed site did not have adequate water and gas supplies. Too, the representatives of Kellwood felt that the reception city officials give them was, generally speaking, poor.

Upon learning of Kellwood's indecision to locate in Amite, Mayor John LaRock of Independence, Louisiana, asked the Kellwood officials for an opportunity to present the advantages of constructing the plant in his city, located six miles south of Amite. Mayor LaRock's presentation was built around the following points:

1. The city of Independence had an existing industrial park. If that location was unsatisfactory, another 17.5-acre site could be purchased.
2. Independence was closer to the population centers of Hammond and Ponchatoula. Because of the greater supply of labor, workers could more easily be employed.
3. The 17.5-acre site located on the southwest corner of the city was close to a ten-in. water main.
4. A general bond referendum in the amount of $800,000 would be presented to the citizens of Ward 6 to be voted on. The estimated cost of constructing a 40,000 sq. ft. facility was $400,000. The balance of the proceeds from the bond sale would be used to expand the original facility at a later date.

5. Firms coming to Louisiana are exempt from state and local taxes for a ten-year period.
6. The city of Independence wanted and needed the Kellwood satellite plant.

Kellwood representatives were favorably impressed with the desire of state and city officials to have their company locate a plant in Independence. After carefully evaluating and comparing the advantages and disadvantages of all potential site locations, Kellwood agreed to build the manufacturing plant in Independence provided the site could be purchased and the following conditions satisfied:

1. The citizens of Ward 6 must vote in favor of the bond referendum, from which the proceeds would be used to buy the land and construct the building.
2. The site would be adequately prepared. (Site preparation essentially involved bringing in fill-dirt and dozer work.)
3. The nearby ten-in. water main and sewer lines would be laid to the site. (Garment manufacturers require an adequate supply of water to reduce fire risks and related insurance premiums.)
4. The use of natural gas could be arranged. Through discussions between the Federal Power Commission and state/local governmental officials, a supply of fuel (either natural gas or low-sulfur fuel oil) was guaranteed.

The proposed 17.5-acre site was purchased by the community Industrial District, an organization comprised of local citizens which was established to facilitate such negotiations. Fourteen city leaders who were members of the Industrial District signed personal notes in order to secure the property. Kellwood, thereafter, purchased the land from the Industrial District.

The citizens of Ward 6 approved the bond issue; Tangipahoa Parish constructed a parking lot on the plant site at a cost of $30,000; the state of Louisiana funded an 8-month worker-training program at a cost of $30,000 and provided a training facility (the rental on the facility, $1,250 per month, was borne by the state); and the Federal Power Commission agreed to allow Kellwood to use natural gas as a source of energy.

Kellwood agreed to provide the necessary manufacturing equipment to be used in production operations and to purchase water and sewage services from the city. In addition, the company signed a 20-year lease on the building.

Construction of the new facility began in April, 1973, and manufacturing operations began January, 1974.

Discussion Questions

1. Evaluate the methods used to persuade a major company to locate a branch plant in a small town.

2. What risks were incurred by the city of Independence? By Kellwood Company?

3. Discuss the responsibilities that the respective parties must assume in future years. What recommendations would you make to small towns which desire to attract industry?

case 16

Southern Recreational
Vehicle Company

In October, 1977, top management of Southern Recreational Vehicle Company of St. Louis, Missouri, announced its plans to relocate its manufacturing and assembly operations by constructing a new plant in Ridgecrest, Mississippi. The firm, a major producer of pickup campers and camper trailers, had experienced five consecutive years of declining profits as a result of spiraling production costs. The costs of labor and raw materials had increased alarmingly; utility costs had gone up sharply; and taxes and transportation expenses had climbed upward steadily. In spite of increased sales, the company suffered its first net loss since operations were begun in 1963.

When management initially considered relocation, they closely scrutinized several geographic areas. Of primary importance to the relocation decision were the availability of adequate transportation facilities, state and municipal tax structures, an adequate labor supply, positive community attitudes, reasonable site costs, and other financial inducements. Although several communities offered essentially the same incentives, the management of Southern Recreational Vehicle Company was favorably impressed by the efforts of the Mississippi Power and Light Company to attract "clean, labor-intensified" industry and the enthusiasm exhibited by state and local officials who actively sought to bolster the state's economy by enticing manufacturing firms to locate within its boundaries.

Two weeks prior to the announcement, management of Southern Recreational Vehicle Company finalized its relocation plans. An existing building in Ridgecrest's industrial park was selected (the physical facility had previously housed a mobile home manufacturer which had gone bankrupt due to inadequate financing and poor management); initial recruiting was begun through the State Employment Office; and efforts to lease or sell the St. Louis property were initiated. Among the inducements offered Southern Recreational Vehicle Company to locate in Ridgecrest were:

1. Exemption from county and municipal taxes for five years
2. Free water and sewage services

3. Construction of a second loading dock — free of cost — at the industrial site
4. An agreement to issue $500,000 in industrial bonds for future expansion
5. Public-financed training of workers in a local industrial trade school.

In addition to these inducements, other factors weighed heavily in the decision to locate in the small Mississippi town. Labor costs would be significantly less than those incured in St. Louis; organized labor was not expected to be as powerful (Mississippi is a right-to-work state); and utility costs and taxes would be moderate. All in all, management of Southern Recreational Vehicle Company felt that its decision was sound.

On October 15, the following announcement was attached to each employee's paycheck:

> To: Employees of Southern Recreational Vehicle Company
> From: Gerald O'Brian, President

The management of Southern Recreational Vehicle Company regretfully announces its plans to cease all manufacturing operations in St. Louis on December 31. Because of increased operating costs and the unreasonable demands forced upon the company by the union, it has become impossible to operate profitably. I sincerely appreciate the fine service which each of you has rendered to the company during the past few years. If I can be of assistance in helping you find suitable employment with another firm, please let me know. Thank you, again, for your cooperation and past service.

Discussion Questions

1. Evaluate the inducements offered Southern Recreational Vehicle Company by community leaders in Ridgecrest, Mississippi.

2. What problems would a company experience in relocating its executives from a heavily populated, industrialized area to a small, rural town?

3. Evaluate the reasons cited by Mr. O'Brian for relocation. Are they justifiable?

4. What responsibilities does a firm have to its employees when a decision to cease operations is made?

Jack's
Cookie Corporation

In October, 1973, Jack's Cookie Corporation employed Slaughter, Martin and Associates, a management consulting firm, to conduct a study to determine the most feasible and profitable use of its land and buildings in Baton Rouge, Louisiana. Two tracts of land on which a 55,000 sq ft warehouse, a 3,720 sq ft maintenance shed, and a 3,100 sq ft office facility were affixed were vacated when the company transferred its operations from Baton Rouge to Charlotte, North Carolina. One tract of land, comprising 6.09 acres, was virtually undeveloped. A smaller tract, on which the buildings are located, had significant improvements, some of which dated back twenty-five years. Figures 3–1 and 3–2 show the tracts of land, including buildings, and the surrounding areas.

Figure 3–1   *Riverside North and Choctaw Road*

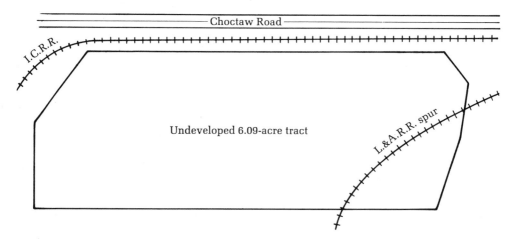

To determine the most profitable use or disposition of the property, Slaughter, Martin and Associates needed information regarding provisions for area improvements, the existing worth of the Jack's Cookie Corporation property, and possible utilization alternatives.

Figure 3–2   *2266 Riverside North*

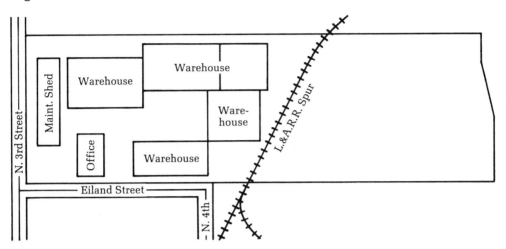

To ascertain whether or not area improvements were being planned, the management consultants interviewed officials of the Capitol Region Planning Commission, City-Parish Planning Commission, Baton Rouge Port Authority, Riverside Association, and the Governor's office of State Planning. All these organizations generally agreed that no plans or provisions existed for immediate area improvements. The representative of the City-Parish Planning Commission, however, stated that an industrial warehousing development had been discussed in long-range planning sessions.

The market value of the undeveloped property was estimated to be about $1.20 per sq ft. Improvements were estimated at $267,500. Total valuation of both tracts of land, including buildings, was $948,446. Estimates were based on the selling prices of similar tracts of property in the area. (The warehouse was appraised at $4 per sq ft, the maintenance shed at $5 per sq ft, and the office space at $10 per sq ft.) Location, visibility, size, frontage, and overall appeal were considered in making the estimates. Replacement costs were not considered.

One potential use of the property was for public warehousing. To generate information about the economic feasibility of the option, a survey of warehouse owners and users in the Greater Baton Rouge area was conducted. The purposes of the survey were to assess the existing and future supply and demand for warehousing space, to determine prevailing storage prices, and to pinpoint the service needed by users and offered by owners of public warehouses.

Discount houses, furniture stores, and other types of retailers typically own their own warehousing facilities; consequently, only manufacturing firms were contacted regarding their need for public warehousing space.

Managers of the traffic, purchasing, or operations divisions of over 100 manufacturing firms in a five-parish (county) area were interviewed. These interviews revealed that eight manufacturers in the Greater Baton Rouge area make extensive use of public warehousing.[1] Table 3–1 shows the space needed, the prices paid, and the warehouse(s) used by these eight firms.

Table 3–1   *Manufacturers Using Public Warehouses in Greater Baton Rouge Area*

Manufacturer	Space Used	Price/Year	Warehouse Used
Allied Chemical— Plastics Division	60,000 sq ft	$1/sq ft	Agway
CIBA Geigy	10M lb	NA*	NA*
Copolymer Rubber and Chemical	100,000 sq ft	NA	Comet, Garig
Dow Chemical	115,000 sq ft	NA	Garig
Ethyl Corp.	60,000 sq ft	$1/sq ft	Garig
Exxon—Chemical Division	400,000 sq ft	Averages 15¢/hundredweight	Wilson (primary) Agway, C & A Comet
Exxon—Plastics Division	2.5M lb	NA	C & A
Goodyear Tire and Rubber	10,000 sq ft	NA	NA
Uniroyal-Geismar	40,000 sq ft	7.5¢/hundredweight	Comet

*Information was considered confidential or was not available.

These manufacturers were optimistic about the potential for public warehousing in the Baton Rouge area. Most of the managers interviewed invited anyone constructing new warehouse space to contact them and submit a price for negotiation or bid.

Interviews with warehouse owners centered around available storage space, pricing policies, and services provided. Public warehouses store two broad categories of goods — household and industrial. Table 3–2 depicts the total space available for storing household goods in the Baton Rouge area.

In addition to the public warehouses that provide storage for household goods, seven commercial warehouses in the Greater Baton Rouge area provide space and services associated with the housing and handling of indus-

---

[1]All eight firms are highly dependent on warehouses. Typically, the warehouser picks up the product(s) from the manufacturer and transports it by rail or truck to its storage facility and ultimately distributes the product to the manufacturer's customers. Service, coupled with price, are the major determinants of warehouse patronage.

trial goods. Table 3–3 lists these industrial goods warehouses and shows the available storage space and planned expansions.

Table 3–2

Warehouse	Total Sq Ft	Committed	Planned Expansion (Sq Ft)
Herrin	75,000	75%	0
All Services	25,000	90%	40,000[2]
AAA	12,000	100%	3,500
Sexton[3]	8,000	50%	0[4]
A-1 Movers	10,000	50%	0
Security Van Lines	15,000	50%	0

Table 3–3   *Industrial Goods Warehouses in Greater Baton Rouge Area*

Warehouse	Total Sq Ft	Committed	Planned Expansion (Sq Ft)
Comet Distributors	100,000	100%	40,000
Garig Warehouse	500,000	100%	*5
C & A Warehouse	50,000	100%	0
Wilson Warehouse	380,000	99%	0
Agway Storage	205,000	75%	75,000
Wells Warehouse	*6	100%	40,000
Baton Rouge Terminals	*7		

[2]All Services was seeking industrial storage. Although the bulk of its work is in household goods, the owner seemed eager to discuss industrial goods storage.

[3]Sexton Transfer and Storage specializes in the moving and storage of electronic equipment.

[4]Sexton Transfer and Storage was actively seeking warehouse space and wanted to talk to Slaughter and Martin's "client" if additional warehouse space were made available Tommy Stiles, manager, indicated a willingness to lease space in client's warehouse if the warehouse facilities met his design needs.

[5]Garig Warehouse readily emphasized that it had seven acres of cleared land and was willing to build as soon as a client would sign a long-term lease.

[6]Wells Warehouse did not disclose this information. A general impression generated from the interview was that the total storage space is in the 200,000 to 400,000 sq ft range.

[7]Baton Rouge Terminals does not seem to want long-term storage. It emphasized that its job is loading and unloading ships, barges, and railroad cars with the idea of quickly moving the materials out of its warehouses.

Two other local warehouses do not fall into the normal classification for warehouse storage. Baton Rouge Automotive Warehouse is a wholesaler for automotive parts, with limited storage space. More notably, G. N. Gonzales Warehouse, which the owner contends is a private rather than a public warehouse, has 500,000 sq ft of covered storage for automobiles, bicycles, motorcycles, and outboard motors. Gonzales Motors acts as a distributor for most of these products.

The pricing policies of public warehouses for both household and industrial goods are presented in Tables 3–4 and 3–5.

Table 3–4   *Pricing Policies of Household Goods Warehouses in Greater Baton Rouge Area*

Warehouse	Cost Per Sq Ft
Herrin	10¢–12¢ per month, depending on volume
All Services	15¢ per month
AAA	$1 per year for large volume users, otherwise 12¢–15¢ per month
Sexton	$25–$30 per month for a 12' x 12' bay
A-1 Movers	12¢ per month

Table 3–5   *Pricing Policies of Household Goods Warehouses in Greater Baton Rouge Area*

Warehouse	Cost Per Sq Ft
Wells	For 5,000 sq ft—$1.25–$1.50 per year
Comet Distributors	12¢ per sq ft per month
Garig Warehouse[8]	89¢–$1 per year for large customers (avoids small customers)
C & A Warehouse	10¢ per month
Wilson Warehouse	About 15¢ per month[9]
Agway	$1.00–$1.50 per year, depending on total area used and the density of material

There are two methods for determining the prices charged by commercial warehouses for storage. One is on the basis of sq ft used, and the other is on the basis of hundredweight (100 pounds of storage). Prices can be quoted

---

[8]Although Garig had 500,000 sq ft of storage, seven additional acres of land were available for future expansion.

[9]During the interview, the manager of Wilson gave the general impression that his price could easily be adjusted to a 10¢–12¢ range for a very large customer.

either way, but the two methods are actually interrelated. Prices by sq ft used are straightforward, such as 10¢ per sq ft per month. The prices may be constant or may diminish as one uses more space, a longer time of storage, or a particular material. Generally, price is a function of weight and/or storage area and/or the length of the contract. Most warehouses that handle household goods, however, do not quote discounts, since they have few volume customers. (Nearly all the warehouse managers contacted mentioned a minimum usage, such as a 4′ × 12′ bin for household goods or 600 sq ft for palletized industrial products.)

Hundredweight pricing is frequently used for industrial products, and the prices vary according to the density of the material stored. For example, Uniroyal at Geismar pays 5¹/₂ cents per hundredweight per month on palletized materials of very low density.

To calculate hundredweight prices, the amount of storage space a material of a particular density will take is determined. Using this information, one calculates a storage cost per hundredweight. Beyond this, a 14-cent to 15-cent nonrecurring charge per hundredweight for handling is added. Since hundredweight prices are generally used in conjunction with leased storage, the approximate time that the materials will stay in the warehouse is known, and the handling charge is prorated over the expected period of storage.

In addition to the availability of storage space and the pricing policies of warehouses in the area, the interviews generated some other pertinent information. Most of the managers of industrial goods warehouses emphasized that they were operating at near-capacity levels and expected their businesses either to continue at the same level or to grow. Owners of firms planning expansion felt confident that they could easily fill the additional space. Wells Warehouse and Garig Warehouse emphasized that they would build necessary storage space if a client would commit himself to a long-term contract. Garig, in particular, pointed out that its long-range plans were to construct storage facilities on a seven-acre tract of land owned by the company.

The industrial storage warehouses are generally congregated in the downtown Baton Rouge area, close to both the interstate highway and the Baton Rouge port, but none of the firms emphasized this location as a selling point. In the interviews, managers and owners gave the impression that price and service are their primary competitive weapons.

The services offered by the warehouses are essentially similar. Every warehouse has a rail spur and loading docks for both rail cars and trucks. In fact, most of the warehouses serve as distribution centers and are in direct contact with their client's customers (referred to as *drop shipping*). In addition, all of the warehouses could arrange insurance for the users of their space, but none included insurance in their quoted prices. Finally, all of the warehouses have available freight-handling equipment to move either pallets or drums. Baton Rouge Terminals (also called Ramsey-Scarlet Contracting Stevedores) has direct access to the Mississippi River as well as to rail and motor modes of transport.

Discussion Questions

1. Based on the information provided, should Jack's Cookie Corporation give further consideration to public warehousing as an alternative use of its property?

2. What additional information is needed by Jack's Cookie Corporation in order to make a sound decision regarding the use and/or disposition of its property? How would profitability estimates be developed?

3. Discuss the effect of economic cyclical fluctuations on warehousing utilization.

4. Jack's Cookie Corporation could build approximately 300,000 sq ft of additional warehouse space on its property (based on an average of 30,000 sq ft per acre). Revenue from this space is estimated to be $2 per sq ft. As a management consultant, advise Jack's Cookie Corporation on the most profitable use and/or disposition of its property. How would Jack's investment criteria affect your decision?

Trident Valve & Manufacturing Corporation

On July 3, 1977, R. J. Northridge, President and Chief Executive Officer of Trident Valve & Manufacturing Corporation, was reviewing the financial statements of his company's operations for the fiscal year which had ended June 30. These financial data revealed that Trident was becoming one of the fastest growing valve manufacturers in the country. Presently, the firm manufactured a complete line of both pressure-seal and mechanical-seal valves, ranging in size from 2″ to 36″ and having pressure capacities of 250 psi to 6,000 psi. (Illustrations of Trident's two-piece and three-piece ball valves are presented in Figures 3–3 and 3–4. Included are material specifications for each component part.) These valves are commonly used in gas transmission, pipeline production, and a variety of other industrial operations.

Practically every major company engaged in the producing, refining, and transporting of oil, gas, and chemicals is a customer of Trident. Its valves are widely used because their sealing elements are suitable for handling practically all liquids and gases, including aromatic hydrocarbons, acids, metals, alkalies, and solvents. Also, with proper metals, the valves are suitable for use throughout a temperature range of $-60°$ to $+450°$ F.

The major purchasers of Trident valves are petroleum exploration firms which operate both within and outside the continental United States. Due to the demand for fossil fuels and the resulting surge of exploration activities by these petroleum companies, 1977 had been Trident's most successful year ever. Revenues reached an all-time high, profits had increased by 60 percent over the previous year; and Trident's market share had improved slightly. The demand for high-pressure valves had necessitated the employment of additional engineering and operating personnel and the conversion to around-the-clock manufacturing operations. Even so, Trident had been unable to meet the demand for its product and had accumulated a backlog of orders. This backlog was expected to grow unless manufacturing capabilities were physically expanded or unless demand declined.

Beneath the financial statements on Northridge's desk was a purchase requisition for a high-speed, computer-controlled lathe which, in the opinion

Figure 3–3

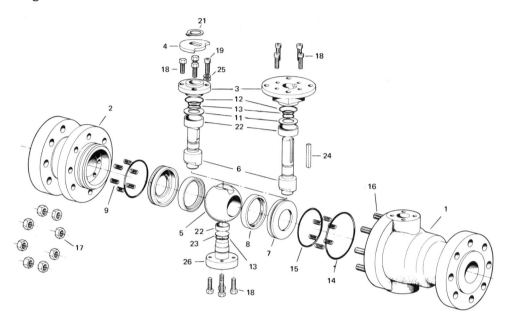

TWO PIECE BALL VALVE 2″ thru 4″

Special trim and body materials available for extremely low temperature service and high temperature service to 400°F. Trim available in 316 Stainless Steel and Electroless Nickel plating (Nye-Kote) as well as other materials for all service applications.

ITEM	QUAN.	PART DESCRIPTION	STANDARD TRIM	ITEM	QUAN.	PART DESCRIPTION	STANDARD TRIM
1	1	Body	Steel ASTM A-216 Grade WCB	14	1	O-Ring	Buna "N"
2	1	Adapter	Steel ASTM A-216 Grade WCB	15	2	O-Ring	Buna "N"
3	1	Bonnet	Steel ASTM A-216 Grade WCB	16	16	Stud	Steel ASTM A-193 Grade B7
4	1 *	Stop Plate	Aluminum-Bronze ASTM B-30-50-9A	17	16	Nut	Steel ASTM A-194 Grade 2
5	1	Ball	ASTM A216 WCB	18	7*	Bolt	Steel ASTM A-193 Grade B7
6	1	Stem	Steel Type AISI 4140 Heat Treated	19	1*	Stop	Steel AISI 4140 Heat Treated
7	2	Seat Holder	Steel AISI 8620	20	1*	Vent Plug	Alloy Steel-Heat Treated
8	2	Seat	Nylon	21	1*	Retaining Ring	Spring Steel SAE 1075 Parkerized
9	12	Spring	Stainless Steel Type 302	22	1	Bushing	Polytetrafluoroethylene with Steel Backing (TFE)
10	1*	Wrench	Cast Steel and Steel Tubing	23	1	Thrust Washer	Polytetrafluoroethylene with Steel Backing (TFE)
11	1	Thrust Bearing Stem	Polytetrafluoroethylene with Steel Backing (TFE)	24	1*	Key	Steel AISI 4140 Heat Treated
12	1	O-Ring	Buna "N"	25	2*	Stop Spacer	Mild Steel
13	3	O-Ring	Buna "N"	26	1	Trunnion	Steel AISI 4140 Heat Treated

* Item 4 needed on Lever Operated Valve only
* Item 10 not shown
* Item 18 only 4 needed on gear operated valves
* Item 19 only 4 needed on gear operated valves

* Item 20 not shown
* Item 21 Lever operated valve only
* Item 24 Gear operated valve only
* Item 25 Lever operated valve only

of the General Production Manager, Ralph Taft, was needed to assure Trident of its continued growth in the valve manufacturing industry. The

Figure 3–4

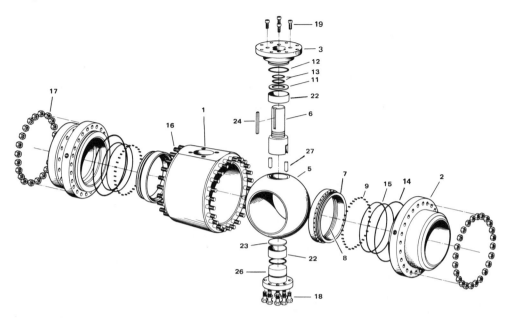

THREE PIECE BALL VALVE 6" thru 36"

ITEM	QUAN.	PART DESCRIPTION	STANDARD TRIM −20° F TO 180° F	ITEM	QUAN.	PART DESCRIPTION	STANDARD TRIM −20° F TO 180° F
1	1	Body	ASTM - A105 - II	16	48	Studs	ASTM - A193 Grade B7
2	2	Adapter	ASTM - A216 - WCB ASTM-A105-11	17	48	Nuts	ASTM - A194 Grade B2
3	1	Bonnet	AISI 4140 HT				
4	1	NA	NA	18	8	Bolt	ASTM - A193 Grade B7
5	1	Ball	ASTM - A105 - II Nye - Kote	19	4 or 8	Allen Screw	Alloy Steel
6	1	Stem	AISI - 4140 - HT	20		NA	NA
7	2	Seat Holder	ASTM - A105 - II Steel AISI - 8620	21		NA	NA
				22	2	Bearing	TFE
8	2	Seat	Nylon	23	1	Thrust Bearing Trun.	TFE
9	60	Spring	302 ST. ST.				
10		NA	NA	24	1	Key	AISI - 4140 - HT
11	1	Thrust Bearing Stem	TFE	25		NA	NA
				26	1	Trunnion	AISI - 4140 - HT
12	1	"O" ring Bon.	Buna-N	27	2	Dowel Pin	Alloy Steel
13	3	"O" ring Tr. & Stem	Buna-N	28	2*	Check Valve	Alloy Steel
14	2	"O" ring Adap.	Buna-N	29	4*	Grease Fitting	Alloy Steel
15	4	"O" ring Seat Holder	Buna-N	30	2*	Body Bleed Plug	Alloy Steel HT

<small>* Item 28 not shown   *Item 29 not shown   * Item 30 not shown</small>

purchase of this $200,000 piece of equipment would enable Trident to eliminate the backlog of orders and to expand its production efforts. A failure to buy the lathe, Taft contended, would ultimately result in a loss of customers and a corresponding decline in profits. Success in valve manufacturing, he asserted, is a function of prompt delivery, competitive pricing, and quality materials. Delayed deliveries would result in cancellations of orders, irate customers, and a bad corporate image.

Prior to his approving a $200,000 expenditure of funds for the high-speed lathe, however, Northridge wanted additional information which would influence his decision. Company policy governing capital budgeting decisions required a rejection of any proposed investment in manufacturing equipment having a payoff period which exceeded five years. In order to ascertain the economic feasibility of purchasing the lathe, a cash flow statement was required. (Table 3–6 shows the projected cash flows from a $200,000 investment outlay with 10-year life and straight-line depreciation, as computed by John Truax, financial analyst for the corporate division.)

Following a brief analysis of the projected cash flow statement, Northridge sent the following note, attached to the purchase requisition, and a copy of the cash flow statement to Ralph Taft:

> Due to the uncertainties surrounding technological innovations and future demand for our product, corporate policy requires that all investments in machinery be recovered within five years from date of purchase. At this time, such an investment would create a financial strain due to our cash-short situation. Requisition is herewith voided. Please consider other alternatives.

After carefully reading the note which rejected the request for the purchase of the lathe, Taft asked for a private meeting with Northridge in order to present "additional data which would support his contention that such an investment was in the best interest of the company and was economically sound."

During the meeting with Northridge, Taft argued that the payback method used as a basis for accepting or rejecting the expenditure of funds was inappropriate. His argument was based on the following logic:

1. Payback ignores the time value of money.
2. It does not consider cash flows over the project's entire life. Once payback has occurred, subsequent flows are ignored.
3. The cost of capital is not considered.
4. Payback is not a measure of profitability; it is a measure of the speed of capital recovery.

Finally, Taft stated that cash flow estimates should not be viewed too precisely. If a 10 percent error factor had been included in the predictions, the equipment expenditure would have been acceptable. He further suggested that the decision be postponed until the financial analysts could compute various rates of return on the proposed investment.

Table 3–6 Expected Cash Flow 1976–1985

	1977	1978	1979	1980	1981	1982	1983	1984	1985	1986
Earnings Before Interest, Depreciation, and Taxes*	45,000	45,000	50,000	50,000	60,000	50,000	45,000	40,000	40,000	35,000
Less: Interest on Bonds	5,000	5,000	5,000	5,000	5,000	5,000	5,000	5,000	5,000	5,000
Less: Depreciation	20,000	20,000	20,000	20,000	20,000	20,000	20,000	20,000	20,000	20,000
Earnings Before Taxes	20,000	20,000	25,000	25,000	35,000	25,000	20,000	15,000	15,000	10,000
Less: Taxes (50%)	10,000	10,000	12,500	12,500	17,500	12,500	10,000	7,500	7,500	5,000
Earnings After Taxes	10,000	10,000	12,500	12,500	17,500	12,500	10,000	7,500	7,500	5,000
Add: Depreciation and Interest on Bonds	25,000	25,000	25,000	25,000	25,000	25,000	25,000	25,000	25,000	25,000
CASH FLOW	35,000	35,000	37,500	37,500	42,500	37,500	35,000	32,500	32,500	30,000

Note: As presented in this table, cash flow is the sum total of cash which an investment returns to replace the cash outlay and to pay a reward to the equity and debt capital providers for use of their money.

*Cash flows are generated through increased production and sales, reductions in waste, lower maintenance costs, and fewer down-times.

The next morning, additional financial data which Taft requested were forwarded to Northridge. The following estimates of profitability, complete with notations and mathematical formulas, were included:

Table 3–7   *Proposed $200,000 Expenditure of Funds for Lathe*

(1)	Average Rate of Return After Taxes on Average Investment	$=$	$\dfrac{\text{Average Income After Taxes}}{\text{Original Outlay}/2}$
	Average Rate of Return	$=$	$\dfrac{\$\,10,000}{\$100,000}$
	Average Rate of Return	$=$	10.5 percent
	Average Rate of Return Before Taxes on Average Investment	$=$	$\dfrac{\text{Average Income Before Taxes}}{\text{Original Outlay}/2}$
	Average Rate of Return	$=$	$\dfrac{\$\,21,000}{\$100,000}$
	Average Rate of Return	$=$	21 percent
	Average Rate of Return After Taxes on Total Investment	$=$	$\dfrac{\text{Average Income After Taxes}}{\text{Original Outlay}}$
	Average Rate of Return	$=$	$\dfrac{\$\,10,500}{\$200,000}$
	Average Rate of Return	$=$	5.25 percent
	Average Rate of Return Before Taxes on Total Investment	$=$	$\dfrac{\text{Average Income Before Taxes}}{\text{Original Outlay}}$
	Average Rate of Return	$=$	$\dfrac{\$\,21,000}{\$200,000}$
	Average Rate of Return	$=$	10.5 percent

Northridge immediately recognized that the average rate of return method incorporated shortcomings identical to those of the payback method — the time value of money and cost of capital were ignored. The average rate of return method, however, included returns over the entire life of the project. After making a mental notation of these similarities and differences, Northridge proceeded to the following caculations and notation:

(2)   Internal Rate of Return[1]: $PV = \displaystyle\sum_{i=1}^{n} \dfrac{CF_t}{(1 + k)^i}$

where

PV = present value of project outlay
CF = each cash flow

---

[1]Sometimes called the *marginal efficiency of capital*, a project's *internal rate of return* is the discount rate that equates the present value of its cash inflows (returns) with its cash outflows (outlays).

$$k = \text{internal rate of return}$$
$$i = \text{year in which each flow occurs}$$
$$n = \text{life of project in years}$$
$$t = \text{each year}$$

Mathematically, the internal rate of return (k) can be solved by using the following equation:

$$\$200,000 = \frac{35,000}{(1+k)^1} + \frac{35,000}{(1+k)^2} + \frac{37,500}{(1+k)^3} + \frac{37,500}{(1+k)^4} + \frac{42,500}{(1+k)^5} +$$

$$\frac{37,500}{(1+k)^6} + \frac{35,000}{(1+k)^7} + \frac{32,500}{(1+k)^8} + \frac{32,500}{(1+k)^9} + \frac{30,000}{(1+k)^{10}}$$

However, one can obtain the same answer more readily by using present value tables which show the present value of future inflows of cash.

Table 3-8 shows the use of present value data as they apply to the proposed $200,000 expenditure of funds for the high-speed lathe.

Table 3-8

Year	Cash Flow	CF (k = 12%)	Present Value	CF (k = 13%)	Present Value
1977	$35,000	.893	$ 31,255.00	.885	$ 30,975.00
1978	35,000	.797	27,895.00	.783	27,405.00
1979	37,500	.712	26,700.00	.693	25,987.50
1980	37,500	.636	23,850.00	.613	22,987.50
1981	42,500	.567	24,097.50	.543	23,077.50
1982	37,500	.507	19,012.50	.480	18,000.00
1983	35,000	.452	15,820.00	.425	14,875.00
1984	32,500	.404	13,130.00	.376	12,220.00
1985	32,500	.361	11,732.50	.333	10,822.50
1986	30,000	.322	9,660.00	.295	8,850.00
			$203,152.50		$195,200.00

Interpolation[2]: $\dfrac{\$3,152.50}{\$7,952.50} = 0.4$

Internal Rate of Return $= 12.4$ percent

[2]At 13 percent, the present value of future inflows is $195,200; at 12 percent, the present value is $203,152.50. The difference is $7,952.50. From the higher *PV* figure (calculated at 12 percent), the internal rate of return must be increased by 0.4 percent (i.e., $3,152.50/ $7,952.50).

(3) Net Present Value = Present Value of Inflows — Present Value of Outlays. The present value of cash inflows discounted at 10 percent[3] is presented in Table 3-9.

Table 3-9

Year	Cash Flow	CF (k = 10%)	Present Value
1977	$35,000	.909	$ 31,815.00
1978	35,000	.826	28,910.00
1979	37,500	.751	28,162.50
1980	37,500	.683	25,612.50
1981	42,500	.621	26,392.50
1982	37,500	.564	21,150.00
1983	35,000	.513	17,955.00
1984	32,500	.467	15,177.50
1985	32,500	.424	13,780.00
1986	30,000	.386	11,580.00
			$220,535.00

Present Value of Inflows:	$220,535.00
Present Value of Outlays:	−200,000.00
Net Present Value	$ 20,535.00

Taft's final notation which appeared below the net present value computation was:

As shown by this computation, Trident should be willing to pay up to $220,535 for the lathe. The figure of $20,535 represents the "bargain" the company would obtain if the equipment were purchased for $200,000.

Northridge again analyzed the computations and then pondered his decision.

Discussion Questions

1. Critique the capital budgeting methods presented by the financial analysts of Trident. Which method is most suitable for use in managerial decision making involving the expenditure of funds for plant expansion and/or equipment purchases?

2. What other factors, if any, should be considered before the request to purchase the lathe is approved or rejected? How would these factors affect the decision?

3. What action should Northridge take?

---

[3]Trident's cost of capital has been calculated at 10 percent.

Acadian
Airlines, Inc.

On April 25, 1970, Acadian Airlines, Inc. had been granted a series of Route Awards by the National Transportation Board to expand its short-hop service between primary and secondary air transportation points in Louisiana. The Route Awards were embodied in a 'Certificate of Public Convenience and Necessity,' which is required by the Federal Transportation Regulations before a transportation company can expand or contract its services.

Acadian Airlines was originally formed in Louisiana in 1923 as a combination crop dusting-air mail company. Its operations were profitable during the Great Depression, and by the mid-1960s it had expanded into one of the country's leading airlines with services extending north and south from Philadelphia, Pennsylvania, to Caracas, Venezuela, and east and west from the Pacific to the Atlantic Coasts. The company's operations were noted for being progressive. In 1940, it moved its home office to Atlanta, Georgia, which was the center of the airline industry, and it was always one of the first to adopt the latest methods and equipment. Thus, Acadian Airlines became one of the most profitable companies in the industry, as evidenced by its ability to pay a dividend in the 1962 recession when other companies were unable to do so.

The company's success at the National Transportation Board hearings, which had begun in 1964 when the company had filed an application to expand its services between Louisiana cities, was primarily due to the increased popularity of jet air transportation. The commercial jet which virtually all large airlines now operate is noted for being the fastest, safest, and most comfortable passenger plane ever devoted to public service. The problem with its use, however, is its requirement for long runways and large airport facilities, such as hangar and loading space. Because of the lack of space at some of the smaller airports and lack of funds with which to expand, many of these smaller airports were unable to accommodate large jet aircraft. As a result, numerous cities were without jet service, and airlines forfeited revenues to companies with propeller-driven aircraft. Aircraft manufacturers, of course, were aware of the problem. By 1964, two manufacturers had introduced smaller jets designed for short hops which were able to operate on the same size runways as the conventional propeller aircrafts. It was on the basis of Acadian Airlines' proposal to provide jet service to smaller Louisiana airports (which had previously not had jet service) that the Route Awards were granted. These awards were subject to certain limitations, including rates and the number and time of flights between the five designated cities.

Since it had been granted an exclusive right to extend this service, Acadian Airlines was confronted with the type of airplane to purchase. As a public transportation company, its rates were regulated by the National Transportation Board, which coordinated the rates and services of all domestic (U.S.) commercial transportation companies. As a result, the company's revenue was strictly limited. It couldn't lower the rates to gain business or raise the rates later to cover a loss without the Board's special permission. The rate schedule, once approved, would have to be adhered to exactly. For this reason, it was essential for the company to make the proper decision about equipment.

The company evaluated several aircraft to determine which would provide the largest present value of net cash flows (its standard selection guide). Each airplane under consideration was estimated to have a life of five years for airline service before becoming technically obsolete as competitive equipment. The resale value to minor airlines was estimated at one-third of the original purchase price. The aircraft under consideration were the CD 9 in both the 70- and 89-passenger model and the Fair Turbo-prop. The CD 9 is a small two-engine jet capable of landing and taking off in relatively small spaces while carrying a good pay load. The 70-passenger model sells for $3 million, and the 89-passenger model sells for $3.5 million. The Fair Turbo-prop is a well-known British-designed plane in which the technical characteristics can best be described as a jet power driven propeller model which combines the low fuel cost of (kerosene rather than gasoline) the jet engine with the handling characteristics of the propeller models. These airplanes cost $2.5 million and are capable of carrying 55 passengers. Although the Turbo-prop is technically a jet in fulfilling the Certificate requirements, it does not possess the same speed as the jet.

Costs of operating the three planes differ considerably, too. Fuel consumption on the CD 9 is 600 gallons of kerosene per hour as compared with the Turbo-prop's 400 gallons per hour. In 1970, kerosene cost Acadian Airlines $0.11 per gallon. Captain's pay on the CD 9 was $0.5633 per minute; and captain's pay on the Turbo-prop, $0.466 per minute. Co-pilot's pay on the CD 9 was $0.375 per minute as compared to $0.308 per minute on Turbo-prop. (Federal law allows a pilot to fly only 75 hours per month.) A flight attendant's pay ran $500 per month on the CD 9 and about $400 on the Turbo-prop, with a limit of 85 hours per month. On the CD 9 70-passenger and the Turbo-prop planes, the number of required crew members is one captain, one co-pilot, and two flight attendants. On the 89-passenger CD 9, an additional flight attendant is required. Crew expenses included meals and hotel fees of $21 per day when flight attendants were required to spend the night away from home. The training costs for the CD 9's crew were $10,000 per captain, $5,000 per co-pilot, and $400 per flight attendant. Training costs for the Turbo-prop were $7,000 per captain, $3,000 per co-pilot, and $300 per flight attendant. (These costs were based on the assumption that qualified pilots would be trained to fly particular airplanes, and not on the basis of training new pilots.)

Estimated maintenance cost is approximately one-fourth of the purchase price of an airplane per year. This estimate is based on past experiences and manufacturers' statistics. The average life of a set of tires is only a few landings because they hit the concrete at about 175–200 knots (100 knots equal 115 mph). In addition, the oil must be changed every eight hours of operational time. (Each engine holds $5^1/_2$ gallons of oil at a cost of $2.50 per quart.) Included in the estimated maintenance cost is the maintenance staff which must be on duty 24 hours per day at the New Orleans airport. This necessitates four crews, one of which is a reserve unit sent to smaller fields to make repairs where it is not economically sound to set up a repair station. Maintenance training is included in the purchase price of the airplane and is provided by the manufacturer in special schools.

The service equipment required on the Turbo-prop includes a special converter for the electric current of the ground power from A/C to the airplane's D/C current to be used to start the engines at each station. Since a plane must shut off its wing engines while loading and unloading, one power converter is required at each base. Converters for the Turbo-prop cost $20,000 each. (Due to the technical conditions of operation, only one type converter can be used.) The Turbo-prop also requires the use of proper-height, motorized, movable passenger stairs which cost $5,000 each. One set of these stairs is required at each base served by the plane. Although the CD 9 is the more expensive plane, it has the distinctive feature of being a completely self-contained unit. No special service equipment is required. The CD 9 has a special jet-driven generator in the tail section, which eliminates the need for ground power and thus for a converter for starting. Since it also carries its own light-weight, telescoping stairway, no ground units are required.

In consideration of other airport facilities, equipment hangars, offices, ticket counter space, cargo carriers, and station personnel, the company felt that its existing facilities and employees were adequate to handle the increased number of flights per day. An analysis revealed that these costs would be the same in either case, so the company decided to apply a percentage of the total operating cost of each station in the system to the cost calculations of each plane. (See Table 3-21 for estimates.) The company estimated from previous experience with propeller-driven airplanes in the same service area that the load factor (number of passengers to total passenger capacity) would average 95 percent Monday and Friday, 75 percent Saturday and Sunday, and 55 percent Tuesday, Wednesday, and Thursday on the 70-passenger CD 9. On the 89-passenger model, the load factor would run about 90 percent Monday and Friday, 70 percent Saturday and Sunday, and 50 percent on Tuesday, Wednesday, and Thursday. On the Turbo-prop, the load factor was expected to run at 100 percent on Monday and Friday, 85 percent on Saturday and Sunday, and about 65 percent on Tuesday, Wednesday, and Thursday.

The Route Award required Acadian Airlines to provide four flights per day to each city; early morning, late afternoon, early evening, and late night flights were mandatory. The exact time tables for the flights were to be worked out by the company and the Board after the company has decided upon the type of equipment to place into service. The engineering department estimated that the company would have to purchase three additional CD 9's to operate 12 air/hours per day operating at an airspeed of 550 knots per hour or 5 Turbo-props to operate at 14 air/hours per day with an airspeed of 350 knots per hour in order to provide the additional service required in the award.[1] (An air/hour is the basic unit for airline cost and pay calculations. It refers to actual time in the air.) The 'Certificate of Public Convenience and Necessity' provided that if the company was unable to fill the service requirement, the part unfilled could be awarded to another airline.

The preceding data, along with Tables 3-10 through 3-21 from the Engineering Department and the Legal Department, were transmitted to the Finance Department so that the requested schedules and estimates could be prepared. The Board of Directors could then evaluate the proposed equipment alternatives in terms of present value of the cash flow. The company used a cost of capital factor of 8 percent in its calculations.[2]

Discussion Questions

1. Compute the net present value for each model of aircraft under consideration.

2. Which, if any, of the airplanes satisfies the company's investment criterion?

---

[1]Loading, unloading, and changing altitudes are more time consuming on Turbo-props than on jets.

[2]An 8 percent return on the rate base (equipment plus cost of service) is the maximum allowable return in total company operations.

Table 3–10 *Projected Revenues from Operations (based on established rates and estimated load factors)*

	CD 9 89-Pass.	CD 9 70-Pass.	Turbo-prop
Passenger Service Revenues[1] (weekly)	$ 82,659	$ 74,439	$ 49,724
Freight Revenues[2] (weekly)	41,330	37,219	24,862
Air Mail Revenues[3] (weekly)	1,250	1,250	1,250
TOTAL ESTIMATED WEEKLY REVENUES	$ 125,239	$ 112,908	$ 75,836
TOTAL ESTIMATED ANNUAL REVENUES	$6,512,428	$5,871,216	$3,943,472

Table 3–11 *Comparison in Terms of Purchase Price and Depreciation Charges (Assuming straight-line depreciation and one-third resale value at the end of 5 years) (in 1,000's)*

Airplane	Price	Salvage Value	Accumulated Depreciation	Annual Depreciation
CD 9 70-Passenger Model	3,000	1,000	2,000	400
CD 9 89-Passenger Model	3,500	1,167	2,333	467
Fair Turbo-prop	2,500	834	1,666	333

Table 3-12 *Daily Comparison in Fuel Cost for Required Service*

Plane	Burns per Hour	Number Air/ Hours	Number Planes	Total Daily Consumption	Cost per Gallon	Daily Fuel Cost
CD 9	600	12	3	21,600	$0.11	2,376
Turbo-prop	400	14	5	28,000	$0.11	3,080

[1]Cities to be served with four flights daily from New Orleans were Baton Rouge, Shreveport, Alexandria, and Lake Charles.

[2]Air Cargo rates vary with the commodity and its characteristics. Generally, air cargo rates tend to average one-half passenger revenues.

[3]The contract established with the U. S. government was for $250 per city/per week, regardless of volume.

Table 3–13   *Crew Required per Month on the CD 9 70- and 89-Passenger Models*

Air/Hours per Day	12
30-Day Month	30
Air/Hours per Month	360
÷75 (max. captain and copilot time per month)	(4.8) or 5
Crews per month required Captain and Copilot	6
Reserve Crew	1
Crews per Plane	7
Planes in Fleet	× 3
Captain and Copilot Crews Required	21
Air/Hours per Month	360
÷85 (max. flight attendant hours per month)	
Crews per Plane/Month	4¹/₂

CD 9 70-Passenger Model		**CD 9 89-Passenger Model**	
Flight Attendant per Plane	2	Flight Attendant per Plane	3
Crews per Plane	4¹/₂	Crews per Plane	4¹/₂
Flight Attendants/Plane mo.	9	Flight Attendants/Plane mo.	13
Number Planes	3	Number Planes	3
Total Flight Attendants	27	Total Flight Attendants	39

Table 3-14   *Crews Required per Month on the Turbo-prop*

Air/Hours per Day	14
Days per Month	30
Total Air/Hours per Plane per Month	420
÷75 (max. captain and co-pilot time per month)	
Crews per Month Required (captain and co-pilot)	5.6
Reserve Crew	1
Total per Plane	6.6
Number of Planes in Fleet	5
Total Crews Required (captain and co-pilot)	33
Total Air/Hours per Month	420
÷85 (max. flight attendant hours per month)	
Crews Required per Month per Plane	5
Planes in Fleet	5
Total Flight Attendant Crews Required per Month	25

Table 3-15   *Crew Flight Pay Calculations*

Turbo-prop

Captain's Pay

Pay per Hour = $0.466 per Minute × 60	$27.96
Max. Number Hours Can Work	75
Pay per Month	2,097.00

Annual Pay ($\times$ 12)	25,164.00	
Captains Required	$\times$ 33	
Annual Rate		$ 830,412

Co-pilot's Pay

Pay per Hour = $0.308 per Minute $\times$ 60	$18.48	
Max. Number Hours per Month	75	
Pay per Month	1,386	
Annual Pay ($\times$ 12)	16,632	
Total Co-pilots Required	33	
Annual Cost		$ 548,856

Flight Attendant's Pay

Pay per Month	$ 400	
Flight Attendants Required (25 crews $\times$ 2)	50	
Pay per Month	20,000	
Annual Pay ($\times$ 12)		$ 240,000
Total Crew Cost for the Turbo-prop		$1,618,788

CD 9 70-passenger Model

Captain's Pay

Pay per Hour = $0.5633 $\times$ 60	$33.80	
Max. No. Hours per Month	75	
Pay per Month ($\times$ 12)	2,535	
Annual Pay ($\times$ 12)	30,420	
Number Required	$\times$ 21	
Annual Cost		$ 638,820

Co-pilot's Pay

Pay per Hour = $0.375 $\times$ 60	$22.50	
Max. No. Hours per Month	75	
Pay per Month	1,687	
Annual Pay ($\times$ 12)	20,244	
Number Required	21	
Annual Cost		425,124

Flight Attendant Pay

Pay per Month	$500	
Required per Month on 70-passenger Model	27	
Pay per Month	13,500	
Annual Pay ($\times$ 12)		$ 162,000
Total Pay on the 70-passenger Model		$1,225,944

CD 9 89-passenger Model

Total pay on 70-passenger Model		$1,225,944

Additional Flight Attendant Pay

Flight Attendant Pay per Month	$500	
Additional Flight Attendants Required	12	
Monthly Pay	6,000	
Annual Pay ($\times$ 12)		$ 72,000
Total Pay on the 89-passenger Model		$1,297,944

Table 3-16   *Crew Expense Allowance*

(Assumption: Each crew member will spend 10 days per
               month, or $1/3$ month, on expense account.)

CD 9 (3) 70-passenger Model

Captains	21	
Co-pilots	21	
Flight Attendants	27	
TOTAL CREW MEMBERS PER MONTH	69	
Expense Allowance on each at $21.00 per Day $\times$ 10 Days	$ 210	
TOTAL CREW EXPENSES PER MONTH	$14,490	
ANNUAL CREW EXPENSES ($\times$ 12)	$\times$ 12	
		$173,880

CD 9 (3) 89-passenger Model

CD 9 70-passenger Model Expense		$173,880
Additional Flight Attendants Required	12	
Expense Allowance per Month	210	
TOTAL ADDITIONAL ALLOWANCE PER MONTH	$ 2,520	
ANNUAL CREW EXPENSE ($\times$ 12)		$ 30,240
		$204,120

Turbo-prop

Captains	33	
Co-pilots	33	
Flight Attendants	25	
TOTAL CREW MEMBERS PER MONTH	91	
Monthly Crew Allowance	$ 210	
MONTHLY CREW EXPENSE	$19,110	
ANNUAL CREW EXPENSE ($\times$ 12)		$229,320

Table 3-17   *Training Cost of Crew Members**

CD 9 70-passenger Model

Cost per Captain	$10,000	
Number Required (Table 3–13)	21	
Cost		$210,000
Cost per Co-pilot	$ 5,000	
Number Required (Table 3–13)	21	
Cost		$105,000
Cost per Flight Attendant	500	
Number Required (Table 3–13)	27	
Cost		$ 13,500
Crew Training Cost on CD 9 70-passenger		$328,500

*Figures are based on the assumption that the company will train qualified pilots and crews to fly the new airplanes and will not hire new unqualified employees.

CD 9 89-passenger Model

Cost of Crew Training on 70-passenger Model		$328,500
Training Cost per Flight Attendant	500	
Additional Flight Attendants Required	12	
Additional Training Cost		$ 6,000
Crew Training Cost on CD 9 89-passenger		$334,500

Turbo-prop

Cost per Captain	7,000	
Number Required (Table 3–14)	33	
Cost		$231,000
Cost per Co-pilot	3,000	
Number Required (Table 3–14)	33	
Cost		$ 99,000
Cost per Flight Attendant	300	
Number Required (Table 3–14)	25	
Cost		$ 7,500
Crew Training Cost on Turbo-prop		$337,500

Table 3-18 *Maintenance Cost (in '000's)*

Airplane	Price	Maintenance Fraction	Maintenance Cost per year	Number Planes in Fleet	Maintenance Cost
CD 9—70	3,000	1/4	750	3	2,250
CD 9—89	3,500	1/4	875	3	2,625
Turbo-prop	2,500	1/4	625	5	3,125

Table 3-19 *Service Equipment Requirements*

CD 9's

None required; plane is a self-contained unit

Turbo-prop

Power Converter Cost	$20,000	
Number Stations Requiring the Equipment (New Orleans already has one)	× 4	
Total Cost of Converters		$ 80,000
Stairs Cost	5,000	
Number Required (New Orleans has one)	× 4	
Total Cost of Stairs		20,000
TOTAL COST OF SERVICE EQUIPMENT		$100,000

Table 3-20   *Depreciation of Service Equipment*

Assume: Service life is the same as that of the airplane — 5 years with 1/5 salvage value under the straight-line method.

Cost of Equipment	Salvage Value	Balance to Depreciate	Period	Annual Charge
Converters	16,000	64,000	5 yrs.	12,800
Stairs	4,000	16,000	5 yrs.	3,200
TOTALS	20,000	80,000		16,000

Table 3-21   *Proportionate Cost of Airport Facilities*

Station	Monthly Cost	Annual Cost	Fraction Charged	Share of Cost
New Orleans	10,000	120,000	1/20	$ 6,000
Baton Rouge	4,000	48,000	1/5	9,600
Shreveport	7,000	84,000	1/2	42,000
Alexandria	5,000	60,000	1/2	30,000
Lake Charles	3,000	36,000	1/2	18,000
Share of Airport Cost to Allocate to the New Equipment				$105,600

Circle Chemical
Corporation

In February, 1977, Mr. Don Davis, Director of Product Planning for the Inorganic Chemical Division of the Circle Chemical Corporation, was reviewing the manufacture of anhydrous caustic soda at the firm's Wichita, Kansas, plant.[1] Within three weeks, he had to make a recommendation to the President of the Inorganic Chemicals Division concerning the future of this operation at the Wichita location. The president, in turn, would suggest the final disposition of the product to the Board of Directors at the March meeting. The decision was essentially whether to rehabilitate and modernize the existing production facilities or to discontinue the production of anhydrous caustic soda.

Circle Chemical Corporation, founded in 1900, was the result of the merger of three "heavy chemical" companies. These companies, after the merger, remained highly autonomous divisions with a parent corporation exercising only "loose" control. Circle Chemical enjoyed great success from 1900 to 1925 because it owned basic manufacturing patents, had prime locations with regard to markets and raw materials, and was dominant in its product lines. The firm fared quite well during the Great Depression due to its lack of debt. (The firm had virtually no debt because of a low expenditure of funds for research and development.) During World War II, the firm prospered by supplying chemicals to the armed forces.

As more companies entered the "heavy chemical" market after World War II, competition depressed the price for Circle's products. Wages and expenses, however, increased rapidly. Hence, Circle was caught in a cost-price squeeze. In an attempt to diversify its product base, Circle increased its number of divisions to seven through mergers and acquisitions in the early 1960s. Poor control, however, was maintained over these autonomous divisions.

In 1970, the firm moved toward greater centralization. The Chairman of the Board stated that the step toward centralization was to "streamline

---

[1]Anhydrous caustic soda is sold in a flake, ground, or pellet form. It is used primarily as a mud chemical in oil well drilling operations and as a drain cleaner.

management and take advantage of functional economies." The centralized organizational structure reduced the number of divisions back to three — Inorganic, Fertilizers and Plastics, and Consumer Products. To streamline the corporation further and improve profitability, each of the three divisions scrutinized its operations to eliminate unprofitable products. The anhydrous caustic operation was included in this examination.

Anhydrous caustic soda is produced from a 50 percent solution of caustic soda. Historically, anhydrous caustic soda has been produced by evaporating all of the water from a 50 percent solution of caustic soda in huge, gas-heated, cast iron pots. The liquid anhydrous caustic soda is pumped to a water-cooled flaker where it is solidified. The solid matter adheres to the water-cooled flaker drum. Then, it is shaved off the flaker drum to form sheets which are broken up in a mill into particles. The particles pass over a screen which separates them according to size. The product is then packed into bags and drums for shipment. (A portion of the product is fed to a pelletizing tower to form pellets which are also loaded into bags and drums.)

In 1965, the cast iron pots were replaced by a dehydration unit which removes the water from the 50 percent solution in two steps — from 50 percent to 70 percent and from 70 percent to anhydrous, or 100 percent. The first step uses steam heating to concentrate the caustic soda from 50 percent to 70 percent; the second step converts the 70 percent to anhydrous, or 100 percent, through evaporation or dehydration. (A liquid heat transfer material is heated by natural gas to convert the 70 percent to anhydrous caustic soda.) In both steps, the evaporation process is performed under a vacuum to enhance removal of water. This dehydration unit was installed at a cost of $300,000. Primary justification for the unit were large fuel savings and lower maintenance costs.

Although the cast iron pots were discarded, management retained the old flaking material handling facilities that had been installed in 1937. However, several equipment manufacturers had developed new "chilled-type flakers" which discharge flake and ground particles at 120° F. (The old flaker discharges particles at 400° F.) The cooler temperature is very important because the flake from the old flaker could not be packed into bags directly. (At 400° F., the bag liners would melt.) In order to ship the product in bags, the flake had to be stored and cooled in steel drums for two weeks. The drums with the cooled material were dumped in a hopper, which fed the bags. These drums were often bent and damaged in this operation and were eventually discarded. Discarded drums were replaced at a cost of $4 each. On the average, 300 drums were discarded each month.

Moreover, the flake from the old flaker would form lumps upon cooling and would not pour out of the drums easily. (This problem was more acute with the ground product.) Consequently, all the ground product had to be re-milled and re-packed after cooling, which resulted in the discarding of an additional 150 drums per month. Product from the new chilled-type flaker could be packed directly into bags and would not form lumps. Moreover, the particles were more uniform and had a superior color.

As competitors began to install the new chilled-type flaker, Circle's competitive position began to decline. Because the new flaker produced a higher quality product, demand for Circle's anhydrous flake and ground began dropping rapidly. In response to this situation, an investment proposal for $600,000 was prepared to modernize and rehabilitate the anhydrous caustic soda flaking, material handling, and warehousing facilities at Wichita. (The proposal is shown in Table 3-22.) The dehydrator, installed in 1965, had a capacity of 60 tons per day of anhydrous caustic soda. The old flaker had a capacity of only 40 tons per day. The proposed new chilled-type flaker would meet the dehydrator capacity of 60 tons per day so that total production capacity would be increased by 20 tons per day.

Table 3-22 *Proposed Investment. Anhydrous Caustic Soda.*
Rehabilitate Flaking, Handling and Warehousing Facilities

Investment	Cost
Flaking Building Expansion	$110,000
Minor Expansion of Warehouse	8,000
Flaker, Storage Bins, Material Handling, Equipment, etc.	271,000
Power Requirements	29,000
Fork Truck	8,000
Engineering and Construction Overheads	110,000
Contingency	64,000
Total Investment*	$600,000

*Useful life - 10 years
Straight-line depreciation; salvage value - 10 percent

Also included in the proposal was the installation of storage bins to store the material from the new chilled-type flaker, which operates three shifts per day. With the installation of these bins, the product would be packed into bags and drums on the day shift only. The flake from the chilled-type flaker would be 120° F. and could be put directly into bags without melting the liners. Flake and ground can be put into drums without any lumping problems. This procedure would eliminate using drums to store the product while it cooled. Moreover, storage and handling costs would be significantly reduced.

The new proposal included storage racks and conveyors to handle the containers more efficiently. An industrial engineering study was made to determine the manning requirements; the results of the study which compared the existing and proposed facilities are presented in Table 3-23.

The marketing department believed that the demand for anhydrous caustic soda was expanding. This belief was based on the acceleration of oil well

Table 3-23   *Packaging and Shipping Manning Requirement*

	Existing	Proposed
Packagers	16	3
Loaders	13	6
Fork Truck Drivers	1	2

Reduction of manpower on shutdown — 30 Packagers-Shippers
1 Foreman
1 Head Loader

drilling operations and the use of anhydrous caustic soda in drilling mud chemicals. Demand was forecasted at 60 tons per day; forecasted price for anhydrous caustic soda was $100 per ton.

The Wichita plant maintenance department checked the condition of the old flaker and concluded that it was extremely poor. Repairs costing $75,000 were required, or the old flaker would cease operation within six months.

Because of an extreme shortage of investment capital, management of Circle Chemical was reluctant to engage in expansion or modernization programs. Only those projects that would generate a discounted cash flow rate of return of 20 percent or greater were considered. Additional financial and production data are presented in Tables 3-24 and 3-25.

Table 3-24   *Production and Expense Related to Anhydrous Caustic Soda Production*

	Existing	Proposed
Production	14,000 tons/year	21,000 tons/year
Expenses		
Raw Material (50 percent caustic soda) and Treating Agents	$ 40/ton	$ 40/ton
Production Labor	62,000/year	62,000/year
Supplies	14,000	14,000
Maintenance	120,000	120,000
Power	19,000	20,000
Tests and Inspection	23,000	23,000
Plant Administration*	49,000	31,000
Depreciation	42,000	70,000
Taxes	10,000	17,000
Insurance	1,000	2,000
Selling Expense	$ 1.51/ton	$ 1.51/ton

*Reduce due to net reduction of 19 people with new facilities.

Table 3-25   *Miscellaneous Production and Financial Data*

Wage Rate (Packagers and Loaders)	$3.00/hour
Wage Rate (Fork Truck Driver)	$3.50/hour
Wage Rate (Head Loader)	$4.00/hour
Foreman's Salary	$10,000/year
Fringe Benefits (Hourly Paid Employees)	17%
Fringe Benefits (Foreman and Salaried Employees)	20%
Basic Tax Rate (with Investment Credits and Write-offs)	40%
Ratio of Flake Production to Ground Production	3 to 1
Percent Production in Bags (50 pounds)	60%
Percent Production in Drums (400 pounds)	40%
Price of 50-pound bags	$0.50/bag
Price of 400-pound steel drum	$4.00/drum

Discussion Questions

1. What course of action would you recommend for this facility?

2. Cite the factors which have a bearing on the decision.

chapter 4

Maintenance

Wayland Refinery

Al Sparkman, the production superintendent, and Fred Grimes, the maintenance superintendent, of Wayland Refinery, Port Arthur, Texas, were engaged in an ongoing debate over the assignment of evening, night, and weekend maintenance crews. The debate was intensified by the traditional separation or polarization of maintenance and operation departments within a plant. While the two groups worked closely on plant problems, they had parallel line organizations that merged only at the general manager level at the refinery. The general manager delegated a great deal of authority to his departmental superintendents. He expected them to resolve interdepartmental conflicts among themselves. In fact, he became very irritated if conflicts were appealed to him for resolution. Often, the resolution by the general manager was unsatisfactory to both of the conflicting department heads. Hence, they tried earnestly to work out interdepartmental problems without appealing to the general manager.

Departmental Objectives

Attempts at resolution of conflicts were hindered greatly by the objectives established for the production and maintenance departments respectively. Wayland Oil Company has instituted a management-by-objectives (MBO) program, and performance appraisals were subsequently based on the extent to which each individual achieved his or her objectives. Sparkman's objectives were related to production level, yields, power consumption, and general operating costs. Grimes' objectives were based solely on budget and POJ measurements. POJ is "productivity-on-the-job" and is defined as the number of visibly productive observations divided by the total number of observations. The observations are of the maintenance crews throughout the refinery and are taken by industrial engineers. The different maintenance crews have color-coded hard hats to designate their respective group for

POJ determination. A major problem arises because Sparkman's objectives and Grimes' objectives are not necessarily compatible.

Grimes was determined to meet his objectives as established in the MBO program. He religiously monitored direct maintenance spending. Overtime by maintenance personnel had to be approved by Grimes and only after elaborate justification by operating personnel. Often, he chose not to work overtime to repair spare equipment when it was obvious that the main equipment was defective and that a total breakdown and production outage was imminent. His rationale was that the overtime would be worked after the outage occurred, not on a forecast of an outage.

Grimes also controlled direct maintenance spending by assigning maintenance crews to work on capital projects. The capital projects were part of the refinery capital budget; as such, any work performed on capital jobs was charged against the capital budget. Hence, Grimes could reduce his direct labor expense by transferring maintenance crews from routine plant maintenance to the capital projects. The operation department determined maintenance priorities, but Grimes controlled the manpower allocation between capital jobs and routine refinery maintenance.

Grimes' other measure of performance was POJ. He and other maintenance superintendents with Wayland Oil Company were very concerned about POJ measurements. The corporate headquarters circulated a monthly summary sheet of the POJ measurement at all Wayland refineries. Last month, the highest POJ measurement (58 percent) in the company was recorded at the Wayland Refinery at Marcus Hook, Pennsylvania. The lowest was Grimes' department with a measurement of 38 percent. This situation greatly embarrassed Grimes, and he was absolutely determined to improve his POJ rating. He held a meeting of his maintenance supervisors and foremen and heatedly criticized their lack of attention to crew productivity. Furthermore, he cited a lack of planning of maintenance jobs as attested by a high percentage of "forced idle" time waiting on equipment, supplies, and preliminary work to be done by special crafts (for example, electricians must tag out a motor before work could begin on a pump). Finally, Grimes berated the foremen for spending too much time in air-conditioned offices and not enough time in the field supervising their crews.

The maintenance supervisory group countered with a condemnation of the supervision of the shift maintenance personnel. The shift maintenance crew reported to the refinery shift supervisor on duty for the evening, night, and weekend shifts. Maintenance supervision normally worked straight days. The shift supervisors reported to the production superintendent. Selected maintenance supervisors were on call during the weekend but came to the refinery only if a large maintenance problem developed. The criticism of the supervision of shift mechanics stemmed from allegations that shift mechanics were allowed to rest and sleep in maintenance shops unless a breakdown occurred. It was reported that the shift operating supervisor condoned this action because he knew where the crew could be located if a maintenance problem developed and operational problems could be minimized by swift action by the shift mechanics. The maintenance group alleged that the idle shift mechanics were responsible for the low POJ measurement. (POJ measurements did include the shift and weekend mechanics.)

The Issue

After the meeting, Grimes conferred with the industrial engineers who had performed the work sampling. They confirmed the fact that idle shift mechanics could substantially lower POJ measurements, but they could not determine the extent to which it could be lowered. As Grimes went back to his office, he walked into the shift mechanic shop. The evening shift mechanics had been on duty for approximately one hour. All six mechanics were seated around a table playing cards. Grimes quietly asked them if they were on duty. They replied, "Yes, but we haven't gotten any calls yet. It looks like it might be a quiet evening." The next morning Grimes related to Sparkman what had happened the previous afternoon and informed him that he was reassigning all shift mechanics to the regular day shift. All breakdowns on the evening, night, and weekend shifts would be handled on an emergency basis. Overtime would be worked if justified.

Sparkman became very upset over Grimes' announcement. Sparkman also had objectives that he was having a great deal of difficulty achieving. Despite having all of the products sold out by marketing, the refinery was operating at only 85 percent capacity. While he had a sizeable proportion of young and inexperienced operators, he attributed most of the output deficit to frequent equipment failures and substandard performance of equipment in operation. Moreover, his raw material yields were poor due to inability to maintain control points because of poorly functioning instruments and automatic controls. This was aggravated by leaks that were so severe that the refinery had been cited twice recently by the Environmental Protection Agency for water pollution. Some of the leaks involved corrosive compounds that spilled over equipment, adding to the maintenance problems. Operators had threatened to call for an OSHA inspection of the refinery. Operating labor costs had been very high due to extra manning for unit start-ups following equipment failures.

Grimes knew Sparkman's position. Often Sparkman had pleaded to Grimes to upgrade the maintenance effort by establishing a sound preventive maintenance program. Sparkman reasoned that such a program would eliminate "fire-fighting" and in the end improve the position of both operation and maintenance. Grimes retorted that the operating department established maintenance priorities and that if Sparkman was sincere in establishing a preventive maintenance program he should give it a high priority in order to allocate the necessary manpower to such a program. Sparkman quipped, "With all the crises we face, the refinery would drop to 50 percent rates before benefits are derived from such a program." Hence, the circular argument was complete.

Sparkman did not advocate hiring more maintenance personnel to alleviate the problems. Rather, he advocated an all-out effort to increase the productivity of the existing maintenance group. He cited the traditionally low POJ measurement for the maintenance department. Sparkman also bewailed the high frequency of repeat work due to poor initial repairs. Grimes countered with the argument that the operators were so inattentive to their work that equipment failure resulted. He cited numerous cases where tanks had overflowed on pumps, burning up motors; dryers had overheated, causing cracking of the shells; and newly repaired plastic piping was "hammered" by a sudden surge of flow (instead of a gradual build-up), resulting in glued sections blowing apart.

Sparkman was particularly furious over the reassignment of the shift mechanics to the regular day shift. His shift supervisors assured him that the shift mechanics were "saving the plant" by their valiant efforts on the evening, night, and weekend shifts. Moreover, they complained that the shift mechanics spent half their time "re-doing" work done by the day crew. When Sparkman confronted the shift supervisors with incidents of idle crew time, they retorted, "Sure, they may be idle a few minutes, but most of the time they are so busy keeping the refinery on stream that they do not even get a chance to eat." The shift supervisors suggested that the list of "work accomplished" should be a better performance measure than the company-wide standard of POJ.

Both Sparkman and Grimes knew that they were approaching "open warfare." They also realized that such a war would jeopardize both of them in the eyes of the refinery general manager. Over a beer at the Hurricane Lounge, they discussed how they could rationally resolve their problems.

Discussion Questions

1. How can Sparkman and Grimes resolve their seemingly incompatible objectives?

2. What factors led to the problem?

Alutex Aluminum Company

In January, 1975, Alutex Aluminum Company, located in Denver, Colorado, was in the process of revising its maintenance work scheduling procedure. The primary product at Alutex is alumina, and the process of alumina extraction from bauxite ore is considered to be maintenance intensive. The process uses numerous pieces of rotating equipment, bulk conveyors, and calciners (dryers) to produce several grades of alumina. Proper maintenance of this equipment is absolutely essential for plant viability.

Because maintenance represented such a significant percentage of operating cost (approximately $1/3$), management of the Denver plant was continuously scrutinizing the efficiency (or productivity) of the maintenance work force. Close scrutiny was a necessity in 1975 because of generally poor economic conditions and the acute cost-price squeeze confronting the aluminum industry. Manufacturing costs had risen sharply because of soaring energy costs and required pollution control. Environmental protection was particularly costly because of the necessity of installing solar evaporation ponds to dispose of the spent bauxite ore and dust collection systems to contain the ever-present reddish-orange bauxite dust that "coats" all aluminum plants.

Work Sampling

The economic well-being of the Denver plant depended on gaining high efficiencies in the so-called "controllable" cost areas, such as maintenance. In January, 1975, a work sampling procedure was instituted at the plant to measure the productivity of the maintenance work force. (The efficiency measure is called *productivity-on-the-job,* or *POJ.*) POJ is the ratio of the number of "productive" observations to total observations taken by the work sampling staff. A "productive" observation is defined as activity by the observed mechanic which visibly advances a job to completion.

The results of the initial work sampling survey highly alarmed management at the Denver plant. The survey indicated a POJ of 26 percent for the maintenance work force. The industry standard was 42 percent. Consequently, the maintenance manager demanded details that would help to explain the low POJ measurement. The work sampling staff had categorized the "unproductive" observations as follows: idle-on-the-job, idle-off-the-job, and traveling. (Traveling is defined as movement by the observed worker, either walking or riding, which is not in the immediate area of the job or which does not directly advance the job to completion.) The survey indicated that idle-on-the-job and traveling were the primary reasons for the low POJ measurement.

When confronted with the low POJ statistics and the apparent reasons, the maintenance foremen tended to substantiate the same conclusions as those reached by the work sampling staff. They were generally surprised that the POJ measurements were so very low, but after some deliberation, they offered the following explanations:

1. Mechanics were often required to wait long periods of time on a job site because operating personnel had not shut down and secured the equipment for maintenance.
2. Many jobs required supporting services (carpenters for scaffolds, electricians to red-tag rotating equipment, crane operators to make lifts, insulators to strip insulation, etc.), and there were numerous delays in obtaining these services.
3. The mechanics were not certain which spare parts were required on a given job, so they spent much time traveling from the job site to the maintenance storeroom.
4. Numerous jobs required special tools (impact wrenches, flange spreaders, knock-wrenches, allen wrenches, mauls, cutting torches, etc.).

As a result, trips were required between the job site and the maintenance shanty. Consequently, an intolerable number of man-hours were wasted on "unproductive" activity.

The maintenance manager was deliberating resolution of the low productivity of his work force when he received POJ statistics from a recent maintenance turn-around on one of the plant's digesting units. The consensus POJ measurement on the turn-around crew was a remarkably high 68 percent. The maintenance manager called a meeting of his superintendents to investigate the differences between turn-around maintenance and routine maintenance. The significant difference was that all turn-around jobs were "planned and scheduled," but only the larger routine jobs were "planned and scheduled."

Planning and Scheduling

At Alutex Aluminum Company, planning and scheduling was a work procedure whereby work orders written by the operating foremen were routed to a maintenance planner. The planner then discussed the job with the operating foreman on duty. This discussion was followed by an estimation of the required spare parts, special tools, and supporting services for the job. If the maintenance storeroom did not stock the required spare parts, the planner contacted the appropriate vendor and sent a requisition to the purchasing department. Also, he rented special equipment if the plant equipment was not adequate for a special job. After he received a delivery date for parts and equipment, he met with the appropriate operating supervisor to schedule the date to perform the job. The operating supervisor made arrangements to have the equipment secured for maintenance at the scheduled time. Finally, the planner met with the crew maintenance foreman to discuss the plan. The result of effective planning and scheduling was a low level of unproductive man-hours and a high stream factor for equipment. Additional statistics from planned and scheduled turn-arounds indicated POJ measurements greater than 50 percent.

Based on these observations, the maintenance manager proposed a "total planning and scheduling system." Under this system, all maintenance jobs (turn-around and routine) were to be planned and scheduled. Each work order would be routed to a planner, who would execute the previously listed steps. To insure that the system was being implemented, he proposed a policy that deviations (emergency jobs) from the daily schedule had to be approved by the area maintenance supervisor. Putting the concept into operation would require hiring or promoting (from the hourly ranks) additional planners. Also, it was suggested that each operating department add a production-maintenance coordinator to its staff to work full time with the planner in preparing daily schedules of planned jobs. The coordinator would schedule the job to minimize the effect upon production rates and would issue instructions to the operating foremen on the details of securing the equipment for maintenance.

The objective of total planning and scheduling was to improve the productivity of the maintenance work force. Expected benefits were an immediate improvement of the condition of the plant equipment and a long-range reduction of the maintenance crew size. (The long-range reductions in manpower were expected to more than offset the additions to the plant staff to implement total planning and scheduling.)

The production foremen, however, were almost unanimously opposed to total planning and scheduling. They offered the following objections:

1. Plant stream factors would suffer if they were required to "chase down" the area maintenance supervisor to sign an emergency work order.
2. Many believed that total planning and scheduling would proliferate the enormous amount of paper work and red tape which confronted supervision.
3. They enjoyed having the flexibility of "in-house" mechanics who could be quickly assigned jobs that often prevented shut-downs and/or equipment damage.

4. Many believed that total planning and scheduling represented "empire building" within the maintenance department.
5. They perceived total planning and scheduling as a challenge to their authority because the assignment of maintenance priorities would be one of the functions performed by the new production-maintenance coordinator.
6. They resented being required to write work orders for minor jobs (changing light bulbs, lubricating pumps, repairing small leaks, etc.) as would be required under a total planning and scheduling system.

Moreover, approximately one-half of the crew maintenance foremen also resented total planning and scheduling. They believed that the system would diminish their own roles in performing the maintenance function. They suggested that increased P●J could be accomplished if they were given an opportunity to correct some of their own bad practices. The maintenance manager pondered his course of action.

Discussion Questions

1. What recommendations would you make to the maintenance manager?
2. Evaluate the criticisms of total planning and scheduling offered by the production foremen.
3. How would you "sell" total planning and scheduling to the plant supervision?

MAJOR PROBLEM –

TRYING TO IMPLEMENT TOTAL PLANNING AND SCHEDULING.

FORMEN – DECREASING RESPONSIBILITY AND INCREASED WORK LOAD

RECOMMEND A TRIAL PERIOD

MAYE SOME KIND OF SCHEDULE ACCEPTABLE TO THE PRODUCTION FORMAN AND TO THE SUPERVISOR.

National Garment
Factory
(Part A)

*MONUS
,2 SECTION
of CHAP. 11*

The National Garment Factory of Milwaukee, Wisconsin, manufactures a complete line of men's and boy's wearing apparel, including shirts, slacks, coats, suits, all-weather top coats, jeans, and sweaters. The company began operations shortly after World War II and has experienced steady, uninterrupted growth since that time. Today, National is one of the nation's leading clothing manufacturers. Among its customers who sell its apparel under private labels are many of the country's leading department stores, specialty shops, and chain stores.

Throughout its years of operation, National has continually upgraded its equipment by purchasing and installing modern, high-speed sewing machines which incorporate new time-saving devices. As advanced techniques are built into sewing machines, the management of National adds them to its production lines. As a result, over 80 percent of the machines currently in operation are less than 10 years old.

National has its own maintenance department which repairs the sewing machines as breakdowns occur, replaces worn parts from inventory kept on hand or from old, discarded machines, and installs new or replacement machines whenever an on-line machine becomes temporarily or permanently inoperable. Whenever all machines are working satisfactorily, the maintenance personnel rebuild and modify scrapped machines, which are sometimes temporarily put into service to meet a surge in demand for the company's product or to facilitate production when a newer machine is being overhauled.

Even though the sewing machines purchased by National Garment Factory are heavy-duty and constructed of the highest quality materials, their parts wear out because of the excessive demands made on them. Each machine has literally hundreds of parts that are subject to wear and malfunction. Among the more common problem areas are the shuttle assembly (levers, hook rings, shuttle race, etc.), motor belts, pressure regulators, switch controls, and the electric motors.

Recently, Julia Rothcliff, production manager, has seriously deliberated over the question of preventive maintenance versus remedial maintenance.

Under National's present system, a machine is fixed after a breakdown occurs. The corrective maintenance costs associated with such a remedial maintenance policy include lost production time, the costs of performing the maintenance, and the cost of replacement equipment. Preventive maintenance, on the other hand, encompasses periodic inspection, adjustment, and needed repair prior to a breakdown. Preventive maintenance costs include the cost of such inspections, adjustments, and the lost production time resulting from these activities.

Ms. Rothcliff's overall objective is to minimize maintenance costs by formulating a new policy — if needed — and by implementing it immediately. To determine which maintenance policy (remedial or preventive) is best for National Garment Factory, Ms. Rothcliff closely scrutinized pertinent records of the accounting and maintenance departments. The information provided by the cost accounting section revealed that the cost of servicing a machine breakdown typically amounted to $80. After discussing the activities of preventive maintenance with maintenance personnel and following consultation with the accounting department, the cost of providing preventive maintenance was estimated to be $15 per machine. In addition to these costs figures, the probability of a machine breakdown following maintenance was determined by analyzing data recorded during the six preceding years. Table 4-1 shows the probability distribution as a function of time since previous maintenance.

Table 4-1

Month following Maintenance	Probability of Breakdown
1	.20
2	.10
3	.05
4	.10
5	.20
6	.35

Analysis of Remedial Maintenance

The cost of remedial maintenance was computed by dividing the total cost of repairing all machines (200) by the expected number of months between breakdown:

$$\text{Remedial Cost} = \frac{(\$80)\,(200)}{1(.20) + 2(.10) + 3(.05) + \ldots + 6(.35)}$$

Analysis of Preventive Maintenance

To determine the total cost of preventive maintenance, the cost of such maintenance for one month, two months, three months, and so forth, was first calculated. To do this, the expected number of breakdowns for each time frame was computed. Hence, the expected number of breakdowns (designated NB) if preventive maintenance is performed on all machines each month is equal to the number of machines (200) times the probability of a breakdown one month following maintenance.

Therefore,

$$NB_1 = (200) \ (.20)^1$$
$$= 40$$

$$NB_2 = 200(.20 + .10) + 40(.20)$$
$$= 68$$

$$NB_3 = 200(.20 + .10 + .05) + 68(.20) + 40(.10)$$
$$= 87.6$$

$$NB_4 = 200(.20 + .10 + .05 + .10) + 87.6(.20) + 68(.10) + 40(.05)$$
$$= 116.32$$

$$NB_5 = 200(.20 + .10 + .05 + .10 + .20) + 116.32(.20) + 87.6(.10) +$$
$$68(.05) + 40(.10)$$
$$= 169.42$$

$$NB_6 = 200(.20 + .10 + .05 + .10 + .20 + .35) + 169.42(.20) +$$
$$116.32(.10) + 87.6(.05) + 68(.10) + 40(.20)$$
$$= 264.70$$

---

[1]The probabilities stated here are derived from life testing data; i.e., each probability is based on the original population and not solely on the remaining units subjected to that period's risk. Consequently, for period 1 a probability of breakdown of $p = .20$ with a population of 200 gives an expectation of 40 breakdowns. For period 2, the expected number of breakdowns for the remaining 160 machines is *not* .10 $\times$ 160, but rather .10 $\times$ 200, or 20. For period 3, the number of original units still in service is 140, and the expected number of breakdowns is .05 $\times$ 200, or 10.

Once the expected number of breakdowns occurring by the end of each period was calculated, the total cost of maintenance for the six periods was computed. Table 4-2 shows these cost computations.

Table 4-2

(a) Time Period	(b) Expected Number of Breakdowns to date	(c) Average Number of Breakdowns per period	(d) Expected Monthly Cost ($80 × c)	(e) Preventive Maintenance Monthly Cost	(f) Total Monthly Cost (d + e)
1	40	40	$3,200.00	$3,000.00[2]	$6,200.00
2	68	34	2,720.00	1,500.00	4,220.00
3	87.60	29.20	2,336.00	1,000.00	3,336.00
4	116.32	29.08	2,326.40	750.00	3,076.40
5	169.42	33.88	2,710.40	600.00	3,310.40
6	264.70	44.12	3,529.60	500.00	4,029.60

[2]Formula for calculating expected preventive maintenance cost per month:
$(1/a) \times \$15 \times 200$

Discussion Questions

1. Calculate the maintenance cost associated with a remedial maintenance policy. Which policy should National Garment Factory implement? What is the cost differential?

2. If National Garment Factory chose the preventive maintenance policy, how often should maintenance be performed?

3. Explain the high likelihood of breakdown during the first month following maintenance.

4. What additional maintenance policy might National Garment Factory consider? Explain such a policy.

Midwestern
Tractor and Combine

A major assembly plant of Midwestern Tractor and Combine is located in Omaha, Nebraska. Machinery assembled at the plant includes tractors of all sizes, harvesters and combines, bailing machines, large spraying machines and fertilizer spreaders, and sowers. The component parts are manufactured at Midwestern foundries located in Ohio and Pennsylvania and are shipped to the assembly plants located in the United States and Canada. The Canadian plants are under a subsidiary, Midwestern-Canada, Ltd. The foundries also produce a wide variety of tractor attachments that are shipped directly to Midwestern's distributors. Too, attachments for certain competitor tractors are produced at the foundries. Other parts, such as engine assemblies, transmissions, tires, electrical components, etc., are located in the Detroit, Michigan area.

The primary function of the Omaha assembly plant is to assemble the farm equipment and ship it to regional distributors who service the nearby wheat belt. Also, the assembly plant serves as a large warehouse for specialized spare parts for its equipment. Hence, a vital spare part can be delivered promptly to a farmer to effect crucial repairs to equipment. Such speedy repairs may actually make or break a harvest. Midwestern service representatives or assembly plant couriers often personally carry these parts directly to the farmer to prevent intolerable delays in shipping. Service mechanics dispatched from the nearest distributorship make the repairs.

The assembly plant also operates a large repair shop to overhaul larger equipment. Flat-bed trucks typically deliver the equipment to the repair shop. Repairs are made only on Midwestern equipment. The shop is operated on a break-even basis.

Service and reliability have been the keys to success for Midwestern. A guiding principle that pervades the entire organization is "closeness" to the farmer. A highly successful sales promotion strategy is to take the farmer co-ops, associations, 4-H clubs, and Future Farmers of America clubs on guided tours of the assembly plant while it is in full operation. In fact, the Omaha assembly plant is recognized throughout the industry as a "showcase factory." Two Russian premiers have toured the plant as have a score of federal and state agricultural officials.

Henry Barnes, the plant superintendent, accepts the fact that one of the functions that the Omaha plant provides is sales promotion. He also realizes that his paramount objective is to achieve a relatively high level of manufacturing efficiency. Recently, Barnes has been somewhat unsuccessful in achieving that objective. In 1975 and 1976, the Omaha plant had substantial unfavorable cost variances. (Please note Table 4-3.) Moreover, Barnes had already informed Midwestern management to expect a 1975 unfavorable cost variance of $600,000.

Table 4-3   *Manufacturing Cost Variances*

Year	Variances*
1972	$ 65,847
1973	450,985
1974	41,112
1975	(383,629)
1976	(466,728)

One of the reasons that manufacturing costs were above budget was an unfavorable variance for maintenance. The Omaha assembly plant was incurring expenses totaling 7.2 percent of total invested capital for maintenance. (Total invested capital of the Omaha plant equals $50 million.) This percentage was compared to an industry standard of 6.2 percent of total invested capital. (Maintenance is an important function at the assembly plant. It is performed primarily on the central conveyors and special-purpose tools used to assemble the component parts. Numerous pieces of rotating equipment and power transmission units require intensive maintenance. The assembly plant is mostly single-train, so a shutdown of one unit typically requires an outage of the entire plant.)

The maintenance superintendent, Barry Chester, suspected that the productivity of the maintenance staff was low. This low productivity was believed to partially explain a high level of overtime and the necessity of an above-budget crew census. Overtime percentage was totaling 8.0 percent compared to an industry standard of 5.0 percent. Budgeted crew size was 100 workers, and existing crew census was 118 workers. The additional workers were hired in an attempt to reduce the high overtime level. It was also believed that the condition of the equipment would have quickly deteriorated if the 18 additional workers were not added to the crew. (Current percentage down time was 1.5 percent compared to an industry standard of 2.0 percent.) There were expectations that the additional 18 workers would

---

*( ) denotes an unfavorable variance

be laid off within the near future. However, Chester believed that improvements in maintenance labor productivity must precede reductions in overtime requirements or crew size.

To implement the necessary controls, Chester investigated a widely used standard to measure maintenance labor productivity. This standard was the ratio of the cost of maintenance labor (hourly workers only) to the cost of maintenance materials. The recognized standard for this ratio was 1:1. This standard was based on the belief that assembly plants should consume an equivalent expense for maintenance material given an equivalent production rate. The major variable was the cost of labor to install or use standard materials. For example, it was expected that $1,000 in labor would be required to use $1,000 in material. (If the labor cost was greater than $1,000, the labor productivity was suspected to be low. On the other hand, if the labor cost was less than $1,000, the labor productivity was suspected to be high.)

Chester examined the labor to material ratio over the past five years and the monthly ratio for 1977 (year to date) as shown in Table 4-4. From these

Table 4-4   *Maintenance Labor to Material Ratio*

Year/Month	Labor	Material	Ratio
1972	$1,300,000	$1,450,000	0.897
1973	1,525,000	1,640,000	0.930
1974	1,580,000	1,585,000	0.997
1975	1,700,000	1,615,000	1.053
1976	1,730,000	1,608,000	1.076
Jan. (1977)	85,000	60,000	1.417
Feb.	92,000	81,000	1.136
Mar.	84,000	55,000	1.527
Apr.	82,000	73,000	1.123
May	81,000	70,000	1.157
June	105,000	82,000	1.280
July	89,000	63,000	1.413
Aug.	79,000	77,000	1.026
Sept.	86,000	75,000	1.147
Oct.	77,000	70,000	1.100

data, Chester concluded that improvements in crew productivity were a necessity. He called a dinner meeting for all maintenance supervision at a local motel. Chester presented these statistics and cited the unfavorable cost variance incurred by the maintenance department and the necessity to improve crew productivity. Then, he asked for suggestions on how productivity might be increased. A veteran maintenance foreman, "Iron-Head"

Birdwell, quipped, "Don't you guys in the ivory tower know that we have implemented a material savings program? We don't scrap large speed increasers, sprockets, conveyor links, etc. anymore. We send them out and have them reconditioned. A local outfit has a metalizing spray that makes them good as new. We even send our small electrical motors out to be rewound. They used to be scrapped. But if you guys want that ratio 'improved,' we can sure do it." (This comment was followed by light applause and general agreement by the foremen at the meeting.)

Discussion Questions

1. Evaluate the approach to maintenance cost control at the plant.

2. What was the implication of Birdwell's remarks?

3. What maintenance problems are associated with being a "showcase" plant?

4. What recommendations would you make to improve maintenance cost control?

Prescott
Plastics, Inc.
(Part A)

Prescott Plastics, Inc., a manufacturer of plastic sandwich bags, trash can liners, shopping bags, and bags used for protective covering, opened its Cape Girardeau, Missouri, branch plant in 1973. Essentially, the manufacturing operations at the Cape Girardeau plant are identical to those in Des Moines, Iowa, and Chattanooga, Tennessee, but production capacity is restricted by a limited number of machines (20) and poor space utilization.

When the plant opened in 1973, twenty new machines were purchased and placed in service. Six months later, a stand-by unit was purchased to be used whenever an on-line machine experienced a breakdown. Presently, Charles Good, the plant's production superintendent, is contemplating the purchase of one or two additional stand-by units because of the high frequency of breakdowns resulting in lost production. His primary goal is to minimize the cost of machines being out of service. Past records indicate that on the average two machines are out of order. The cost of a stand-by unit is $15 per day, and the cost of lost production resulting from a machine being out of service is $200 per day. If six or more machines are out of order at the same time, total operations cease.

Table 4-5 shows the probability of a given number of machines being out of order at one time. (The probabilities are based on the Poisson Distribution.)

Table 4-5

Number of Machines Out of Order	Probability
0	.135
1	.271
2	.271
3	.180
4	.090

[1]For additional information regarding manufacturing operations, see case 35, "Prescott Plastics — Part B."

Table 4–5 (continued)

Number of Machines Out of Order	Probability
5	.036
6	.012
7	.003
8	.001

Discussion Questions

1. What is the expected cost of maintaining one stand-by unit? Two units? Three units?

2. How many stand-by machines should be used to minimize total costs?

3. What assumptions were required in answering questions 1 and 2?

4. How many stand-by machines would you use if you were the plant's production superintendent?

chapter 5

Production Planning

case 26

Cumberland Ford
Company

In January, 1977, Tom Fisk, owner and general manager of the newly created Ford dealership in South Tampa, supervised the ribbon-cutting ceremonies which signaled the opening of his business. On hand for the gala were the mayor, two city councilmen, and a host of area businessmen and towns-people, including representatives from local banks and savings and loan associations. Also participating in the grand opening were the families of Cumberland Ford's employees.

Tom Fisk was especially proud of the people who had chosen to work for his company. Both Frank Simmons, manager of the Sales Department, and Benjamin Addison, manager of the Service Department, were natives of the Tampa area. Before resigning his position to work for Cumberland Ford, Simmons had served for ten years as sales manager of the local Lincoln-Mercury dealership. Benjamin Addison, on the other hand, had worked as both mechanic and shop foreman of service departments in Orlando, Talla-hassee, and Sarasota. The combined experience of Simmons and Addison in selling and servicing Ford automobiles totaled 28 years. Henry Owens, manager of the Parts Department, had previously worked for a local NAPA outlet. His decision to join Cumberland Ford was based on the higher salary and shorter hours (the Parts Department would be closed on Saturday) that Fisk had offered. Office Manager of the dealership was Mary Tilly, a highly competent bookkeeper who had worked for Fisk in his earlier business ventures for a total of 15 years. The only department manager who was considered relatively inexperienced as a supervisor was Jesse Jarman, man-ager of the Body Shop.

Jarman was known throughout the city as an excellent "body man." For 20 years, he had perfected his skills in reshaping metal, repairing fiberglass, spray-painting, and all the other functional areas identified with body and fender repair. On one occasion, he entered into business for himself, but his limited funds prohibited him from purchasing the infra-red baking equipment needed to "turn out like-new repair work." Consequently, he returned to his previous employer, Haney's Body Shop, as a craftsman who took exceptional pride in his work.

Having been in business for himself temporarily and having repaired hundreds of wrecked automobiles, Jarman was adept at estimating repair costs and supervising the physical operations of Cumberland Ford's Body Shop. However, he felt that he was doing an inadequate job of scheduling repair work because employees were often idle, queues would form at the painting station, and deliveries to car owners were not being made on time. He knew that other body shops with similar equipment and personnel were turning out more cars in less time than his department. Within the first three months of operation, five irate customers complained to Tom Fisk that repair work on their cars had not been completed when promised.

On Monday morning, April 19, Jesse Jarman arrived at work at 7:30 a.m. and discovered that the firm's wrecker service had towed in five automobiles involved in weekend accidents. In all cases, the owners had authorized Cumberland Ford to make all necessary repairs. Jarman carefully analyzed the extent of damage to each car and noted the amount of time (in hours) that each car would require at each station in the Body Shop. Table 5–1 shows these time estimates.

Table 5–1

Automobile	Metal Work and Replacement of Parts	Sanding and Masking	Painting and Baking
1972 LTD	9 hours	8 hours	2 hours
1972 Galaxie	12	6	3
1973 LTD	10	3	5
1975 Pinto	8	7	4
1976 Granada	14	2	1

Jesse Jarman wanted to minimize waiting time and total time consumed in repairing the five automobiles. However, he was uncertain about the priority to give each car to accomplish this objective. After re-checking his time estimates for accuracy, he pondered his decision.

Discussion Questions

1. In what sequence should the cars be routed through the various operations to minimize waiting time and total time consumed?

2. Suggest a scheduling method which Jarman could substitute for his "trial-and-error, hit-or-miss" sequencing decisions. Illustrate.

case 27

Merriwell Bag
Company
(Part A)

Merriwell Bag Company is a small, family-owned corporation located in Seattle, Washington. The stock of the company is equally divided among five members of the Merriwell family (husband, wife, and three sons), but the acknowledged leader is the founder and patriarch, Ed Merriwell. Ed Merriwell formed the company 20 years ago when he resigned as a mill supervisor for a large paper manufacturer. Ironically, the same manufacturer formed a container division five years ago and is presently one of Merriwell's competitors.

Company Strategy

The family attributes the success of Merriwell Bag Company to the fact that it has found a market niche and has no "serious" competition. Merriwell supplies stock bags to many small chain stores scattered over a wide geographical area. It ships the bags directly to small regional warehouses or drop ships directly to the individual stores. The family reasons that the large bag manufacturers cannot profitably provide service to accounts on that small of a scale. In fact, Ed Merriwell formed the business with one second-hand bagging machine to provide bags for a small discount store chain and a regional chain of drug stores. These two organizations have grown tremendously over the years, and Ed Merriwell proudly points out that the bag company has grown with them. Today, these two original clients are Merriwell's largest customers.

The Merriwell family does not want its business to be too heavily reliant on any one customer. Hence, they have a policy that no single customer can account for over 15 percent of sales. In fact, Merriwell Bag Company encourages its major customers to establish alternative sources of bag supply for insurance against stock outs because of paper shortages, freight line difficulties, local trucking/warehousing strikes, and production problems that may locally affect Merriwell's ability to supply bags.

Merriwell does not aggressively pursue new bag customers, yet it has over 500 customers. The smallest customers order five bales per year (smallest order processed and shipped), and the largest order 15,000 bales per year. The number of bags per bale varies according to the weight of paper used and the size of the bag. Merriwell manufactures only pinch-bottom general merchandise bags, ranging in size from small $2^{1}/_{2}'' \times 10''$ pencil bags to large $20'' \times 2'' \times 30''$ bags used for larger items sold in discount stores. They make no flat bottom (grocery) bags or bags that require sophisticated printing (specialty bags). Bag labels are restricted to 20 percent face coverage and one-ink color placed on one side only. Hence, Merriwell's central strategy is built around low unit cost production due to standardization which allows a selling price that is competitive with the large bag manufacturers. At the same time, Merriwell provides the shipping and inventory services that are on too small of a scale for most of the large manufacturers. The Merriwell family takes great pride in "taking care of" a customer who has an emergency need for additional bags or who would like Merriwell to warehouse a bag order for a given time because of storage problems at the customer's warehouse.

Forecasting Demand

Providing this personal service requires tight inventory control and production scheduling at Merriwell's bag plant. A highly accurate demand forecast allows Merriwell to service the special customer requests by use of Merriwell's own warehouse facilities and routing schedules of the company's truck line. Heretofore, Ed Merriwell could manage the demand forecasting and production scheduling by "feel." Because of the ever-growing number of accounts and changes in personnel in customer purchasing departments, the accuracy of Merriwell's forecasting has been rapidly declining. The percentage of short-shipped accounts for particular types of bags is increasing alarmingly. Conversely, the warehouse is becoming overstocked with other types of bags. As a result, a severe demurrage penalty on three boxcars of incoming rolls of paper was recently paid because the paper warehouse was partially used to store finished bags that spilled over from the finished bag warehouse. This caused a delay in unloading the boxcars until space could be created in the raw material warehouse.

Demand forecasting has historically been difficult due to the seasonal nature of the product. There is always a surge in demand for bags prior to a holiday season. The exact timing of the surge in demand for particular types of bags depends upon customer stocking policies and the dates that holiday promotional activities begin.

The Merriwell family needs a forecasting method that would take this seasonal factor into consideration. Moreover, they want a method that exhibits stability, because their market is relatively stable with a large number of repeat customers. Finally, they want a forecasting method that anticipates the growth patterns of their respective customers. A forecasting method with these specifications would greatly enhance the company's ability to service its market profitably. It is believed that if such a method could be applied to forecasting aggregate demand, the same method could be used to gain additional accuracy by forecasting demand of its larger customers. By having an accurate forecast of aggregate demand and demand of larger customers, the requirements of the smaller customers could be processed within the existing warehousing and shipping flexibility.

To develop such a method, the Merriwell family compiled the following aggregate demand data:

Table 5–2

Month	Sales (in no. of bales)				
	1972	1973	1974	1975	1976
January	2,000	3,000	2,000	5,000	5,000
February	3,000	4,000	5,000	4,000	2,000
March	3,000	3,000	5,000	4,000	3,000
April	3,000	5,000	3,000	2,000	2,000
May	4,000	5,000	4,000	5,000	6,000
June	6,000	8,000	7,000	6,000	6,000
July	6,000	4,000	7,000	10,000	8,000
August	6,000	8,000	10,000	14,000	10,000
September	10,000	12,000	15,000	16,000	20,000
October	12,000	12,000	15,000	16,000	20,000
November	14,000	16,000	18,000	20,000	22,000
December	8,000	10,000	8,000	12,000	8,000
	77,000	90,000	99,000	114,000	112,000

Actual demand through the first quarter of 1977 was 14,000 bales.

Discussion Questions

1. Develop and justify a forecasting method that fulfills the company's specifications.

2. Forecast aggregate demand for the balance of 1977 and the first quarter of 1978.

3. In addition to forecasting demand of larger customers and aggregate demand, how might the accuracy of the forecast be improved?

4. What role should Ed Merriwell's "feel" of the market play in establishing new sales forecasts?

Merriwell Bag
Company
(Part B)

One of the major problems Merriwell Bag Company faces is procuring an adequate supply of raw materials (paper) and maintaining an acceptable level of finished goods inventory in order to meet both expected and unexpected demand for stock bags.

Prior to the shortage of pulp and paper in 1973, Merriwell purchased approximately 95 percent of its paper from National Paper Company of Seattle, Washington. The remaining sources of paper were firms in various Scandinavian countries. Because of the uncertain delivery dates of imported paper and the dwindling price advantage of foreign-produced goods, Merriwell decided to purchase only domestically produced paper. Also, because of the increasing difficulty in getting enough paper of different weights and colors, Merriwell began buying raw materials from three suppliers — Ragsdale Paper Company, Savannah Paper Company, and West Coast Paper and Products, Inc.

In the latter part of 1973, the shortage of paper became critical. In August of that year, management decided to reduce its bag offerings from five colors (green, gray, blue, natural, and white) to two colors (natural and white). In addition, orders for 25-pound weight paper were discontinued, thereby restricting the company's offerings to 30- and 40-pound weight bags. Because Merriwell's competitors were experiencing identical problems, Merriwell did not suffer a loss of sales as a result of its restricted offerings. In fact, Merriwell was forced to reject new customers during this time because of the shortage of paper. (For the first time in the company's history, sources of raw material supplies became more critical than customers.) All attempts were made, however, to supply established customers with the quantity of bags ordered, but often in different colors and weights. Table 5–3 shows the different combinations of paper bags (color and weight) sold prior to and following the decision to restrict offerings.

Ironically, prosperity of bag-producing firms varies inversely with that of the automobile and home-building industries. Throughout 1974 and 1975, when the home building and auto industries faced one of the most severe

Table 5–3   *Production of Bags According to Color and Size*
                (percent of total production)

Color	25 lb	Weight 30 lb	40 lb
Prior to August, 1973			
Natural (brown)	5	55	5
White	5	5	5
Green	2	5	3
Gray	—	5	—
Blue	1	3	1
August, 1973 — Present			
Natural (brown)	—[1]	85	5
White	—	5	5

economic slumps of their histories, greater amounts of wood were available for the manufacture of wood-based products.

During this time, Merriwell expanded its storage capacity for both raw materials (paper) and finished goods inventory (printed and plain bags). Total storage capacity for raw materials following the expansion amounted to one million pounds of paper, which constituted approximately a two-month supply.[2] Physical facilities for finished goods inventory were doubled. (A large amount of space was required for finished goods inventory because most of Merriwell's customers — small chain stores — do not have storage facilities and because the storage order per customer is small (approximately ten bales.[3])

Prices and quantity of finished goods are basically the same among paper bag manufacturers throughout the country. Competition, then, is in the area of service to customers. Essentially, the focal point of customer service is the delivery of bags in the right quantity at the right time. To make certain that it is able to fill the orders of customers on schedule, Merriwell attempts to keep its raw material inventory at 100 percent of capacity at all times. (With an average price per pound of sixteen cents, Merriwell's investment in raw material inventory amounts to approximately $160,000.)

---

[1]Because of the higher costs associated with the production of 25-pound weight paper, greater supplies of 30- and 40-pound paper were available from suppliers at lower prices. Customers were willing to accept bags of natural color provided they were printed with name identification or other insignia to identify the retail outlet. One-color name identification bags are priced 5 percent higher than plain bags. Printing is limited to 20 percent face coverage (one-fifth of one side of a bag).

[2]The standard diameter of a roll of paper is 40 in. Widths vary according to the size of bag to be produced. Merriwell produces bags ranging in size from $2^{1}/_{2}'' \times 10''$ to $20'' \times 30'' \times 2''$.

[3]One bale equals 55 lb.

Not only is Merriwell concerned with maintaining an adequate supply of paper on hand, but it is equally concerned with storing correct amounts of different weight and color paper. Delivery of raw materials, therefore, is particularly critical to Merriwell's operations. Since delivery dates are not guaranteed by suppliers of paper who ship by rail, Merriwell uses its own truck to pick up supplies of raw material whenever its routing schedules permit. (Usually, Merriwell's truck departs the Seattle plant filled with bags and returns with paper.) If Merriwell chooses to allow the suppliers to ship the paper (by either rail or truck), the delivery date is approximately one month from date of order.

Nearly 85 percent of all raw material purchased is shipped by truck. However, West Coast Paper and Products, Inc., one of Merriwell's suppliers, frequently ships its supplies by rail. To facilitate such delivery, Merriwell's expansion program included a rail spur adjacent to its warehouse. Figure 5–1 shows Merriwell's existing floor plan.

Figure 5–1

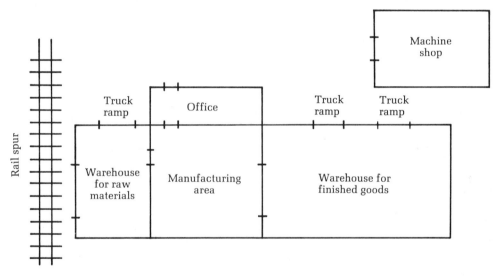

Typically, regular customers request Merriwell to keep on hand a specified number of bales (or pounds) of paper against which they will make purchases in the form of finished goods. Hank's Dollar Store, for example, has requested Merriwell to keep 30,000 pounds of 30-weight, natural color paper on hand at all times, thereby assuring Hank's of a supply of paper bags in the event of a paper shortage.

In addition to the inventory kept on hand for regular customers, Merriwell buys paper to satisfy the needs of new and irregular customers. Approximately 80 percent of its annual sales are to repeat (regular) customers.

Merriwell uses a simple Cardex system of inventory control. For each regular customer, a different card is maintained for each color, weight, and size bag ordered. Each card shows the quantity and date of raw material purchases and each reduction in inventory as a result of filling orders. This system allows Merriwell to know the quantities of various colors and weights of paper it has in stock for all customers at any given time. Whenever an order is filled, Merriwell systematically submits a purchase requisition to one of its suppliers in order to bring the inventory back up to the desired level.

Physical inventory is taken quarterly. Comparisons are then made to see if the physical inventory agrees with the Cardex balances.

Discussion Questions

1. Evaluate Merriwell's Cardex system of inventory control.

2. What changes would you recommend in the firm's procurement of raw materials? In its offerings of finished goods?

3. Merriwell considers its suppliers of raw materials to be more valuable than its customers. Since potential customers outnumber producers of paper, is this philosophy sound?

Gulfside
Terminal
(Part B)

Don Harris was the manager of Gulfside Terminal and tank farm located on the east bank of the Mississippi River thirty miles south of Baton Rouge, Louisiana. Gulfside was owned and operated by Union Petro-Chem and serviced three Union chemical complexes in the area. The operation of Gulfside was becoming increasingly difficult with expansion of product lines and capacity at the three manufacturing complexes. This situation was complicated by a broadening of customer services at the terminal, such as dissolving bulk shipments of sodium nitrite and loading the solution into tank trucks for shipment to local rubber plants.

The storage and shipment of additional quantities and types of products as well as the use of terminal facilities for customer services were not accompanied by an increase in tank farm capacity or in manpower at the terminal. Harris's capital appropriation requests for additional storage tanks were given a low priority. It was difficult to demonstrate how the additional terminal facilities would meet company profitability goals. There always seemed to be capital projects that involved plant expansions that were projected to be more profitable than additions to Gulfside Terminal. In fact, a Union Petro-Chem executive related to Harris that he was always opposed to increases in storage capacity because that "took the pressure off marketing." His rationale was that the salespeople always seemed to find customers if faced with a plant rate reduction caused by high inventories. The marketing manager dreaded having to admit to the president that production curtailments were due to lack of sales. Additional storage capacity would postpone rate reductions and reduce the pressure upon marketing personnel.

The Contract

Harris knew that there was a great deal of truth in the marketing manager's argument. He also had a "gut feeling," however, that very costly incidents would develop if Gulfside's facilities were not significantly expanded.

This premonition was based on a new contract recently signed between Union Petro-Chem and aluminum producers located in the West Indies. The contract was for 20,000 tons (short tons or 2,000 pounds) per month shipments of 50 percent caustic soda from the Gulfside terminal via tanker to the West Indies. The caustic soda would be produced by an expansion of caustic/chlorine facilities at one of Petro-Chem's area complexes. The new expansion was projected to come on-stream within three months and would boost caustic soda production to 1200 tons per day.

The terms of the contract were as follows:

1. Duration of the contract was three years.
2. The price of the caustic soda was $20 per ton with a 10 percent increase in price at the end of each year.
3. Minimum cargo weight per shipment was 20,000 tons, maximum weight to be dictated by tanker capacity and approval of Union's management; a freight penalty of $8 per ton would be paid by Union for tonnage less than 20,000 tons for each shipment.
4. The tanker would arrive between the 18th and the end of each month; if possible, the aluminum producer would attempt to schedule the arrival of the tankers within the period to accommodate the plant production schedule and the terminal's inventory levels.

Such a long-range, high-volume contract was considered desirable by Union's management. Caustic soda was a co-product of chlorine, and traditionally its demand was not as strong as that of chlorine. The two products are produced on approximately a one-to-one basis. In fact, the chlorine produced by Union's expansion was mostly captive, i.e., it was to be used as a raw material in the production of ethylene dichloride (EDC), vinyl chloride monomer (VCM), and assorted chlorinated solvents at new and expanded facilities within the three area complexes. The demand for these products is strong and considered to be growing.

Caustic soda, however, must be marketed directly, and the demand has traditionally lagged behind that for chlorine and chlorine products. If markets cannot be found for the caustic soda, producers must incur the heavy expense of deep ocean disposal or reduce plant rates to meet existing markets. A rate reduction automatically means a curtailment in the output of the highly profitable chlorine. Besides incurring losses of direct manufacturing and transportation expenses, deep ocean disposal of caustic soda is under heavy scrutiny from regulatory agencies who frown upon such pollution. Hence, a long-range reliable outlet for a high percentage of the complex caustic soda production was desirable. The balance of the caustic soda production was to be marketed commercially in barge and railroad tank car quantities. The price for the domestic shipments was much higher than the tanker shipments, but demand was somewhat erratic.

The Problems

To meet the monthly tanker commitments, Harris foresaw a number of difficulties. First of all, the tank farm had only 30,000 tons of storage capacity for caustic soda (See Figure 5–2 for a layout of the terminal and tank farm facilities). The effective storage capacity was less, however, because solid salt

Figure 5–2

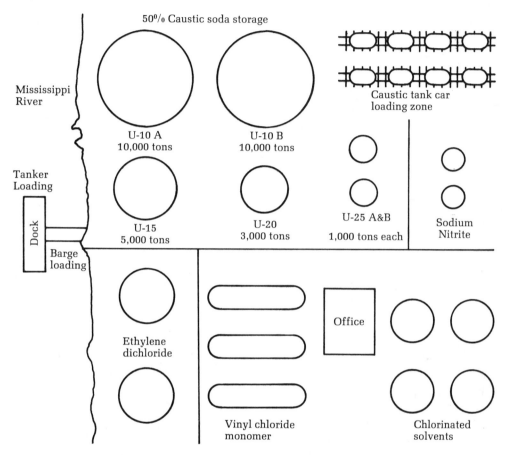

50% Caustic soda storage

U-10 A
10,000 tons

U-10 B
10,000 tons

Caustic tank car
loading zone

Mississippi
River

Tanker
Loading

Dock

Barge
loading

U-15
5,000 tons

U-20
3,000 tons

U-25 A&B
1,000 tons each

Sodium
Nitrite

Ethylene
dichloride

Office

Vinyl chloride
monomer

Chlorinated
solvents

(sodium chloride) would settle out of the caustic soda in storage. The salt build-up in the bottom of the storage would reduce the capacity of each storage by 2 percent per month. For example, a 10,000-ton storage would lose 2 percent of 10,000 tons, or 200 tons per month, due to the salt displacement. The removal of the salt bed in the bottom of the storage tank required one day of cleaning per 100 tons of capacity displaced. In this example, the 200-ton displacement would require two days of cleaning time. Obviously, the tank would have to be empty during the cleaning to restore full use of the storage.

A second problem was the erratic arrival pattern of tankers. Whereas the contract dictated arrival between the 18th and the end of each month, it was almost impossible to schedule the arrival within that period to best accommodate the terminal inventory position. This was due to many complex variables encountered at sea as well as fog and traffic conditions faced on the trip up the Mississippi to Gulfside Terminal. Also, the tanker may require cleaning upon arrival, depending on the nature of return cargo from the West Indies. This was determined by inspectors from the aluminum producers after the tanker arrived at Gulfside Terminal. Cleaning normally took two days. Hence, the tankers could be expected to arrive approximately on the 24th of each month, with a wide standard deviation of three days.

If the tanker arrived before the 18th, it was required to lay at anchor in the Mississippi River unless called in by the terminal for loading. If the tanker arrived after the 18th and was declared fit for loading by the inspectors, the terminal had 48 hours of "free time" to load the tanker. A demurrage penalty of $200 per hour had to be paid if the tanker was detained by the terminal over the 48-hour "free time". Terminal loading rates were approximately 600 tons per hour. Hooking-up and disconnecting loading hoses normally took a total of one hour for both functions.

If the tanker arrived after the loading period (the end of the month), the aluminum producers were required to pay a penalty of $8,000 per day for each late day. The penalty began accruing at 12:01 a.m. the first day of the next month.

A third problem that Harris recognized was that plant production rates were subject to interruptions due to operational upsets and maintenance problems. The plant typically produced 1200 tons per day of caustic soda, but they averaged two and one-half outages per month. The outages averaged 30 hours in duration, with a standard deviation of 8 hours.

The Assessment

Harris recognized that Gulfside Terminal could not be held accountable for plant outages or for the erratic arrival of tankers. He did realize, however, that management of the terminal could have a profound impact upon profits. Harris had the assignment of allocating caustic soda production between the domestic and West Indies markets. The marketing department informed him that they could sell all tonnage produced in excess of that committed for export to the West Indies. Moreover, they informed Harris that profit and overhead contribution was $6 per ton for domestic caustic soda and $4 per ton for export caustic soda. Profit and overhead contribution for the co-product, chlorine, was $10 per ton after it was used in the manufacture of the previously mentioned chlorine-based compounds. As indicated previously, chlorine is produced on a one-to-one basis with the caustic soda.

For domestic shipment of caustic soda, the terminal has the loading stations for ten 50-ton railroad tank cars per day. Also, domestic marine markets and availability of barges indicate that the terminal could load two 1,000-ton barges per month if desired. Due to the dock layout, a barge could be loaded at the same time that a tanker is being loaded.

Hence, Harris had a complex task. If he allocated too much caustic soda for domestic markets, a freight penalty for short tanker shipments might result. If he allocated too much caustic soda for export to the West Indies, a tanker's late arrival might cause high inventory levels and a reduction of plant production rates to match the loading rates for domestic shipments. This would cause an equal reduction in chlorine production. Harris pondered his plan of action.

Discussion Questions

1. Develop a framework for analysis to aid Harris in terminal inventory control and shipping scheduling.

2. What subjective factors bear upon this analysis?

case 30

T. H. Burton and Sons, Wholesalers

Thomas Burton, Sr., founder of T. H. Burton and Sons, Wholesalers, began his distributorship as a tobacco jobber in Terre Haute, Indiana, in 1949. Initially, tobacco products were sold and delivered to local independent grocery stores, service stations, and restaurants. In the mid-1950s, other product lines were added, including paper products (cups, plates, and napkins), food products (catsup, salad dressings, pickles, etc.), detergents, shampoo, candy, gum, and other consumer/household items. By early 1957, T. H. Burton and Sons had become a full-fledged wholesaler, distributing a wide range of consumer products including Coca-Cola, Dr Pepper, and Seven-Up soft drinks. Its customers had expanded to include area hospitals, drive-ins, chain stores, and motels.

By 1970, Thomas Burton, Sr., had begun relying heavily on the knowledge and assistance of his sons, Tom, Jr., and Ben. The wholesale business grossed $1.2 million in sales in 1970, and its inventory amounted to $125,000. Upon the recommendation of Tom, Jr., the warehouse was expanded to a total storage capacity of 25,000 sq ft., and most slow-turnover items were dropped. Mark-ups ranged from 2 percent on tobacco products to 50 percent on other goods.

The company owns its own warehouse, valued at $225,000, and two new delivery trucks. Typically, Tom, Sr. manages in-house operations, including taking and placing telephone orders, supervising the unloading of trucks and rail cars from suppliers, determining storage locations for merchandise, taking inventory, handling all business correspondence, and supervising office operations. Ben and Tom, Jr. drive the delivery trucks, supervise the loading of merchandise for delivery, and take orders from route customers, which are turned in to the office daily. Delivery routes have been established which permit the firm to call on high-volume customers daily and all other customers three times each week. To accommodate regular customers who face emergency shortages, special deliveries are made. Commonly the wholesaler assures one- or two-day delivery. Rarely do derailments, work stoppages, or other circumstances beyond the control of T. H. Burton and Sons prohibit delivery within a day or two after an order is received.

The major problem facing the wholesale establishment generally, and Thomas Burton, Sr., specifically, is associated with the maintenance of a perpetual inventory system. Physical inventory of fast-moving items is taken weekly, and slower-turnover items are counted monthly. Thomas Burton, Sr., counts and records all items delivered to the warehouse, and Ben and Tom record all items removed from the warehouse for delivery. The company has no predetermined re-order points or quantity requirements. Decisions as to "when and how much" of an item to purchase are made by Thomas, Sr., who bases such decisions on his feel for the operations and his 25 years of experience in the wholesale business. Yet, he readily admits that he sometimes gets overstocked with certain items and understocked with others.

In 1974, Janis Pledger, a representative of Small Business Data Systems (SBDS) of Indianapolis, contacted the Burton family and explained how her firm could develop a management information system for the wholesale company. The proposed computer-augmented information system would provide the Burtons with the following data:

- instantaneous inventories of all items handled
- inventory re-order points and economic order quantities
- proper assignment of merchandise to warehouse locations
- delivery routes which would minimize time, mileage, and associated costs
- data on which to base expansionary decisions (trucks, inventory items, warehousing space, and so forth)

At that time, the Burtons generally agreed that they did not need the management information system. However, they realized that unless they operated more efficiently in the future their company would be unable to continue growing and providing the services on which their business depended.

Between 1974 and 1976, sales of T. H. Burton and Sons, Wholesalers, increased 20 percent. Commensurate with the increase in sales was an increase in the volume of merchandise handled and the number of man-hours required to operate the business. Faced with a massive expansion program, including additional personnel, or a curtailment in the number of customers served, the Burtons deliberated over the best choice.

Discussion Questions

1. On what basis should the decision to use the SBDS management information systems be made?

2. What recommendations would you make to the Burton family regarding its inventory system? Its overall business operations?

3. Assume the Burton family agrees to purchase a tailor-made MIS which is implemented through a time-sharing computer operation located in Indianapolis. Assume, also, that the Burtons want to minimize costs by obtaining only the most essential information. What should be included in the system?

case 31

Brunswick
Business Machines

Brunswick Business Machines, located in Cleveland, Ohio, is a regional distributor of business machines and office equipment, including typewriters, calculators, duplicating machines, and office furniture. The firm sells and services Monroe, Remington, and Ditto (Bell and Howell) brand machines. Among its customers are governmental agencies (to which competitive bids are submitted), universities, and a multitude of business firms located within a 100-mile radius of Cleveland.

One of the major problems confronting Brunswick is the determination of an adequate inventory of each machine sold. Management does not want to overstock because of the carrying costs associated with inventory, but it wishes to minimize stockouts during lead times (the time between placing an order to replenish stock and the receipt of the goods). To avoid stockouts, the company maintains a safety stock. Even so, because demand varies from day to day, shortages occasionally occur. (For example, a shortage would occur if the orders received during the lead time exceeded the safety stock of a particular item.)

Figure 5-3 depicts the uncertain demand for Remington Electric Standard typewriters. As illustrated by the graph, the lead time is constant (five days) because a regional warehouse located in Cincinnati regularly delivers requisitioned machines to area distributors. (The re-order point (R) is based on units remaining in stock. The safety stock is the amount by which the re-order point exceeds the average sales during lead time.)

Management of Brunswick Business Machines wishes to minimize inventory costs by establishing optimal re-order quantities and appropriate re-order points. The company feels that it should be able to satisfy 95 percent of the customers who place orders for Remington Electric Standard typewriters during the re-order period. A review of the firm's accounting records reveals the following information:

1. The daily demand for this particular typewriter is normally distributed with a mean of 30 and a standard deviation of 3.
2. Procurement costs total $10 per order.

3. Annual carrying costs are $1.50 per unit.

Moreover, there are no stockout costs, and all unfilled orders are filled immediately upon delivery of requisitioned typewriters. The firm is open for business 300 days each year.

Figure 5–3

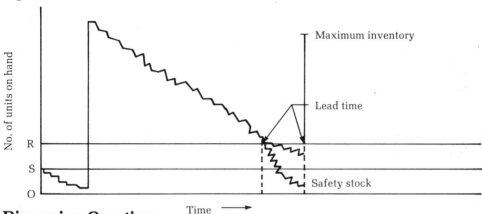

Discussion Questions

1. Determine the optimal number of Remington Standard electric typewriters that Brunswick Business Machines should requisition on each order.

2. Compute the re-order point at which 95 percent of all customer orders during the re-order period could be filled. (The standard deviation of sales during the total lead time of five days depends on the variance of the individual days.)

3. In layman's terminology, state the inventory procurement policy which Brunswick Business Machines should implement.

case 32

Sturdivant
Sound Systems

Sturdivant Sound Systems manufactures and sells stereo and quadraphonic sound systems in both console and component styles. All parts of the sound systems, with the exception of turntables, are produced in the Rochester, New York, plant. Turntables used in the assembly of Sturdivant's systems are purchased from Morris Electronics of Concord, New Hampshire.

Jason Pierce, purchasing agent for Sturdivant Sound Systems, submits a purchase requisition for the multispeed turntables once every four weeks. The company's annual requirements total 5,000 units (20 per working day), and the cost per unit is $60. (Sturdivant does not purchase in greater quantities because Morris Electronics, the supplier, does not offer quantity discounts.) Rarely does a shortage of turntables occur because Morris promises delivery within one week following receipt of a purchase requisition. (Total time between date of order and date of receipt is ten days.)

Associated with the purchase of each shipment are procurement costs. These costs, which amount to $20 per order, include the costs of preparing the requisition, inspecting and storing the delivered goods, updating inventory records, and issuing a voucher and a check for payment. In addition to procurement costs, Sturdivant Sound Systems incurs inventory carrying costs which include insurance, storage, handling, taxes, and so forth. These costs equal $6 per unit per year.

Beginning in August of this year, management of Sturdivant Sound Systems will embark on a company-wide cost control program in an attempt to improve its profits. One of the areas to be closely scrutinized for possible cost savings is inventory procurement.

Discussion Questions

1. Compute the optimal order quantity.

2. Determine the appropriate re-order point (in units).

3. Compute the cost savings which the company will realize if it implements the optimal inventory procurement decision.

4. Should procurement costs be considered a linear function of the number of orders?

chapter 6

Job Analysis

case 33

Pasadena
Toys, Inc.

Pasadena Toys, Inc., a manufacturer of a complete line of toys for preschool children, began operations in an abandoned warehouse in Pasadena, California, in 1956. Initially, the firm was a family-owned business in which all members of the Lawrence Rosenberg family worked. Mr. Rosenberg, an unemployed cabinet maker, first began building and selling "tinker" toys, building blocks, and alphabetical-numerical learning blocks. Later, he added wooden puzzles, peg boards, and animated animal toys to his product line which was marketed under the Kiddie Kare brand name.

Until 1960, Mr. Rosenberg personally promoted, displayed, and sold his toys to area retailers. As his business prospered, he added additional production and sales personnel, purchased a small fleet of delivery vans, and expanded his market to include most of southern California. Expansionary needs for larger physical facilities (manufacturing area, office facilities, and warehouse) and new tools and equipment forced the Rosenberg family to incorporate in 1963. Since that time, the business has experienced remarkable success, as measured in gross sales and after-tax profits. Today, Pasadena Toys, Inc., employs nearly 200 people and is one of the largest manufacturers of wooden toys in the country. Its customers include major chains, specialty shops, discount houses, and individually owned retail firms located throughout the western and southwestern United States.

Mr. Rosenberg attributes his success to hard work, capable employees, and the use of the most modern production methods and equipment available. When the firm was incorporated in 1963, Mr. Rosenberg implemented sound quality and cost control programs. In addition, he employed specialists to design a system for forecasting demand for the company's products, to determine proper inventory levels, and to design a complete work system, including process planning and layout of facilities. Too, he implemented a wage incentive program based on sound work measurement principles.

In 1977, Pasadena Toys added Kiddie Kare Karpenter Kits to its product line. The kit, designed especially for four-to-six-year olds, included four "tools" made entirely of wood. The manufacture of the kit was simple, and early feedback indicated that it would be a hot item during the Christmas season.

As with all other products manufactured by the firm, methods analysis of each operation was undertaken to establish the optimum methods and procedures for doing the work. Once the proper procedures were established, work measurement studies were conducted to determine standards of performance. (Pasadena Toys used motion-and-time study as a basis for setting production standards.) Several operations performed in the manufacture of the kit necessitated motion-and-time study. One of these operations was the boring of four $1/4$-in. holes in a piece of wood on a drill press. Another operation which required motion-and-time study was the assembly of four dowel rods into the bored holes.

Rodney Barnett, a recent college graduate with a major in industrial technology, eagerly accepted his first job assignment as an employee of Pasadena Toys — a stopwatch time study of the drill press operation required in the manufacture of the Karpenter Kit. Since the results of the study would ultimately be used in setting production standards, Rodney carefully planned the study and divided the work into its basic elements. He was somewhat uncertain, however, about the number of cycles he should time. The size of the sample, he knew, was a function of the variations in times recorded. Table 6–1 shows the variations in times that Rodney recorded after ten cycles:

Table 6–1

Element Times in .01 Minutes	X	22	20	18	21	23	24	19	19	20	24
	X^2	484	400	324	441	529	576	361	361	400	576

A quick glance at his production management textbook told Rodney that the following formula, based on the standard error of the sample mean time, could be used to determine the number of observations required:

$$N' = \left(\frac{c/p \sqrt{N\Sigma X^2 - (\Sigma X)^2}}{\Sigma X}\right)^2$$

where:

N' = number of required cycles
c/p = confidence-precision ratio
X = elemental times observed
N = number of observed individual elemental times

Discussion Questions

1. At a 95 percent confidence level and at ± 5 percent precision factor, compute the minimum number of cycles Rodney should observe.

2. Discuss the procedures Pasadena Toys should have gone through before the actual drill press operation was "clocked." What activities follow the time study?

3. Indicate the relationships among motion-and-time study, production standards, and wage and salary administration. How are employees affected by motion-and-time study? The employer?

National Garment Factory[1]

(Part B)

When the National Garment Factory began operations in 1946, all workers were employed under an hourly wage system. In the company's infancy, management chose to implement a wage plan based on time worked rather than on the basis of goods produced (incentive system) because adequate work procedures had not been analyzed and work measurement techniques had not been conducted. In the mid-1950s, the firm adopted a profit sharing plan in which all production workers participated. Profit sharing was initially begun to create a proprietary interest on the part of the employees. Management surmised that if a sense of ownership could be fostered, employees would be motivated to work harder and to become more cost conscious, thereby reducing scrap. Other possible benefits would include higher morale, improved employee relations, and greater company loyalty. The share of net profits to be distributed to employees varied from year to year (depending upon the economic status of the firm); each person's share was based upon annual earnings and length of service.

Today, management of National Garment Factory is contemplating a wage incentive plan in lieu of profit sharing. Four consecutive years of high costs and low profits caused the workers to become disenchanted with the profit sharing plan. As a result, they (through union representatives) began bargaining for higher and higher wages to offset the inflationary spiral which had significantly cut into their purchasing power. During this time, management found the profit sharing plan to be less useful as a "weapon" during contract negotiations with the Amalgamated Clothing Workers Union.

An incentive wage plan seemed appropriate, since the sewing operations satisfied the following conditions:

1. The work was standardized; that is, the work methods, materials, and operations were uniform from one unit to the next.
2. There existed a positive relationship between the amount of skill and effort exerted by the worker and the physical output.

---

[1]For additional information regarding the operations of National Garment Factory, see case 23 "National Garment Factory — Part A."

3. Units of production could be counted and credited to the proper person.
4. Increased productivity would result in lower unit cost.
5. Employees who produced the greatest number of acceptable units would receive the highest compensation.

Management seriously considered two different incentive pay plans — "straight piecework" and "piecework with a guaranteed minimum wage." Before a decision was made, the company's industrial engineer conducted methods analysis of each operation and applied appropriate work measurement techniques (motion-and-time study) in determining production standards.[2] To compute the per unit pay for the plans, the industrial engineer set a time standard for each unit. Then, the number of units per hour was calculated. Finally, the number of units per hour was divided into the base wage rates (as determined by job evaluation[3]), thereby giving the per unit rate.[4]

Under a "straight piecework" plan, the direct labor cost per unit remains constant as the quantity produced increases. This relationship is shown in Figure 6–1.

Figure 6–1

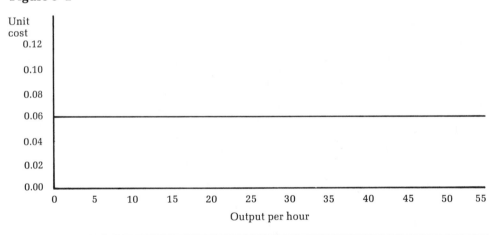

---

[2]Production standards are not based on past performance. Even so, standards which are based on time study or some other work measurement technique are frequently too "loose" or "tight." In time study, the worker selected to "time" may not be typical of the work force. Too, he or she may attempt to fool the industrial engineer because he or she knows that recorded times will be used to set standards which will directly affect future earnings. In addition, the industrial engineer feels pressure from both management and workers. Management wants efficiency, high productivity, lower costs, etc. "Tight" rates would serve these goals. Workers, on the other hand, will file grievances if they consider the standards too high.

[3]National Garment Factory uses the point system of job evaluation.

[4]For example, a standard time of 0.025 hours per unit was set for sewing on a shirt pocket (40 per hour). By dividing the base rate of pay ($2.40/hr.) by 40, the rate per unit, $0.06, was established.

After plotting on the graph the relationship between direct labor cost and output, the industrial engineer noticed that the relationship differed from that of the company's time-based pay system whereby direct labor cost per unit was curvilinear as productivity increased.

Under the "piecework with a guaranteed minimum wage" plan, direct labor cost per unit decreases as productivity increases up to a point and remains constant thereafter. The relationships among earnings, output, and unit labor cost are shown in Figure 6–2.

Figure 6–2

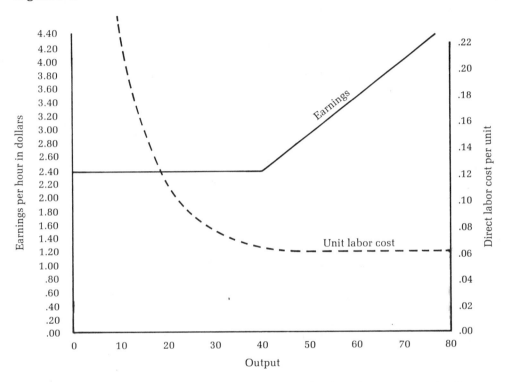

For the job of sewing on pockets, the standard is $0.06 per unit. For an output of 40 units or less, the employee would earn $2.40 per hour, the base rate of pay. For productivity over 40 units, the worker would earn an additional $0.06 per unit.

The management of National Garment Factory felt that the "piecework ·with a guaranteed minimum wage" plan was somewhat superior to its existing plan, but it, too, failed to discriminate among workers who produced "at average" and those who produced "below average." Yet, management also recognized serious shortcomings of the "straight piecework" plan.

P.C, w/ MIN, WAGE - PRODUE UP TO CERTAIN

PECES OR LESS YOU GET CERTAIN RATE, ANY MORE
THAN THAT YOU GET CERTAIN AMOUNT/P.C.

Discussion Questions

1. Which plan would you recommend for National Garment Factory? Why?

2. List specific drawbacks of each incentive pay plan.

3. Does an incentive pay plan have an effect on overhead costs? Explain.

4. Explain the problems commonly encountered with incentive pay plans.

5. Can you design another wage incentive plan that would be better for the National Garment Factory? Explain why you favor your plan.

1) PIECE WORK WITH GUARANTEED MINIMUM WAGE.

2) STRAIGHT PIECEWORK—
   WORKING TOO FAST COULD MEAN NOT AS HIGH QUALITY
   DOES NOT ACCOUNT FOR BREAKDOWNS, MATERIAL RUN OUT

   P.W. W/MIN. WAGE—
      TAKES FAILURES INTO CONSIDERATION

3) OVERHEAD COST/UNIT COME DOWN BECAUSE
   COST REMAINS THE SAME AND PRODUCTIVITY INCREASE

4) SUPERVISORS DON'T LIKE IT, MORE PAPERWORK
   MANY JOBS ARE MACHINE CONTROLLED (PACE IS CONTROLLED
   BY MACHINE AND NOT BY HOW FAST THE WORKER WORKS)
   MACHINE BREAKDOWNS
   MATERIAL RUNOUT

5) STANDARD HOUR PLAN
   PROFIT SHARRING

Prescott Plastics, Inc.[1]

(Part B)

Prescott Plastics, Inc., a manufacturer of plastic sandwich bags, trash can liners, shopping bags used by department stores, and bags used by dry-cleaners and retail apparel stores for protective covering, opened its first plant in Des Moines, Iowa, in 1970. The demand for Prescott's product necessitated around-the-clock operations and, ultimately, an expansion program which doubled the production capacity of the plant. In 1972, the company opened a second plant in Chattanooga, Tennessee, followed by another in Columbia, South Carolina, the following year.

Basically, employee relations in all three plants were considered good. A constant complaint leveled against management in the Des Moines plant, however, was voiced by workers who checked, counted, and packed the bags into cardboard boxes for shipment. Each worker folded boxes from pre-cut cardboard, randomly checked the bags for proper sealing and coloring, packed 200 bags in each box (the size of the cardboard boxes depended upon the size bag produced), certified the quality of the batch by placing an individually numbered inspection sticker in each box, closed and sealed the box, and placed it on a pallet for delivery to the finished goods warehouse. Each machine produced three bags simultaneously and automatically counted and stacked the bags. (Whenever the counter read 50, for example, the machine had produced three 50-count stacks, or 150 bags.) While the stacks were forming, each worker performed other job duties (preparing boxes, checking for quality, packing and sealing boxes, and so forth). Whenever the plastic became twisted in the machine rollers or whenever the quality was judged less than satisfactory, the inspector would notify the floor supervisor, who would shut the machine off until maintenance personnel could correct the situation.

The plant production superintendent set the production rates for all shifts. (The rate at which the polyethylene was fed into the machines and, hence, the rate at which finished bags came off the machines were controlled by the production superintendent). Identical production rates for all shifts were set

---

[1]For additional information, see case 25, "Prescott Plastics, Inc. — Part A."

by the production superintendent to avoid complaints that one shift was not carrying its load or that the graveyard shift did not work as hard as the day shift. The complaint which all shifts uniformly voiced was that the plant was a "sweat shop" and the excessive production rates did not allow a worker a chance to "catch his breath" or take care of personal needs.

To determine the percentage of time the inspectors-packers were engaged in productive operations and the percentage of time they were idle (not engaged in productive activities), work sampling was applied. Management of Prescott Plastics agreed that the work measurement program would be performed at a 95 percent confidence level coupled with a 2 percent absolute error factor. Based on an estimate that 75 percent of an inspector-packer's time is spent in actual productive activities, Clyde Forest, the company's industrial engineer, determined that 1,875 observations would be required. (See appendix A.)

The observations were made over a 15-day (3-week) period, with 625 observations per shift. The exact times at which observations were made were selected through the use of a table of random numbers. In addition, to minimize the effect of bias, inspectors-packers were similarly randomly chosen. Table 6–2 shows the results of the work sampling on five different dates. (Periodically, the results were analyzed to determine the adequacy of the sample size.)

Table 6–2

	Total No. Observations	No. of Productive Observations	Percent	No. of Idle Observations	Percent
End of 2nd day	250	175	70	75	30
End of 8th day	1,000	740	74	260	26
End of 14th day	1,750	1,260	72	490	28
End of 15th day	1,875	1,350	72	525	28
End of 16th day[2]	2,016	1,452	72	564	28

Discussion Questions

1. On the assumption that the industry standard for idle time (time not directly spent on a productive activity) for this particular job ranges between 12 and 16 percent, evaluate the results of this work measurement study.

2. Critique the complaints of the inspector-packers.

---

[2]An additional 141 observations were required because estimated productive activities were less than recorded productive activities. Forty-seven additional "readings" were randomly taken on each shift.

appendix A

Percent of Total Time Occupied by Activity or Delay, p	Absolute Error					
	±1.0%	±1.5%	±2.0%	±2.5%	±3.0%	±3.5%
1	396	176	99	63	44	32
2	784	348	196	125	87	64
3	1,164	517	291	186	129	95
4	1,536	683	384	246	171	125
5	1,900	844	475	304	211	155
6	2,256	1003	564	361	251	184
7	2,604	1157	651	417	289	213
8	2,944	1308	736	471	327	240
9	3,276	1456	819	524	364	267
10	3,600	1690	900	576	400	294
11	3,916	1740	979	627	435	320
12	4,224	1877	1056	676	469	344
13	4,524	2011	1131	724	503	369
14	4,816	2140	1204	771	535	393
15	5,100	2267	1275	816	567	416
16	5,376	2389	1344	860	597	439
17	5,644	2508	1411	903	627	461
18	5,904	2624	1476	945	656	482
19	6,156	2736	1539	985	684	502
20	6,400	2844	1600	1024	711	522
21	6,636	2949	1659	1062	737	542
22	6,864	3050	1716	1098	763	560
23	7,084	3148	1771	1133	787	578
24	7,296	3243	1824	1167	811	596
25	7,500	3333	1875	1200	833	612
26	7,696	3420	1924	1231	855	628
27	7,884	3504	1971	1261	876	644
28	8,064	3584	2016	1290	896	658
29	8,236	3660	2059	1318	915	672
30	8,400	3733	2100	1344	933	686
31	8,556	3803	2139	1369	951	698
32	8,704	3868	2176	1393	967	710
33	8,844	3931	2211	1415	983	722
34	8,976	3989	2244	1436	997	733
35	9,100	4044	2275	1456	1011	743
36	9,216	4096	2304	1475	1024	753
37	9,324	4144	2331	1492	1036	761
38	9,424	4188	2356	1508	1047	769
39	9,516	4229	2379	1523	1057	777
40	9,600	4266	2400	1536	1067	784
41	9,676	4300	2419	1548	1075	790
42	9,744	4330	2436	1559	1083	795
43	9,804	4357	2451	1569	1089	800

Percent of Total Time Occupied by Activity or Delay, p	Absolute Error					
	$\pm 1.0\%$	$\pm 1.5\%$	$\pm 2.0\%$	$\pm 2.5\%$	$\pm 3.0\%$	$\pm 3.5\%$
44	9,856	4380	2464	1577	1095	804
45	9,900	4400	2475	1584	1099	808
46	9,936	4416	2484	1590	1104	811
47	9,964	4428	2491	1594	1107	813
48	9,984	4437	2496	1597	1109	815
49	9,996	4442	2499	1599	1110	816
50	10,000	4444	2500	1600	1111	816
51	9996	4442	2499	1599	1110	816
52	9984	4437	2496	1597	1109	815
53	9964	4428	2491	1594	1107	813
54	9936	4416	2484	1590	1104	811
55	9900	4400	2475	1584	1099	808
56	9856	4380	2464	1577	1095	804
57	9804	4357	2451	1569	1089	800
58	9744	4330	2436	1559	1083	795
59	9676	4300	2419	1548	1075	790
60	9600	4266	2400	1536	1067	784
61	9516	4229	2379	1523	1057	777
62	9424	4188	2356	1508	1047	769
63	9324	4144	2331	1492	1036	761
64	9216	4096	2304	1475	1024	753
65	9100	4044	2275	1456	1011	743
66	8976	3989	2244	1436	997	733
67	8844	3931	2211	1415	983	722
68	8704	3868	2176	1393	967	710
69	8556	3803	2139	1369	951	698
70	8400	3733	2100	1344	933	686
71	8236	3660	2059	1318	915	672
72	8064	3584	2016	1290	896	658
73	7884	3504	1971	1261	876	644
74	7696	3420	1924	1231	855	628
75	7500	3333	1875	1200	833	612
76	7296	3243	1824	1167	811	596
77	7084	3148	1771	1133	787	578
78	6864	3050	1716	1098	763	560
79	6636	2949	1659	1062	737	542
80	6400	2844	1600	1024	711	522
81	6156	2736	1539	985	684	502
82	5904	2624	1476	945	656	482
83	5644	2508	1411	903	627	461
84	5376	2389	1344	860	597	439
85	5100	2267	1275	816	567	416
86	4816	2140	1204	771	535	393
87	4524	2011	1131	724	503	369
88	4224	1877	1056	676	469	344

Percent of Total Time Occupied by Activity or Delay, p	Absolute Error					
	$\pm 1.0\%$	$\pm 1.5\%$	$\pm 2.0\%$	$\pm 2.5\%$	$\pm 3.0\%$	$\pm 3.5\%$
89	3916	1740	979	627	435	320
90	3600	1600	900	576	400	294
91	3276	1456	819	524	364	267
92	2944	1308	736	471	327	240
93	2604	1157	651	417	289	213
94	2256	1003	564	361	251	184
95	1900	844	475	304	211	155
96	1536	683	384	246	171	125
97	1164	517	291	186	129	95
98	784	348	196	125	87	64
99	396	176	99	63	44	32

From Ralph M. Barnes, *Motion and Time Study* (New York: John Wiley & Sons, 1968), pp 528–29. Reproduced with permission of publisher.

case 36

Allstate Automotive Analyzers, Inc.

Allstate Automotive Analyzers manufactures a complete line of automobile testing equipment, ranging from basic timing lights and tachometers for the do-it-yourself owner-mechanic to superior quality console testers for the professional. Basic DC-powered timing lights are used to check timing, distributor action, centrifugal and vacuum advance; tachometers measure rpm, point resistance, and dwell angle. Allstate's professional quality analyzer checks the electrical output of alternators, generators, and voltage regulators and measures rpm, air-fuel ratios, and carbon monoxide levels of automobiles. When coupled with an oscilloscope, the tune-up analyzer diagnoses coil output, spark plug voltage, polarity, point bounce, and other aspects of a secondary ignition circuit.

Allstate's products are advertised and sold nationally. Prior to the surge in prices of new cars in the early 1970s, the company was only moderately successful; following several years of significant price increases, Allstate has enjoyed strong demand for its equipment and resultant high profits. (The demand for the firm's analyzers is attributed to car-owners keeping their automobiles longer and a tendency for the owner to save on expensive tune-ups.) Unit price on the firm's testers varies from $25 for the most basic timing lights to nearly $1,000 for the firm's most sophisticated console analyzer.

For several years, management of Allstate has had a number of its manufacturing operations on individual incentives. Before an operation is placed on an incentive wage plan, however, the firm's Industrial Engineering Department thoroughly analyzes the job, establishes standardized methods of performance, and sets production standards based on accepted work measurement techniques. The firm uses motion and time study as a basis for setting productivity expectations, and it has adopted the standard hour[1] wage incentive plan for all operations that lend themselves to incentive pay.

---

[1]The standard hour plan expresses the work standard in terms of time. It incorporates a base rate of pay which workers earn if they fail to meet standards. For all productivity over standards, earnings are directly proportional to the output. For example, assume the base rate of pay for a job is $5/hour and the time standard is $1/2$ hour per unit. If a worker produces 20 units in one day, he or she earns 10 standard hours of pay, or $50. Productivity is 125 percent of standards; hence, earnings are 125 percent of base wages.

Eligible employees of Allstate are represented by a large national labor union which has gained a reputation for hard-nosed bargaining with employers on wages, hours, and conditions of employment. As a result of the union's effective bargaining, the base rates of pay for employees of Allstate are above average for the geographic region and type of work performed. One of the key factors which the union uses in negotiating for higher base rates of pay is the "tight" production standards set by management. Such tight standards, according to the union, restrict employees from earning "bonus" pay.

Basically, the wage incentive program has been a success for the company. With the exception of one department, very few grievances are filed with the union stewards. Whenever a grievance charging unfair standards is voiced, the steward (who has been trained in basic motion and time study) has the right to time the operation himself. Based on his analysis, the steward either processes the grievance or screens it out as being without merit or justification. A majority of the formal grievances and informal complaints over standards originate in the assembly department, where one of the union stewards works. (All stewards are regular employees of the company; each is given six hours each week for the purpose of handling union business. While conducting union business, stewards earn the base rate of pay established for their particular jobs.) This steward recently transferred to the assembly department from another operation which is not on incentive pay because it is machine controlled.

Management of Allstate contends that the existing production standards in all departments, as set by the Industrial Engineering Department, are fair. Moreover, they feel that the steward is bitter because of his inability to earn higher wages than he earned in his former job. (He cannot bump back into his old job because all other workers in that department have more seniority.) As a result of his situation, management argues, the steward continually stirs up trouble and acts as an agitator. To support its contention, management points out that most of the grievances over unjust standards never get to the second stage of the grievance procedure and, hence, are not put in writing as dictated by the union contract. Even so, the steward remains quite popular with many of his co-workers, who feel that he gives them better representation than the other stewards who "bend over backward to get along with management."

Generally, the grievances filed by employees of the assembly department are based on standards which they consider "too tight," excessive down-time resulting from mechanical failures, and the introduction of new electric power drills and other assembly tools with which they must become familiar. In addition, they complain that the motion-and-time-study engineers use their positions to intimidate and harass by continually conducting time studies (with the implied threat of reducing time and increasing productivity requirements).

On two occasions (once in the assembly department and once in a punch press operation), formal grievances led to re-timing of operations and a reduction in standards. Following the change in standards, productivity increased by an average of 20 percent, thereby making the operations more costly for the company. Restriction of output, on the other hand, which results from standards that are too tight makes it difficult for the firm to meet its production schedules. Consequently, management is baffled by the seemingly paradoxical situation.

Discussion Questions

1. Evaluate the strengths and weaknesses of the standard hour plan used by Allstate Automotive Analyzers, Inc.

2. On what basis should production standards be set? Changed?

3. Discuss the handling of grievances which arise because of "tight" standards, new assembly tools, down-time, etc.

1) THE STRENGTHS ARE THAT THE STANDARD HOURLY WAGE GIVES THE EMPLOYEE THE INCENTIO TO WORK, YET IF THE EMPLOYEE IF THE EMPLOYEE TRIES TO PRODUCE TO MANY GOODS IN A GIVEN TIME, HE MAY MAKE MISTAKES WHICH WILL COST THE COMPANY IN THE LONG RUN.

2) STANDARDS SHOULD BE SET ACCORDING TO MACHINERY USED AND THE AMOUNY of SKILL REQUIRED BY THE WORKERS.

S.T. = N.T₁ + ALLOWANCES ON THE AMOUNY oF TIME NEEDED TO COMPLETE A JOB BY A TYPICAL QUALIFIED WORKER USING A STANDARD METHOD + WORK LAYOUT PERFORMING AT A RATE WHICH CAN BE MAINTAINED THROUGOUT THE DAY WITHOUT FATIGUE. STANDARDS ARE CHANGED WHEN METHODS ARE CHANGED.
N.T. = C.T. * R.T.

chapter 7

Management of Human Resources

3) ANALIZE GRIEUANCE, AND FIXID OUT IF THERE IS REALLY A PROBLEM.

case 37

Precision Tool Company

In December, 1976, both the International Association of Machinists (IAM) and the Precision Tool Company of Memphis, Tennessee, were awaiting arbiter Josh McIlveen's award in connection with an unsettled dispute over the misclassification of four employees. Because the union contract called for compulsory arbitration as the final step in the resolution of grievances, the employees of Precision Tool were completing the second year of uninterrupted employment under the provisions of a three-year agreement. Relations between the company and the union were considered fair; employees received slightly higher pay and greater fringe benefits than did their counterparts in nonunion plants, and payroll deductions for union dues revealed that roughly two-thirds[1] of all eligible workers were union members.

The Precision Tool Company manufactures a complete line of hand-held power saws, grinders, and drills marketed under the Skill-Rite brand name. Although 85 percent of its customers are retailers who sell to homeowners, a significant number of industrial manufacturers buy its products for use in their manufacturing operations. The company consists of seven separate, autonomous units located throughout the Southeast, with the home office in Birmingham, Alabama.

In January, 1975, Precision Tool decided to build an experimental stamping machine in the maintenance department of the Memphis plant. The machine would be built from spare parts on hand and the serviceable portions of old, discarded, fully depreciated stamping machines which had been replaced with expensive, new equipment. Management of Precision Tool had decided against the purchase of a new stamping machine because sales forecasts of the not-too-distant future were quite dim. However, additional stamping was presently required to meet the temporary surge in demand.

Since the construction of the stamping machine would be a temporary job, four workers were temporarily hired to work under the supervision of James Duggan, an experienced millwright. Each worker was informed that employ-

---

[1]The state of Tennessee has passed a right-to-work law.

ment was temporary and that the job would be terminated at the conclusion of the project.

All permanent jobs at Precision Tool were classified and had established rates of pay. No provision was made, however, for temporary jobs. Consequently, the four new employees were classified as maintenance mechanics, a classification which most nearly encompassed the skills and duties of the work to be performed. The agreed-upon rate of pay was $3 per hour. This hourly wage rate was $2 less than the established rate for maintenance mechanic positions. The wage differential was incorporated because none of the four new workers possessed all the skills and other qualifications listed in the job specification and none had completed the apprenticeship required for maintenance mechanic classification.

The stamping machine, completed three months after work was initiated, was added to the production line, where it operated perfectly. The cost savings associated with its manufacture were significant. In fact, the total cost was calculated to be only a fraction of the price of a new machine. Because of its successful manufacture and because demand for Precision's products remained unexpectedly strong, management chose to build, repair, and modify other production machinery used in various manufacturing processes. This decision resulted in a continuation of employment of the workers assigned to the maintenance department. Six months after the date of their initial employment, their job status was changed from temporary to permanent as required by the union contract. The rate of pay, job classification, and job duties remained unchanged.

On December 10, 1976, Jerry Frazier, newly appointed personnel manager, discovered the erroneous classification of the four maintenance department employees. Joseph Nettleton, production manager, provided an explanation of the classification. Following their discussion, Frazier and Nettleton agreed to establish a new classification—mechanic helper/maintenance—and to reclassify the workers. The hourly rate of pay for the new classification was set at $3.30. (Ten percent across-the-board pay raises were given January 1, 1976.) As required by the union contract, notification was forwarded to the union.

When Donald Dorsey, the local union representative, received notification of the reclassification, he contacted the four maintenance department employees, explained that they had been underpaid for their classification, persuaded them to join the union, and processed a formal grievance in their behalf.

The grievance asked for a retroactive pay adjustment from the date of employment to the date of reclassification. The union maintained that all workers should be paid according to their classification; a failure to pay them on this basis would constitute a breach in a union contract provision.

Precision Tool contended that the union erred by overlooking the erroneous classification when the employees were initially employed. The union, it was argued, shared the responsibility of proper classification.

Discussion Questions

1. As an arbitrator, what award would you render in this case?
2. On what basis did you make your decision?
3. Discuss the duties and responsibilities of both the company and the union in regard to proper classification.

McKinley Oil
Company

With 25 years of service at McKinley Oil Company, a small, independent producer located in Smackover, Arkansas, Hank Tomlison had seen his employer amass a sizeable fortune in a highly risky business during a period when oil deposits were becoming increasingly difficult to locate. Although Smackover had at one time been one of the country's leading oil production sites, large deposits in the area were being tapped less frequently with each passing year.

Tomlison was initially hired by Charlie McKinley as a roustabout, a maintenance job involving the pulling of parted rods and ruptured tubing, the setting of walking beams and engines for producing wells, the laying of gas lines (the company produced its own feeder fuel for its engines), the hooking up of separators, treaters, and salt-water disposal stations, and other general maintenance tasks associated with oil field operations. Later, he became a pumper, a relatively "soft" job encompassing the daily gauging of oil tanks for the purpose of reporting production, keeping the engines running at all times, and performing routine maintenance on engines, his pick-up truck, and other oil field equipment. Tomlison, however, had spent the bulk of his employment as foreman of the company's water and natural gas operations. His primary duties were to manage pumping stations, supervise the construction of all water and gas lines throughout the field, and locate and repair any leaks which caused losses of fuel and/or water to the wells and to company-owned houses where employees lived.

Although Tomlison did not keep permanent records or diagrams of lines constructed, he invariably remembered where cut-off valves, unions, and tie-in's were located. Within hours after a gas or water cessation was reported, he would have found the leak, shut off the gas to that station, and removed and replaced the ruptured section of pipe. Often, however, lines were difficult to locate because the right-of-ways had grown up with trees and undergrowth. Also, the task of getting an acetylene-oxygen torch and other repair equipment to the job site was quite often frustrating.

During the last three years of his employment, Tomlison began drinking heavily and was often inebriated on the job. It was not uncommon, in fact, for him to carry a bottle in the pocket of his coveralls during normal working hours. His appearance and indifference were attributed to the loss of his wife and to the "dead-end" job to which he was relegated.

Following the merger of McKinley Oil Company with Mid-South Production Corporation, Tomlison was fired for drinking on the job. Within six months after his discharge, his contribution and worth became blatantly apparent—no other employee knew the location of underground lines, shut-off valves, and so forth. Lines constructed two decades earlier were unknown to present employees, and the cost of laying new lines was prohibitive.

Faced with this predicament, top management of the company attempted to re-employ Tomlison temporarily. His job would entail sketching a diagram which would depict all lines and connections throughout the oil field. Also, he would serve as advisor to the Maintenance Department in an effort to help it locate and correct existing problems.

Tomlison refused the company's offer, but stated that he would consider permanent employment in his previous capacity. He stated unequivocally that he had no intention of "putting his knowledge on paper, thereby reducing his job security."

Discussion Questions

1. How did Tomlison become "indispensable?"

2. What recommendations would you offer to resolve the problem?

National Chemical Corporation:
East Texas Plant
(Part A)

National Chemical Corporation is one of the leading U. S. producers of chemicals and related products. Organized in 1923, National has enjoyed many years of success in the chemical industry and has diversified into related areas, such as synthetic apparels, agriculture, and energy (petroleum-nuclear). The company's solid financial position enabled it to survive during the Great Depression of the 1930s. National's product line has always been considered vital to the nation's defense, and the company was one of the leading suppliers of chemicals during World War II. Spurred on by the demand for basic chemicals during World War II, National built the East Texas Plant in 1943. The site chosen was East Texas City, closely linked to a larger metropolitan area supported primarily by the petro-chemical industry. The East Texas Plant was started in 1945 and undertook major expansions approximately every 10 years (1955 and 1967). By 1967, the capital of the plant was approximately $180 million, and there were 1,200 employees. The metropolitan area that encircled the East Texas Plant contained nearly 225,000 people, according to the 1960 census.

The East Texas Plant has become one of the largest plants in National's Basic Chemical Division. The Basic Chemical Division produces bulk, industrial type chemicals and has plants in 22 states and 3 foreign countries. The Division, as well as the Corporate headquarters, is located in New York. National's managerial philosophy has historically been one of decentralization, with the divisions operating with a great deal of autonomy. The divisions do, however, exercise tight control over their member plants, with detailed responsibility reporting of costs, capital performance audits, periodic review of operations, and a high degree of involvement in contract negotiations.

Prior to 1970, the rank-and-file of the East Texas Plant were represented by Local No. 75 of the International Chemical Workers (actual union name is disguised; however, it is a large diversified international union). Local No. 75 was the sole bargaining agent and was somewhat militant, which was characteristic of the union. Grievance levels were extremely high. (For example, one foreman received as many as ten grievances in one day in 1963.)

Many of the grievances were certified to arbitration, resulting in great expense for both the company and Local No. 75.

Local No. 75 — Organization and Political Structure

With this high level of union activity, the leadership of Local No. 75 commanded a significant political regime comprised of its 1,000 members. The president, Charley Stonebraker, was elected by the membership for a two-year term. Charley was recognized as the formal leader, presided over all meetings of the membership, and was the spokesman for the union in daily business with the East Texas Plant management. The vice-president was also elected for a two-year term, but as in many political hierarchies, he possessed neither significant formal nor informal leadership. The Union's recording secretary, Joe Hawkeye, held the third most prestigious position in Local 75's organization structure. Joe kept records and minutes of all meetings, including grievance meetings and disciplinary hearings. He was regarded as the "sea lawyer," or the Union's "legal beagle," because of his access to records, knowledge of past practice, and uncanny ability to discover loopholes or ambiguity in the labor agreement.

The officer with the most political power was the Chairman of the Grievance Committee, Harry Hardline. The Chairman was appointed by the president and was not subject to the electorate. Harry processed all grievances which included setting priorities for meetings at the various steps. He generally accepted or rejected answers from management and was the greatest influence in deciding the merit of certifying any grievance to arbitration.

The balance of the union officials included 17 stewards, each of whom was elected from the designated operating sections or crafts within the East Texas Plant. These stewards were elected for a two-year term by their respective work groups, that is, the section or craft of which they were a member. The stewards, together with the previously mentioned officers, comprised the committee that heard grievances at the second step. The first step was a written reply from the supervision of the section involved in the complaint to the section steward. The second step was a meeting between the section supervision together with representatives of the employee relations department and the grievance committee. The employee relations representative, in turn, submitted the written answer at the second step. The third step was between the East Texas Plant Manager and the president of Local No. 75. The plant manager would render the written answer at the third step, and if rejected, the grievance might be certified to arbitration.

As well as hearing grievances at the second step, the section stewards, local president, vice-president, recording secretary, and chairman of the grievance committee formed the negotiating team. A representative of the International Chemical Workers would normally join the team as the spokesman.

Activity of Union Officials

There was an informal understanding that the union president did not do plant work. Also, the chairman of the grievance committee appeared to be continuously handling grievances. Hence, he was not available for work duty at any time. These officers were paid their regular wages and were eligible for overtime work. The section representatives were all considered full-time workers and were compensated only for the following time off: to attend second stage grievance meetings, to conduct union business within their jurisdiction, and to negotiate contracts. The negotiating members were paid their regular wages, however, by Local No. 75 during a strike in which negotiations had not been indefinitely suspended. The rationale of this policy was that these union officials could not work at second jobs and should not be placed in a comprising position due to their own financial strain during negotiations.

1964 Contract — "Let's Shut It Down"

A strike did occur at the expiration of the contract in 1964. The strike lasted only five days. (It was generally acknowledeged that the opening of deer-hunting season was more of an incentive to "hit the bricks" than any bargaining issue.) At the recommendation of the negotiating team, the membership then ratified the contract. Exactly what the five-day strike gained has remained unclear.

The major provisions of the 1964 contract were as follows:

1. Local No. 75 gained a major medical insurance plan, one of the first issued to hourly employees by National Chemical Corporation. This was the major issue during the negotiations.

2. There would be no wage increases at the signing of the agreement on December 10, 1964.

3. Effective December 10, 1965, the Company would grant a $1^{1}/_{2}$ percent general wage increase computed to the nearest penny on hourly rates then in effect.

4. Effective December 10, 1966, the Company would grant a $1^{1}/_{2}$ percent general wage increase computed to the nearest penny on hourly rates then in effect.

5. Effective December 10, 1966, the Company would increase the shift differential from 6¢ to 7¢ per hour for employees required to work the second shift and from 12¢ to 14¢ per hour for employees required to work the third shift. The contract term was three years (expiration date, December 10, 1967) and contained the standard no-strike, no-lockout provision.

These astoundingly low wage settlements while achieving breakthroughs in benefits were not unusual for the 1964 period. It must be recognized that the fourth postwar recession had started in May, 1960, and had reached its low point in February, 1961. Prices remained somewhat stable through 1964. At the beginning of 1965, however, prices "took off." A great deal of the increase was attributed to activity in the industrial sector of the economy. Construction and expansion booms, coupled with a manpower shortage linked to the war in Southeast Asia, caused an acceleration in the cost of labor throughout the industrial sector.

1965–1967 — "You'd Better Treat Us Right"

The timing of these economic events was most unfortunate for Local No. 75 and the management of the East Texas Plant. Just as the 1964 contract had been signed with negligible increases in wages for the next three years, the cost of living started soaring. Moreover, the metropolitan area surrounding the East Texas Plant was undergoing a tremendous boom, and the local inflationary pressures were greater than the national economic aggregate. As noted previously, the area was supported by the petro-chemical industry. The timing of contracts at the other chemical plants, particularly the petroleum refineries, was such that fellow members of the community were receiving substantial wage increases as well as lucrative fringe benefits. In addition, new plant construction and expansions were flourishing. There was a drain on skilled manpower, with a consequent acceleration of wages for construction workers that were even greater than the refinery wages. These factors all combined to create inflationary pressures in the East Texas area that approximated 4.0 to 4.5 percent per year. The cost-of-living pinch was becoming so pronounced that many workers at the East Texas Plant were joining construction crews while on vacation. Deprived of the benefits of vacations, many of the workers were becoming more and more irritated, and tempers would flare over minor issues and problems. Hence, the three-year contract signed in December, 1964, had become one of deep regret. (Wage comparisons for selected job classifications at the end of 1965 are presented in appendix A.)

Cognizant of the preceding factors, the rank-and-file of the East Texas Plant were generally beginning to question their compensation. Historically, their wages had been lower than the petro-chemical average. The rationale and device by which management throughout the years had "sold" this to the employees was based on the fact that National Chemical Corporation was in the chemical industry and that the East Texas Plant produced chemicals. Hence, it should pay wages comparable to other chemical plants and not comparable to the refineries that were in the area petro-chemical complex. The refineries had historically paid higher wages than the chemical plants.

This rationale, however, was quickly discounted because of the acceleration of the cost of living. The workers expected comparable wages. Moreover, the oil companies were beginning to expand and diversify into chemicals, with construction of new units in the east Texas area. The oil companies retained their philosophy of wages and paid their chemical workers at a rate equal to their refinery workers. The East Texas Plant employees were very much aware of the diversifications of the oil companies simply by the word "chemical" in the name of these oil company subsidiaries. Also, the typical comment was, "Maybe those new units on the main highway are going to produce ice cream." Finally, National Chemical dispelled any industry distinction by its own diversification into the energy sector.

Consequently, the workers at the East Texas Plant were not a "happy family." The local newspapers would often print accounts and details of settlements at the area plants that called for "substantial wage increases." The East Texas Plant employees were constantly agitated by neighbors and relatives. Morale at the plant was considered to be at an all-time low. High turnover, numerous grievances, several reported and an equal number of unreported fist fights, costly waste of supplies and raw materials, numerous slowdowns, and even sabotage were some of the major problems facing supervision.

As indicated previously, the East Texas Plant was targeted for major expansion, with construction to begin in late 1967. This expansion added approximately 300 people to the plant's census and $75 million to its capital. With the attitude and morale of the work force, there was great anxiety on the part of National's management about the consequent effect on the start up of the new area. Also, with the ensuing poor job perception of the East Texas Plant that pervaded the community, recruiting top-notch hourly employees for the expansion was predicted to be difficult, if not impossible. An additional complicating factor was the age composition of the rank-and-file at the plant. There were many older (age 50 and above) workers at the plant, who started the plant in 1945 as young men and returning war veterans. These men had known hard times and appreciated having a job, even though the wages were relatively low. They tended to be happy, productive employees and were the stabilizing influence at the plant. Expansion and attrition, however, had added a majority of younger workers (age 35 and below). The average age of the hourly employees in June, 1966, was 32. These younger people tended to be the most dissatisfied and were the crusaders as well as the troublemakers. They were extremely militant in their views, and the productivity of many was marginal. Management shuddered when contemplating the effect of adding approximately 300 young employees to their ranks to staff the new expansion.

These factors of discontent were self-perpetuating and self-reinforcing, and serious outgrowths seemed imminent. Consequently, in November, 1966, a wildcat strike developed and lasted three weeks. The strike developed because of a seemingly minor issue over work assignment in one of the plant's sections. Management obtained an injunction ordering the employees back to their jobs due to the no-strike provision of the contract. While not officially substantiated, members of supervision believed that it took three weeks to secure an injunction from the local judiciary because of the intense political power held by the unions in the community.

June, 1967 — "You'd Better Give Us Something"

After the wildcat strike, management spent considerable time in deliberating the course of action needed to improve the general employment conditions at the plant. Attention was directed and redirected to section 50 of the 1964 agreement: "The rates of pay as well as individual job classifications may be changed by mutual consent of Local No. 75 and National Chemical Corporation." It appeared at first glance that the East Texas Plant had been quite fortunate to "get away with" the 1964 contract that suppressed wages. Also, the expiration of the contract "would come soon enough"; management knew that they would pay dearly for the next contract. All agreed, however, that something had to be done quickly!

This deliberation over an appropriate course of action consumed a great deal of time. It was not until June 1, 1967, that a decision was reached. The plant manager announced the following memorandum: "Effective June 1, 1967, a general wage increase of 21¢ per hour will be granted to all hourly paid employees at the East Texas Plant. This increase is the response of the management of National Chemical Corporation to the changing needs of its employees." This decision originated at the plant level and was subsequently approved by division and corporate offices.

June, 1967 — "How About Us?"

The plant management proposed an addendum to the decision for division and corporate approval. The compensation plight was certainly not confined to the hourly ranks. Historically, there had been a very slim differential between the salary earned by foremen and that of the highest-paid hourly employee reporting to the foreman. Management desired to maintain the differential at 15 percent for all foremen, with better performers enjoying a larger differential. Due to the timing of hourly contracts and the salary administration program, this differential often disappeared for periods of time. Additionally, the foremen were not paid for any overtime (they were exempt employees). It was recognized, however, that the foremen did not work a significant amount of overtime. An informal arrangement of compensatory time-off for overtime was practiced, but was not guaranteed. The hourly employees did receive numerous overtime opportunities. A standing joke was, "I would like to be a foreman, but I cannot tolerate the cut in pay."

The foremens' response to this quandary was "unhappy resolution." They lost all union seniority rights when promoted to foreman, and they could return to the hourly ranks only on the lowest-rated job *and* if there was an opening. In no case did a foreman ever return to the hourly ranks at the East Texas Plant. Some foremen did quit to join new plants, but the turnover was very low as compared to the hourly workers. Also, in isolated cases, hourly employees did, in fact, refuse offers of promotion to foreman. Experiencing the same inflationary pressure as the hourly workers, the foremen were certainly not satisfied with their salaries. There was scattered talk of a "foreman's union," but the movement was ill defined and had no leaders. Any leader could easily be discharged because there was no protection from a recognized union or a U.S. labor law.

Ironically, the foremen were the greatest asset in the plant. They were competent, patient, and, in reality, "kept the lid on things." Nonetheless, there was growing discontent among the foremen over pay. Their salaries were approximately 15 percent below the average salary for foremen in the area's petro-chemical industry. Their job was unfavorably perceived in the community, too.

The salaries of foremen, like those of all salaried employees, were subject to a salary administration program. (The formulation of foreman merit increases is presented in appendix B.) There were almost no grade "1" or grade "5" performers. The distribution of grades approximated the standard bell-shaped curve, with most foremen receiving a grade "3" rating. There were a number of criteria by which to evaluate performance, but the ratings were mostly based on the subjective judgment of a foreman's superior.

The plant management recognized that a general increase for the hourly personnel must be accompanied by a corresponding increase for the foremen. Hence, management (with the division's and corporation's approval) granted each foreman a $60 per month increase. Included in this general increase were selected second- and third-level supervisors, staff, and technical personnel. The personnel (other than foremen) selected to receive the increase were those most affected by salary compression. The foremen were called in individually by their superiors and informed that the increase was an "adjustment" and an adjunct to the merit increase program.

Most of the increases were well received. In ensuing months, however, the foremen discovered that their increases from the merit plan had, in fact, been adjusted due to the $60 per month increase. The percent increase had not been affected, but the timing was manipulated with no apparent explanation. The date of the merit increase was delayed three to five months for many foremen. This situation caused varying degrees of resentment, depending on the individual involved. Moreover, the foremen's superiors cited historical inequities in the merit increase program and wished to make individual adjustments. This adjustment was not possible with the across-the-board $60 per month increase. Finally, there was definite resentment from the small number of middle-supervision, staff, and technical personnel who did not receive the increase.

December, 1967 — "That Was Just Openers"

After granting the general hourly wage increase of 21¢ per hour, management attempted to poll the effect during the three months prior to contract expiration. They noted that an improvement in morale was evident, but that the overall effect was definitely not what was desired. The following quotations generally described the reaction:

1. "Sure we appreciate it, but this place doesn't give something for nothing. What are they up to?"
2. "They had no choice; they could see they had to pay us a decent wage."
3. "What are they trying to do, buy us off? They have 'nickeled and dimed' us long enough!"
4. "Ha! They give us the change, and the foremen are folding the money."
5. "Why didn't they do this two years ago when it meant something? Who are they trying to kid now?"
6. "That was just openers; wait till we get them at the table in December."

Discussion Questions

1. Discuss the role of compensation in promoting effectiveness and efficiency in the plant.

2. Critique management's resolution of the hourly and salaried compensation problem.

3. Are any weaknesses in the collective bargaining process demonstrated in this case?

4. How could a foreman's salary influence the hourly employees' adherence to work standards?

appendix A
Hourly Wage Comparison — East Texas Area, December, 1965

Job Classification	East Texas Plant	Petro-Chem Plant Average	Construction*
Chief Operator	$3.40	$3.80	$4.50
Operator 1C	3.25	3.65	N.A.**
Operator 2C	3.05	3.40	N.A.
Chief Mechanic	3.50	3.85	4.40
Mechanic 1C	3.30	3.75	N.A.
Mechanic Apprentice	3.00	3.35	3.65
Chief Electrician	3.55	4.00	4.65
Electrician 1C	3.35	3.75	N.A.
Electrician Apprentice	3.10	3.40	3.80
Instrument Mechanic	3.45	3.90	4.65
Carpenter 1C	3.30	3.75	4.50
Truck Driver	3.15	3.35	3.80
Laborer	2.50	2.80	3.10

*Construction wages are trade average estimates, and the job classification comparable to the industrial workers is a judgment of the case writer.

**Not applicable

appendix B
Merit Increase Plan for East Texas Plant Foremen

Performance Grade	Description
1	Excellent
2	Good
3	Average
4	Below average
5*	Minimum acceptable for employment

Grade	Percent Increase	Period between Increases
1	10.0	8 months
2	7.5	12 months
3	5.5	15 months
4	3.5	18 months
5	—	

*Grade 5 performers must achieve grade 4 or above rating within 12 months or be subject to discharge.

case 40

National Chemical Corporation
East Texas Plant[1]

(Part B)

In the latter part of 1967, the management of the East Texas Plant was braced for stiff bargaining upon the expiration of the three-year contract signed December 10, 1964. Their pessimistic expectations were certainly realized. Not only was the union negotiating committee seething over the expiring three-year contract, but the East Texas Plant was in the process of major expansion totaling $50 million. The construction had begun in August, 1967, and was targeted for completion in June, 1968. Following a start-up period of several months, the plant had some significant shipping contracts to fill (toward the latter part of 1968) from the new addition. Failure to meet this production schedule would prove extremely costly; therefore, delays in construction and start up were to be avoided. A strike on December 10, 1967, would stop construction at the plant because the trade unions would not cross *any* picket line, regardless of the identity of strikers or the nature of the strike.

Needless to say, National Chemical Corporation wanted a signed contract on December 10, 1967. Negotiations were completed prior to expiration, but the company paid dearly. A summary of the major provisions was as follows:

1. A one-year contract (no more three-year contracts for Local No. 75 of the International Chemical Workers) with the standard no-strike, no-lockout clause.
2. Two additional paid holidays.
3. Increase in shift differential from 7¢–14¢ to 10¢–20¢.
4. Double-time premium pay for the seventh day worked in a work week.
5. A minimum across-the-board increase of 30¢ per hour.
6. Other wage adjustments to "standardize the rates." (For example, a 1-C mechanic historically earned a higher rate than a 1-C operator or a 1-C carpenter.)

The new contract stipulated that all class designations would earn equal pay, regardless of the nature of the work group. These adjustments, *in addition*

---

[1]For additional details, see case 39, "National Chemical Corporation: East Texas Plant — Part A."

to the 30¢ per hour, ranged from 5¢ to 30¢ per hour. Hence, the percentage increase varied between 10 percent and 20 percent for most of the 1,000 workers in the bargaining unit.

In addition, the union won certain strategic procedural issues, such as direct 1¹/₂ time payment for overtime selection errors. However, the significant feature of the 1967 contract was definitely the wage increase. This contract vaulted the workers at the East Texas Plant to the top wage earner status in the area. A summary of the rates is shown in appendix A.

Another major provision of the 1967 contract was a specific agreement that all hourly workers in the new area would be included in the bargaining unit. This provision ended speculation that the new expansion would be staffed by all salaried personnel.

Salary Program

The 1967 contract was most disheartening to the foremen. They felt that the union had been "given the keys to the plant." Moreover, many foremen were actually earning less than the highest-paid hourly worker. Management did, however, anticipate this condition and made significant changes in its salaried program. Both the percent increase and the timing of increases were accelerated as shown in appendix B.

Even with sweeping salaried adjustments, supervision in general was disconsolate. Agitation and gloating by the union workers further deteriorated the situation.

Personnel Problem Solved?

When the contract was signed December 10, 1967, a period of "high spirits" reinforced by the holiday season pervaded the hourly ranks at the East Texas Plant. This boost in morale ended early in 1968. The union leaders (formal and informal), spurred on by recent contract "victory," were asserting their power in more and more areas. Grievances were again rampant, and effective discipline was almost totally absent. There were constant threats of wildcat strikes on seemingly minor issues.

Meanwhile, the new expansion was completed in mid-1968, and after the usual difficult start-up period, the new units were in full operation. At the end of the start-up period, the 1967 one-year contract expired (December 10, 1968). A new two-year contract was signed, with the following significant provisions:

1. Eight percent general across-the-board increase for all work groups.
2. Wage "re-openers" after one year of the contract had expired to determine the increase for the second year.

3. The standard no-strike, no-lockout clause except for nonagreement on wages for the second contract year.
4. Several upgradings of job classifications from third and second class to first class.

Labor Turnaround

During the first quarter of 1969 (after the new units were firmly on line and in a producing state), the corporate, division, and plant management mapped out strategies for a program termed *labor turnaround* for the East Texas Plant. The objectives of this program were to eliminate the waste and inefficiencies resulting from mismanagement and poor direction of the hourly personnel. Important aspects included the establishment of effective discipline and the improvement of the status of foremen. The first step in this program was to inform the union that conduct which interfered with the normal and efficient operation of the plant would be dealt with in an appropriate, corrective manner.

Strong disciplinary measures ensued, including suspensions without pay. Each of the disciplinary cases was conducted in spite of bristling threats of wildcat strikes. No such strike developed in 1969. Most suspension cases were the result of incidents involving refusal to carry out specific instructions from a foreman or similar conduct that led to work slowdowns or stoppages. Most of these cases were certified to arbitration and resulted in favorable awards for the company.

The wage issue was settled during wage negotiations December 10, 1969, as provided in the 1968 contract. Another 8 percent increase was agreed upon in spite of the union's attempt to bring up other matters, such as reinstatement and back pay for suspension cases.

The labor turmoil at the plant reached a peak in March, 1970, when the union president, recording secretary, and a section steward were discharged following work slowdowns in several departments. Each of these employees had records of suspensions for similar incidents. A wildcat strike immediately followed. Supervisory and staff personnel manned the plant and maintained operations. The strike lasted 16 days, with the hourly forces returning to work after the company agreed to immediate arbitration of the discharge cases (a very slight concession by the company).

The labor turnaround was in progress, and there was no doubt that Local No. 75 of the International Chemical Workers had "lost face" at the plant. The union filed a charge of unfair labor practices against the company, but it was denied by the NLRB.

Enter Local No. 8

Consequently, Local No. 75 was "raided" at the plant during the summer of 1970. A major factor in the success of the raid was the arbitrator's ruling upholding the three discharges in March that precipitated the wildcat strike. Standard NLRB procedures were followed, and Local No. 75 of the International Chemical Workers was replaced by Local No. 8 of the Craftsman Union (again, actual union name is disguised) as the bargaining agent for the 1,000 hourly workers. Local No. 8 had a reputation of being tough and was elected primarily in retaliation to management's crackdown.

To the surprise of many employees at the plant, Local No. 8 also was very tough on its membership. It did not tolerate constant agitation at the plant by "wandering" union officials. All the representatives, as well as the negotiating team for the upcoming contract, were initially appointed, with elections of officers to follow. Also, there were no "nonworking" union officers as had been the case with the president and the chairman of the grievance committee in the previous representative union. The major union official was a business agent paid by the union, not the company. The number of grievances dropped dramatically, with Local No. 8's stipulation that a grievance would be submitted in writing only after three steps to verbally resolve the grievance had failed. Local No. 8 made it clear in a general meeting that it was Local No. 8's job to process union problems and it was the membership's job to *work*, and that many "agitators" were now going to have to go to work.

1970 Contract

After the election certifying Local No. 8 was held, both parties were eager to negotiate a new contract. Hence, negotiations commenced September 15, 1970. Local No. 8's objectives were to secure good wage settlements, reaffirm union security, and eliminate the so-called "side-deals" that many believed existed under the political structure of Local No. 75. In addition, Local No. 8 was eager to neutralize management's disciplinary offensive by establishing procedures whereby the union was to be included in early stages of the procedure. The business agent would be present at all disciplinary meetings, and the practice of suspension pending investigation would be ended.

Management, on the other hand, was eager to eliminate inefficiencies and costs due to craft sovereignty. For example, work on a particular pipeline might include carpenters to build a scaffold, insulators to remove any insulation, and mechanics to repair the pipeline. Hence, management introduced a "flexibility clause" in the 1970 contract. Excerpts from that clause are included in appendix C.

Both parties achieved their specific objectives and signed a two-year contract October 15, 1970. Wage provisions stipulated across-the-board increases of 35¢ per hour effective October 15, 1970, and 30¢ per hour effective October 15, 1971. A summary of the wage schedule is presented in appendix D.

The first half of 1971 was relatively quiet; during that six-month period, all grievances were resolved verbally. Personnel at the latter stage of the disciplinary procedure were aided through stern counseling from Local No. 8 and cooperation by the company. The company slowed down its labor turn-around offensive. Major labor-management problems stemmed from application of the flexibility clause. There were several confrontations, with both parties settling for compromise. To aid in solving such problems, a committee of appointees from Local No. 8 met monthly with a company committee. The union committee prepared the agenda for discussion.

Wage-Price Freeze

While the labor climate at the East Texas Plant was somewhat harmonious, President Nixon proclaimed a 90-day wage-price freeze on August 15, 1971. By this executive order, all wages at the East Texas Plant were frozen. On October 15, 1971, the workers did not receive their contracted 30¢ per hour increase. Both the workers and Local No. 8 anxiously awaited national labor leaders' response to President Nixon's executive order. Just prior to the end of the 90-day freeze and the pronouncement of Phase II of Nixon's economic plan, the business agent of Local No. 8 issued the following memorandum to the membership:

> Dear Brothers:
>
> Who is the company trying to fool? We know that when we signed the October 15, 1970, contract, we gave up certain key issues in return for what we consider was an equitable wage settlement. Now, we have not received that wage settlement. The consideration due us under that contract has been abrogated. This is to let you know that your union will not stand idly by but will very much protect your interests.

Phase II of the wage-price freeze stipulated a ceiling of 5.5 percent on increases. This 5.5 percent was lower than the negotiated increase to have taken place on October 15, 1971, and was much lower than the existing Salaried Merit Increase Plan (appendix B). During the first half of November, prior to the end of the 90-day freeze, the plant management communicated at length with the division and corporate offices on strategy for Phase II. There was the immediate question of whether or not to grant the contracted October 15, 1971, increase to the hourly workers. Also, there was a definite problem attempting to administer the merit salary program in light of Phase II and the effect of granting or not granting the October 15, 1971, increase to the hourly workers. Too, there was the question of what to do about salaried personnel whose merit salary increases were delayed by the 90-day freeze. A sound plan had to be outlined immediately. The East Texas Plant management remembered all too well the turbulent years from 1965 to 1970.

Discussion Questions

1. What are the implications of the governmental restrictions placed on salary merit plans with regard to motivation of foremen to maintain work standards and improve productivity?

2. Evaluate the approach to unionism that Local No. 75 and Local No. 8 followed.

3. Evaluate the labor turnaround which management applied.

appendix A
Hourly Wage Rates at East Texas Plant, December 10, 1967

Job Classification	Rate/Hour
Rated Jobs[2]	
Chief	$4.06
First Class	3.86
Second Class	3.66
Apprentice	3.46
All Laborers	2.80

appendix B
Salaried Merit Increase Plan Effective December 1, 1967

Performance Grade	Description	Grade	Percent Increases	Period between Increases
1	Excellent	1	14.0	6 months
2	Good	2	11.0	9 months
3	Average	3	8.0	12 months
4	Below Average	4	6.0	15 months
5[3]	Minimum Acceptable for Employment	5	No increase	

appendix C
Flexibility Excerpts

1. "On evenings, nights, or weekends, mechanics may erect a prefabricated-sectioned scaffold not over two sections high to facilitate their job. . . ."

2. "On evenings, nights, or weekends, mechanics may operate lift equipment not over 10-ton capacity to facilitate their job. . . ."

3. "On evenings, nights, or weekends, mechanics may remove insulation only to expose necessary flanges on pipelines or work areas on equipment. . . ."

---

[2]Groups include operators, mechanics, welders, electricians, carpenters, instrument technicians, insulators, machinists, lab analysts, painters, tinsmiths, and equipment operators.

[3]Grade 5 performers must achieve grade 4 (or above) rating within 12 months or be subject to discharge.

4. "Meter and instrument mechanics may use a sabre-saw (previously reserved for carpenters) to cut holes in panelboards for installation of instruments. . . ."

5. "Helpers or apprentices in one craft may be reassigned temporarily at any time as helpers in another craft to facilitate a given job. . . ."

appendix D
Hourly Wage Rates

Job Classification	10/15/70	10/15/71
Rated Jobs[4]		
Chief	$5.05	$5.35
First Class	4.83	5.13
Second Class	4.60	4.90
Apprentice or Helper	4.35	4.65
All Laborers	3.60	3.90
Shift Differential	12¢–24¢	15¢–30¢

---

[4]Group is the same as in appendix A.

National Chemical Corporation
East Texas Plant[1]
(Part C)

The wage-price freeze of 1971 was bitterly received by both hourly and salaried employees at the East Texas Plant. The freeze was imposed just at the time when both salaries and hourly wages were beginning to be competitive with those of neighboring plants.

Certain members of supervision were particularly critical of the wage freeze. Their salaries were frozen only because their respective reviews for increases typically occurred after August 15, 1971. A large number of their associates, however, were given substantial increases because their reviews occurred prior to the freeze date. (For a schedule of the salaried merit increase plan, refer to appendix B of case 40.) Some of the fortunate members of supervision who received annual merit increases prior to the freeze often "gloated" in the presence of those who were adversely affected by the freeze. This situation resulted in a great deal of bitterness and poor morale within the supervisory ranks.

On the other hand, hourly workers were not too concerned about the freeze. They were highly confident that their contractual wage increase would eventually be honored and that retroactive increases would be forthcoming. To ensure this, Local No. 8 conferred at length with managers of the company and also with governmental officials.

Phase II

As expected, the hourly workers received their 30¢ per hour increase retroactive to October 15, 1971. Special checks were mailed in mid-December, 1971, to all hourly employees. The ceiling of 5.5 percent as imposed by Phase II did not apply to increases negotiated prior to August 15, 1971.

The ceiling of 5.5 percent, however, was imposed on the salaried ranks, and salaried increases were not retroactive. In fact, increases were not forthcoming until March, 1972. The reason for the delay was not apparent to the

---

[1]Refer to cases 39 and 40 for additional details.

management of the East Texas Plant. All salaried employees, other than those who received a merit rating of No. 5 (minimum acceptable for employment), received the 5.5 percent increase recommended by Phase II. The merit system was temporarily "scrapped."

Management at the East Texas Plant did not immediately announce that the salaried merit pay plan was temporarily suspended. The 5.5 percent increases, granted in March, 1972, were angrily received by members of supervision who had ratings of No. 1, 2, or 3. The superior who passed out the raises did not have the information or the authorization to explain why the increases were 5.5 percent. Consequently, the recipients of the 5.5 percent increases rationalized that their performance ratings had been adjusted downward because "someone was out to get them personally."

Not until June, 1972, was a full explanation given for the 5.5 percent ceiling on wage increases. Much damage, however, was already done. There was a significant relaxation of work standards established during the 1969 "labor turnaround" (see case 40 for details). Particularly damaging was the failure to uniformly apply work flexibility gained in the 1970 contract. Application of the flexibility clause often involved heated confrontations with stewards who feared abuses of the new provision. Foremen, who were adversely affected by changes in the salary plan, readily avoided the hassle in application of flexibility. Other foremen, who had received generous increases prior to wage-price controls, aggressively used work flexibility. Local No. 8 played one foremen against another to minimize the impact of work flexibility and to preserve craft sovereignty.

1972 Contract

The failure to uniformly apply flexibility gained in the 1970 contract adversely affected objectives sought by management in the 1972 contract negotiations. Management's strategy was to totally eliminate the inefficiency and feather-bedding characteristic of craft sovereignty. The company wanted to establish a single "general mechanic" classification for all employees who did maintainance work. This plan would result in elimination of all craft designations and, subsequently, the end of craft sovereignty. Management calculated that maintenance labor costs could be reduced by 20 percent if a "general mechanic" could be called upon to perform (and assist in performing) a wide variety of craft work.

The elimination of craft sovereignty, however, was not accomplished in the 1972 contract. Local No. 8 representatives gloated at the negotiating table that many foremen were not even using the flexibility gained in the 1970 contract. The union condescended, "Why don't you use the tools we have already given you before you ask for more?"

Hence, elimination of craft sovereignty was postponed for at least three years, the duration of the contract signed on October 15, 1972. Changes between the 1970 and 1972 contracts were minor. Local No. 8 demanded and received the 5.5 percent increase sanctioned by the governmental wage-price board. There were to be wage re-openers for the second and third years of the contract. The union also received minor increases in insurance benefits and an additional paid holiday (Washington's Birthday).

Beyond 1972

The restriction of wage increases to 5.5 percent paid to union employees helped alleviate some of the bitterness of those salaried employees who had also been limited to 5.5 percent increases. In fact, a period of harmony prevailed over the East Texas Plant. National Chemical Corporation attempted to improve management skills of its supervisory ranks by adding a training staff and conducting a series of supervisory training programs. An effort was made to improve communications between upper and lower levels of management by holding quarterly foremen dinners, during which informal discussions together with question-answer sessions were held.

As the effects of wage-price controls passed, the merit salaried plan was reinstated. A great deal of debate stemmed over whether or not adjustments should be made to correct past inequities caused by the controls. There was no total resolution of the question. Everyone unanimously agreed, however, that "you better get what you can before new and permanent controls are imposed."

Discussion Questions

1. Discuss the elimination of craft sovereignty and the impact upon productivity at the plant.

2. What implications do wage-price controls have on plant operations today?

3. Should attempts be made to correct past salary inequities caused by wage-price controls?

chapter 8

New Factors in Production/Operations Management

North American
Pipeline Company

On July 18, 1973, Robert Graham, Vice-President of the Engineering Division of United Contractors, Inc., faced one of the most difficult decisions of his career — to fire or retain a welding inspector accused of suggesting to the superintendent of a construction company that he be given a substantial amount of money for each arc burn and "bad" weld overlooked. In the absence of tangible evidence, but in the arena of heated, conflicting testimony, Graham was forced to either "take the word" of the inspector (who he believed was innocent) and suffer a costly shutdown of all construction operations, or accept the testimony of the construction superintendent and release a highly competent welding inspector in order to maintain all ongoing operations involved in the construction of a 30-in. naturtal gas line from Detroit to the intercoastal waterways of south Louisiana.

Background

The construction of one segment of a gas line to transmit natural gas from production sites off the Gulf Coast of Louisiana to large industrialized cities in the eastern and midwestern United States encompassed the functions of four different firms.

North American Pipeline Company would own the line after its completion and had ultimate authority over all phases of its construction. Planning the project, performing all engineering activities, securing access to private property, and subcontracting actual operations were its primary duties. North American was concerned with maintaining exceptional progress in all activities during the summer months. Experience had taught the company's construction personnel that rainfall and bad weather during the fall and winter severely hampered nearly all operations identified with the laying of a pipeline. However, North American was equally concerned with maintaining quality control, especially in the welding and coating functions. Everyone knew that a bad weld or uncoated spot on the iron pipe (causing the iron to rust) could possibly result in an explosion in the future, causing extensive damage and/or death to nearby residents.

Gulf Coast Construction Corporation, a subcontractor of North American Pipeline Company, performed all functions required in the physical construction of the line. These activities included clearing the right-of-way, hauling and stringing the pipe, bending the pipe to fit the contours of the terrain, digging the trench into which the pipe would be placed, welding, coating and wrapping, inspecting the pipe for jeeps (uncoated surfaces), placing the coated pipe in the trench, covering the pipe, inspecting for jeeps after the pipe had been buried, testing, and cleaning up the right-of-way (including the planting of grass).

All construction equipment, with the exception of welding machines, was owned and maintained by the company. This equipment included Caterpillars, lowboys with sidebooms, trucks, floats, tractors, backhoes, and so forth.

United Contractors, Inc., also a subcontractor of North American Pipeline Company, inspected and approved all functions performed by Gulf Coast Construction Corporation. One or more inspectors were assigned to each function, and each reported directly to the Chief Inspector, who in turn was accountable to North American Pipeline Company.

Although the inspectors and construction workers were employed by different firms, inspectors had the authority to accept or reject any work performed under their auspices. This checks-and-balances relationship was essential to the maintenance of quality construction.

All inspectors were veterans of pipeline construction, and all had previous experience in performing the activities which they were now inspecting.

Baton Rouge X-ray Company was employed to x-ray all welds (at both tie-in stations and along the main line), thereby providing welding inspectors with photographs that revealed welding flaws which were often not visible to the naked eye. Whenever a weld was considered unacceptable because of flaws, or whenever a welder accidentally touched the pipe with his rod (causing an arc burn and irreparable damage to the pipe), the welding inspector could require that section be cut out and replaced. Replacing a bad section of pipe was both time consuming and costly for Gulf Coast Construction Corporation. Often, welding inspectors discovered that a welder or a welder's helper would put mud over an arc burn to camouflage or hide it. While such practices may have been frowned upon by the management of Gulf Coast Construction Corporation, they did, nevertheless, save the company money and speed up progress. In addition, welders sometimes employed such practices in an attempt to maintain their jobs. Too many bad welds or too many arc burns resulted in discharge. Turnover of welders was one of many critical problems which Gulf Coast Construction Corporation wanted to minimize. A shortage of competent welders would slow down construction progress considerably.

The Incident

On the morning of July 10, Raymond Biggs, Superintendent of Construction for Gulf Coast Construction Corporation's pipeline division, telephoned Chief Inspector Pete Milton at his temporary residence in Alexandria, Louisiana, and asked him to come to Gulf Coast's field office as soon as possible. Biggs mentioned a serious problem involving one of the welding inspectors who worked under Milton's supervision, but he declined to go into detail over the phone.

Raymond Biggs and Pete Milton had known each other for several years. United Contractors, Inc. had performed inspections on pipelines constructed by Gulf Coast in prior years. Too, both companies had subcontracted several segments of the line presently under construction. Because Biggs was in charge of all on-site construction activities, and because Milton had authority over all inspection duties, it was essential that they cooperate as fully as possible. Typically, they saw each other daily, and frequently they conversed over their car telephones.

Each man had great respect for the other. Over the years, Biggs had developed a reputation for maintaining schedules in all types of terrain and weather conditions. No one questioned his knowledge of pipeline construction. Biggs ran a "tight ship" and expected his construction foremen to do the same. Construction workers were expected to be on the job at the assigned time; they were expected to "earn their pay"; equipment was always maintained adequately; and every construction worker knew that carelessness, indifference, and excessive absenteeism would result in immediate discharge. Biggs' only trait which Milton considered to be a fault was his apparent obsession with keeping ahead of schedule on all construction activities. His reputation had been built and was being maintained by completing projects ahead of schedule.

Pete Milton, too, was well versed in all phases of pipeline construction. His father had been a construction worker, and it was the only life he had ever known. He had worked as a laborer, foreman of the coating and wrapping operations, welder for twelve years, welding inspector, and, for the past three years, Chief Inspector in the Engineering Division of United Contractors, Inc.

Milton handpicked all the inspectors who were currently working under his supervision. In past years, he had worked alongside each of them and, in all cases, considered them to be competent and conscientious.

Pete Milton was shocked when Raymond Biggs told him that Red Whatley, a welding inspector, had approached him and offered to overlook a few bad welds and arc burns "for a price." The price of overlooking a bad weld, Whatley contended, would be less than the cost of repairing it. Also, progress would not be impeded, resulting in a tremendous savings in labor costs and materials.

When queried about his response, Biggs told Milton that he virtually threw Whatley out of his trailer (which was used as an office) after informing him that under no circumstances would he resort to payoffs and corruption to speed up progress on the line.

Following his account of the incident, Biggs asked Milton to fire Whatley. If Milton refused, Gulf Coast Construction Corporation would inform North American Pipeline Company of the incident and then cease all operations until the welding inspector had been replaced. Milton commented that he found it "hard to believe" that Whatley asked for a payoff. Having known Whatley for more than 15 years and having worked with him for 10 of those years, Milton considered him to be honest, dependable, and trustworthy. He had never known Whatley to either ask for or accept graft. In fact, Whatley was the first inspector Milton had chosen at the start of the project because of his competence as a welding inspector and his dedication to quality construction.

Milton wanted to talk personally with Whatley before taking action. At 9:15 a.m., Milton arrived at the tie-in station where Whatley was waiting on a weld to be x-rayed. As Milton drove up, Whatley walked toward his pick-up and greeted him cordially, as he had done every morning since welding operations had begun. After an exchange of light, casual remarks about the hot, humid weather and the plight of the St. Louis Cardinals, Whatley became quite serious and told Milton that he thought he should know about a situation involving the construction superintendent, who got "out-of-line" earlier that morning. Whatley then told Milton that Raymond Biggs had offered him money if he would "help speed up the welding process by ignoring some of the arc burns and begin accepting welds which otherwise would be unacceptable."

According to Whatley, Biggs became enraged when he refused the offer and threatened to "get his job." Whatley then left the superintendent's office, drove to the job site, arriving at 7:00 a.m., and began performing his regular duties. His first impulse, he said, was to inform Milton of the incident, but that would have caused him to be late getting to the tie-in station. Following Whatley's account of the incident, Milton told him that Biggs had accused him of asking for a payoff.

The Decision

Pete Milton realized that there was no tangible evidence which could be used as grounds for Whatley's discharge. He knew also that a refusal to discharge Whatley would result in a costly cessation of all construction activities. There was no doubt that Biggs would never reconsider his demand for Whatley's dismissal. Even if Biggs could somehow be persuaded to withdraw his demand, the working relationship between the welders and Whatley would be severely damaged. Milton believed that his first course of action should be to consult with his immediate superior, Mr. Robert Graham, Vice-President of the Engineering Division of United Contractors.

Bob Graham was sitting in his New Orleans office, reviewing daily progress reports on the North American line when his telephone rang. Milton quickly reviewed the situation and asked for Graham's suggestions on the appropriate course of action. Knowing that the decision would have to be made as quickly as possible, Graham suggested that he fly to Alexandria in the corporate plane, where Milton would meet him. Following his arrival, they would go to the field office of North American Pipeline Company and explain the incident to Henry LeBlanc, Head of Construction and Engineering for his company's regional construction activities. From LeBlanc's office, they would telephone Biggs and ask him to meet them at the job site for a personal confrontation with Whatley. Graham insisted on a face-to-face exchange of accusations and countercharges before a decision was made on discharging Whatley.

Graham and Milton, in their review of the incident with LeBlanc, discussed factors which both supported and refuted Whatley's statement. Among the issues which they discussed and believed to be pertinent were the following:

1. Both Milton and Graham had known Whatley for several years, and neither had ever had reason to question his honesty and integrity.
2. Whatley was experiencing some financial difficulties as a result of his recent investments in real estate. Property which he had bought for resale was difficult to unload due to the tight money market and high interest rates.
3. Raymond Biggs had never previously been accused of attempting to "buy off" an inspector.
4. Gulf Coast Construction Corporation was ahead of schedule in all construction operations, including welding.
5. It was common practice for Gulf Coast Construction Corporation to give inspectors fifths of whiskey and to occasionally pick up gasoline tickets. (Inspectors used their private vehicles on the job and were reimbursed by United Contractors for expenses incurred. Inspectors sometimes submitted expense vouchers to their employer, requesting reimbursement for gasoline actually paid for by Gulf Coast Construction Corporation. Whatley, however, refused to allow the construction corporation to pay for his expenses. In fact, he had mentioned to Milton on several occasions that other inspectors were being reimbursed for costs that they did not incur.)

Biggs arrived at the tie-in station as Graham, LeBlanc, and Milton were parking their car under a nearby tree. Biggs, followed by Whatley, walked over, greeted them, and exchanged pleasantries. Following these initial greetings, the following conversation took place:

> Biggs: "Bob, I hope you came here to fire this s.o.b. who asked me for a payoff for overlooking some bad welds."

Graham: "Now wait a minute, Raymond. My purpose in being here is to determine exactly what the problem is and how best to resolve it. I've known all of you guys a long time, and I hate like hell to see a problem of this nature crop up. First, I want to hear both sides of this argument and then I'll make my decision."

Milton: "Well, Red, why don't you tell us your side of the story?"

Whatley: "Hell, Pete, there ain't much to tell. Raymond called me this morning around 6:00 and asked me to come by his office before going to work. When I got there, he said he wanted me to overlook some arc burns and bad welds. Said he would make it worth my trouble. That's when I told him to go to hell and started to leave. The last thing he said before I left was that he would get my job."

Biggs: "That's a lie, damn it. You came by and asked if I would be willing to pay you to overlook some bad welds. I have no reason to offer you anything. Everyone knows we're ahead of schedule. Besides, everyone here knows that I've never tried to buy anyone off. Isn't that right, Pete?"

Milton: "Yes, Raymond, that's correct. I've never known you to try and buy an inspector off. But, then, I've never known Red to ask for a payoff either."

Biggs: "I have only one more thing to say. If Whatley isn't off this line within the next hour, I will shut down all construction operations and keep them down until he is fired from this job."

LeBlanc: "My concern is that we keep all operations going. You men have contracted to perform this work, and I expect you to meet those obligations. Future contracts depend upon your performances on this job."

Whatley: "Pete, both you and Bob have known me for a long time. We have worked together for more years than I care to remember. Both of you know what kind of person I am. I can't believe that either of you is willing to let this man ruin my life by getting me fired for something I didn't do."

At this point in the conversation. Graham asked Milton to join him in a private discussion, during which he informed Milton of his decision and asked for Milton's reaction. Afterward, Graham walked back to the group and briefly announced his decision.

Discussion Question

1. If you were in Graham's position, what decision would you have made? Cite the rationale for your decision.

National Chlor-Alkali:
Geismar, Louisiana, Plant

H. C. Cardwell, plant manager of National Chlor-Alkali's Geismar, Louisiana, plant, was convening a meeting of the catastrophe committee to investigate the accidental electrocution of a chlorine cell repairman, Jerome Grant, two days earlier. The purpose of the meeting was to determine the cause of the fatality, prescribe corrective measures, and prepare for the Occupational Safety and Health Act (OSHA) investigation that could be expected within a week. As required by law, the plant immediately notified the Department of Labor of the fatality. (For this and other information about OSHA, see appendix A to this case.)

Present at the meeting were Fred Stolts (Safety Supervisor), John Buckner (Production Manager), Gwen Morgan (Personnel Manager), Ed Chaucer (Maintenance Manager), Brett Barlow (Technical Manager), Hank Thornton (Production Superintendent), John Bessels (Cell-Repair Foreman), Jim Stewart (Production Shift-Supervisor), and the presiding Cardwell. Cardwell opened the meeting by asking Bessels and Stewart to review the fatality.

Stewart: It was approximately 5:00 p.m. (shifts at the plant were 6:00 a.m. to 2:00 p.m., 2:00 p.m. to 10:00 p.m., and 10:00 p.m. to 6:00 a.m.) when Bessels came into the control room for a cup of coffee. We had just finished pouring the coffee when we noticed Stoneman and Davis scrambling out of cell room "B" carrying Grant (The cell room is across the main street from the control room. See Figure 8–1 for a plant plot plan.)

Cardwell: Were Stoneman and Davis working with Grant?

Bessels: Yes, that's correct. They were renewing cell no. 38. (For job description and typical crew work assignments, see appendix B.)

Buckner: What was wrong with no. 38?

Stewart: It had high voltage — 4.8 volts (For a description of the chlorine cell and typical operating characteristics, see Figure 8–2.)

Chaucer: How far had the job progressed before the fatality?

Bessels: They were just beginning to hook up the jumper switch (See appendix B).

Cardwell: What was Grant doing?

175

Figure 8–1 Plant Plot Plan

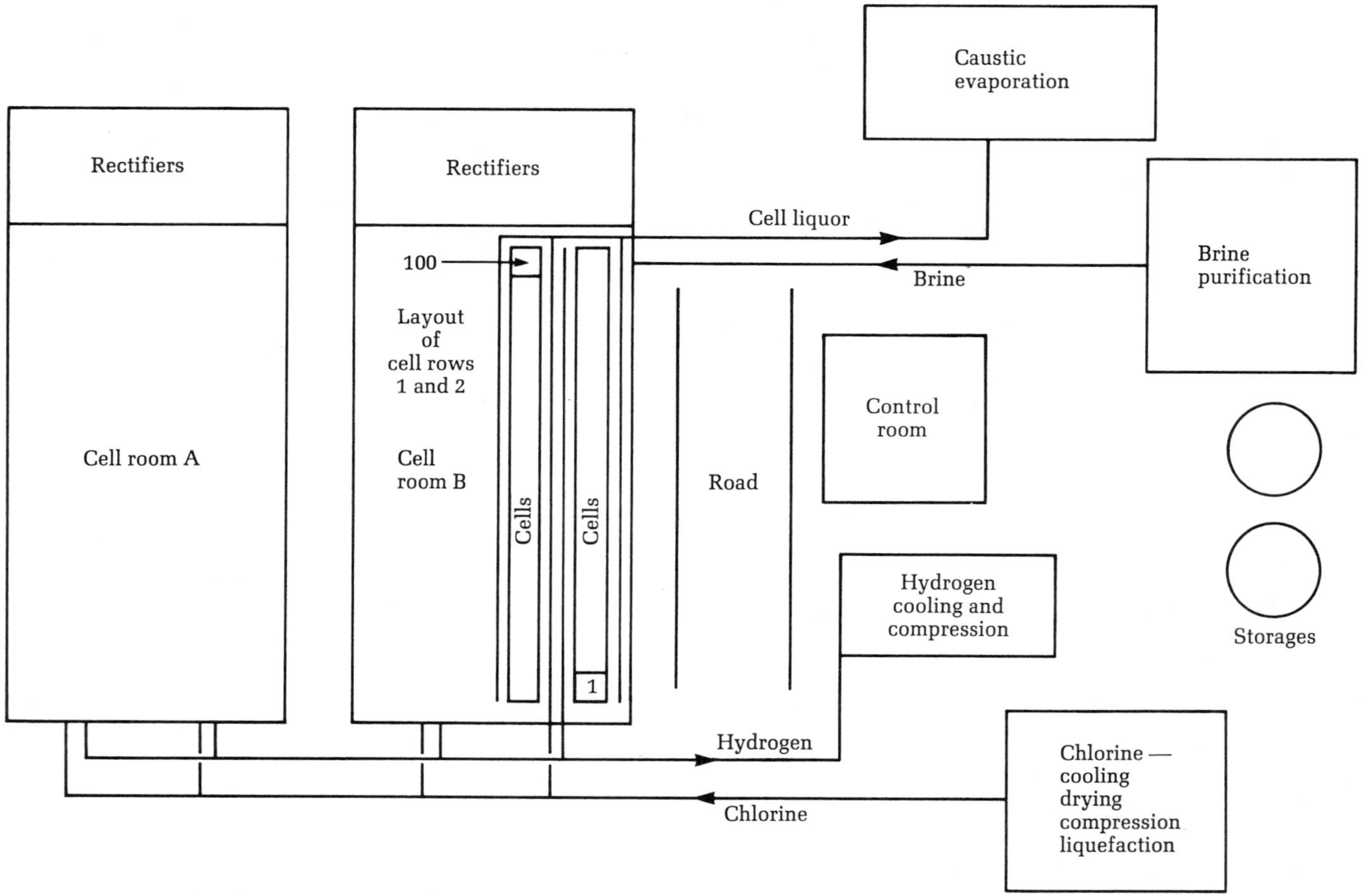

Figure 8-2   *Chlorine Cell*

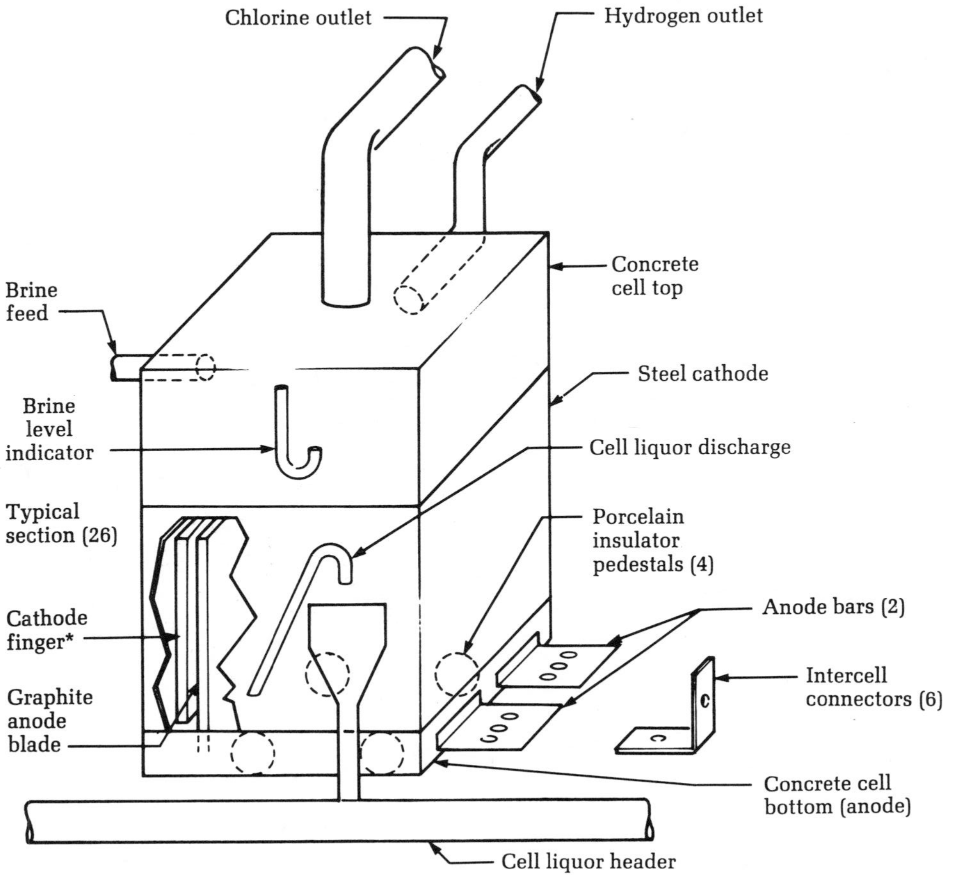

Operating Data

Current: 50,000 amps

Voltage: 4.0 V

Output: 4.0 Tons/day Chlorine
         4.4 Tons/day Caustic soda

Temperature: 250° F

Cell Liquor: 10% Caustic soda
            17% Salt
            73% Water

Chlorine: 98% Chlorine
          0.5% Hydrogen
          1.5% Miscellaneous

Hydrogen outlet

Chlorine outlet

Concrete cell top

Steel cathode

Cell liquor discharge

Porcelain insulator pedestals (4)

Anode bars (2)

Intercell connectors (6)

Concrete cell bottom (anode)

Cell liquor header

Brine feed

Brine level indicator

Typical section (26)

Cathode finger*

Graphite anode blade

*Cathode finger is covered with asbestos diaphragm.

Bessels: According to Stoneman and Davis, Grant was taking off the copper connectors to cell no. 39. He yelled, "It's grabbing me!" Then, he slumped down on the floor in convulsions.

Cardwell: Where did Stoneman and Davis take Grant?

Bessels: They laid him in the back of the pick-up truck and drove to the first-aid station (which is also the patrol office for the main gate).

Cardwell: What first aid was administered?

Stolts: He was immediately given oxygen and a closed heart massage and was put on the resuscitator.

Barlow: Do we have a de-fibrillator (a device designed to restore the heart beat to a normal pattern after electric shock)?

Stolts: No. We considered purchasing one, but discovered that it requires a trained technician to operate the machine safely. Our guards could do more harm than good with such a device.

Cardwell: (bluntly) *Not* in this case!

Stolts: Obviously, that is true. But, even after this tragedy, I still believe we made the correct decision. Our focus should be on prevention of electric shock, not attempting to save someone whose heart had been put in fibrillation due to electric shock.

Cardwell: O.K., what else was done for Grant?

Stolts: Bessels, didn't you try mouth-to-mouth resuscitation?

Bessels: Yes, I learned how to administer it in our first aid training program two weeks ago. But I was unsuccessful.

Cardwell: Any other treatment?

Stolts: Well, the emergency team from Central Hospital tried extensively to revive him, but to no avail. Grant was pronounced dead on the scene by a representative from the Coroner's Office and the Sheriff's Department.

Cardwell: What has been the effect on the work force?

Thornton: Remarkably, the attitude is good, considering what happened.

Chaucer: That's right. Would you believe that the first three men we called out to finish no. 38 accepted the overtime?

Morgan: Did you tell these people who finished renewing no. 38 what had happened to Grant?

Bessels: Yes, we told them exactly what happened. But it didn't affect them at all.

Morgan: What was the rationale? It would have scared the hell out of me.

Bessels: Me, too, but they all shrugged and indicated that Grant just wasn't careful.

Cardwell: Well, let's try to maintain that attitude. The last thing we need is to have a state of panic among our workers. But, we in this room know there *is* something to fear. It is an established fact that we have a very serious problem. We need to examine fully the entire spectrum surrounding this tragedy — work methods and standards, working conditions, training programs, "failsafes", and/or process-equipment design. Can any of you assure me that another tragedy will not occur this very afternoon?

From the attendees: Silence

Cardwell: That's the "fear" I mentioned earlier. Well, our work is ahead of us. Your duties are to remain calm, rational, objective, and reassuring to your crews and to analyze continually each facet of the cell renewal job to make certain that no one else is killed or injured. You will earn your salaries over the next few weeks. O.K., let's discuss why Grant is not alive today.

Background of National Chlor-Alkali and the Geismar Plant

National Chlor-Alkali is a large diversified corporation with a basis in heavy or industrial chemicals. It was formed in the mid-1920s as a result of a merger of three chemical producers.

The Geismar plant was built in 1938 to serve primarily the alkali needs of the developing petrochemical industry in the greater Baton Rouge, Louisiana, area. The plant had major expansions in 1950 and 1966, producing basic chemicals such as soda ash, chlorine, caustic soda, solvents, and also supplying brine to other plants in the industrial area.

The 1966 expansion consisted of the addition of an 800-ton-per-day chlorine/caustic soda complex. Chlorine and caustic soda are co-products, stemming from an electrolytic cell process. In the process, a direct electric current is passed through a brine solution (a solution of sodium chloride). The current decomposes the sodium chloride into the basic chemical elements, chlorine and sodium. The chlorine is released in the cell as a gas. The sodium is hydrolized (reacts with water) to form caustic soda (sodium hydroxide) and hydrogen. The caustic soda comprises 10 percent of the liquid cell discharge called cell liquor. The hydrogen is released as a gas from the cell liquor and is partitioned from the chlorine by a diaphragm that separates the cell anode and cathode (See Figure 8–2). The chlorine gas is dried by cooling and scrubbing with sulphuric acid. This is followed by compression and liquefaction. The liquid chlorine is loaded into tank cars and barges for shipment.

The cell liquor, which consists of 10 percent sodium hydroxide, 17 percent sodium chloride (salt), and 73 percent water, is evaporated to remove some of the water. The evaporation continues until the sodium hydroxide concentration increases to approximately 50 percent. The evaporation also precipitates (solid formation in a solution) out almost all of the salt, which is removed by cooling and filtration. The salt that is removed is redissolved to form brine, which is fed back to the electrolytic cells. The 50 percent sodium hydroxide is loaded in tank cars, barges, and large tankers for shipment.

The hydrogen generated in the cell as a by-product is cooled, compressed, and used to supplement the natural gas used as boiler fuel in the generation of steam and electricity. The hydrogen and chlorine must be separated at all times because together they form a highly explosive mixture. The chlorine gas is analyzed continuously for traces of hydrogen. If the chlorine gas has a high percentage of hydrogen (greater than 1 percent by volume), the individual cells are checked for high hydrogen. The high hydrogen may come from diaphragms that have holes or that are too "loose" (allowing passage of hydrogen through the diaphragm into the chlorine gas).

The rates at which the electrolytic cells generate chlorine, caustic soda, and hydrogen are directly proportional to the electric current passing through the cell. To produce 800 tons of chlorine and caustic soda per day requires a continuous flow of 50,000 amps of current through the cells at the Geismar plant. With electric current of that magnitude, plant personnel must be constantly on guard for electrical shock hazards. A passage of 0.050 amp (50 milli-amps) through a human could possibly place the heart into fibrillation and cause death. Electrical shock and high hydrogen in the chlorine gas are the foremost concerns of all personnel in a chlorine/caustic soda plant. Prevention of electrical shock is attributed to the design of the chlorine cell, the wearing of personal safety equipment, and the caution exercised by personnel.

Design of the Chlorine Cell

A general description of the chlorine electrolytic cell is in Figure 8–2. The Geismar Plant had two cell rooms, each containing 200 of these electrolytic cells. The 200 cells constitute a continuous circuit, such that direct current flows from cell to cell from the rectifiers. (A rectifier is a device that converts alternating current from the power generating plant to direct current used in the cell.) The breaking of current in any one of the 200 cells would result in an outage or loss of current for all 200 cells.

Consequently, renewing or repairing an individual cell requires a jumper switch to maintain the circuit for the duration of such repairs.[1]

One half of the copper intercell connectors are removed from the cell to be removed in order to connect the jumper switch to the adjacent cells. (Cell design allows operation with one-half the intercell connectors for short duration if water sprays are placed on the one-half carrying the current to prevent overheating.) The jumper switch removes the cell to be renewed from the circuit by diverting the electric current from the cell through the switch. Jerome Grant was connecting the jumper switch to cell no. 39 when the fatality occurred.

The fatal electric shock Grant received is normally prevented because of the insulated cell circuit. All 200 cells in each of the two cell rooms are mounted on porcelain insulators. Due to the nature of the cell circuit, the

---

[1]The cells have to be renewed primarily for two reasons: (1) The diaphragm is plugged by impurities such that brine could not flow in sufficient rates through the diaphragm. (2) The graphite anode is consumed to the extent that voltage on the cell would rise and prolonged operation would jeopardize the circuit. A diaphragm is renewed each time the anode is renewed. Hence, a diaphragm renewal is termed a *single*, and an anode renewal is termed a *double*.

"first" ground would not result in a shock to personnel.[2] Shocks occur only when a "second" ground is established by the flow of current through the person to the ground.

For Grant to have been shocked, there had to be a prior ground in the circuit. The operating personnel are constantly on guard for grounds in the cell circuit through monitoring voltage to ground meters placed on the first cell (no. 1) and the last cell (no. 200) in the circuit. The circuit voltage is approximately 800 volts (200 cells × 4.0 v. per cell) and should be equally divided so that voltage to ground readings on cells no. 1 and no. 200 should indicate 400 volts each — if no grounds exist in the circuit. A ground would be indicated by imbalance between the two meters. For example, a ground may cause the meter at cell no. 1 to indicate 100 volts and no. 200 to indicate 700 volts. The voltages to ground meters are on the control room panel board and are monitored by operating personnel. If a ground is indicated, operators scrutinize the circuit and remove or clear the ground.

Wearing of Personal Safety Equipment

Because "first" grounds often do occur in a cell circuit, personnel who operate and repair the chlorine electrolytic cells insulate their bodies from ground by wearing high voltage gloves and boots. Both gloves and boots have ratings in excess of 10,000 volts if they are not defective. A lower voltage rating occurs when a glove or boot becomes worn through use or has a tear or defect.

The practice has been for workers to inspect visually their gloves and boots for defects and receive new pairs if they discover any. Evidence indicates, however, that personnel request new pairs only when they are shocked frequently when working on the cells. Hence, they deduce that their gloves and/or boots are not affording proper protection and request new pairs.

National Chlor-Alkali keeps a large inventory of gloves and boots and normally honors any request for new pairs without question. Recent expenses for gloves and boots have risen sharply, however, and foremen such as Bessels have been instructed to receive detailed explanations before they authorize issuance of new gloves or boots.

Two types of boots have been issued to personnel who operate and repair the cells. One type, which is ankle-length, was recommended by Amalgamated Electrode, the developer of the chlorine cell technology purchased by National Chlor-Alkali. The other type, which is knee-length, was detected being used in one of Amalgamated Electrode's plants where National Chlor-Alkali's supervisory personnel received training on the cells. The discrepancy between Amalgamated Electrode's recommendation and their own use was explained by the fact that the shorter (ankle-length) boot would be cooler in the warm climate of Louisiana. They also stated that the voltage

---

[2]The flow of current from the circuit to the ground may occur through a faulty cell insulator, salt build-up under the cells, or trash that would conduct current such as clamps, welding rods, pipe fittings, misplaced value wrenches, etc.

ratings for both boots were approximately the same. The knee-length boot would, however, give more insulation protection for the calf and shin. National Chlor-Alkali could not determine which boot was better, so it made both types available to personnel. Jerome Grant had a pair of both types, but he was wearing the ankle-length boot at the time of his electrocution.

Personal Caution

After Grant's electrocution, the consensus reaction of the cell repair crew was that "he (Grant) just was not careful." Even though protection was provided by the insulated cell circuit requiring two grounds before electrical shock can occur and additional insulation by wearing high voltage gloves and boots, great care and discretion had to be exercised when working on an electrical circuit that carried 50,000 amps. Hazards were ever present:

1. A steel cell liquor header that collected cell liquor from each cell ran in front of each cell. The header was one foot above the floor and had to be straddled when removing the intercell connectors for attaching the jumper switch to the adjacent cell. Contacting the header with an uninsulated leg while contacting the cells with an uninsulated arm or shoulder could cause a shock.
2. Steel air and water headers run on a pipe bridge behind the cells. Contact with these headers or the bridge could cause shock.
3. Cells were placed in four rows of 50 in each cell room. This layout is to minimize the use of intercell copper connectors and allow a single jumper switch to service two rows, or 100 cells. (See appendix B.) Because of the close proximity of cells, personnel had to be extremely careful not to bridge a tool or their bodies from one row of cells to another. This would result in a severe arc or "short" across the tool or body which results from diverting the 50,000 amps from the cells through the bridged tool or body. The arc compares closely to a bolt of lightning.

The only foolproof protection is to encapsulate personnel in a rubber or insulated suit. Because of the warm climate, this alternative was not considered feasible. Hence, safety depended to a great extent on the discretion and care that personnel exhibited. This included being constantly on guard to prevent shocks from grounds or arcs. Also, personnel were admonished to take minor shocks seriously — checking gloves and boots for defects and searching for grounds in the cell room circuit.

The Investigation

Apparently, Grant did not take minor shocks seriously. According to Stoneman, Grant reported just prior to the electrocution that "he (Grant) was hit (shocked) so hard that he could 'taste' it." This occurred while Grant straddled the cell liquor header, removing the intercell connectors to cell no. 39. Stoneman also related that Grant did not stop to examine why he was being grounded (shocked).

The fatal shock that Grant received did not result from faulty gloves or boots. A local utility company indicated that the gloves and boots withstood in excess of a 10,000 volt potential before "breaking down" (arcing or passing an electric current). The utility company also discussed a boot and glove tester that their linemen use daily before working on high voltage power lines. The autopsy revealed that Grant sustained an arc burn on the left shoulder and on the right leg just above the ankle. This strongly suggested that Grant contacted the cell with his shoulder and the straddled cell liquor header with his leg, consequently becoming fatally grounded (see Figure 8–3).

Figure 8–3   *Contact Points of Fatality*

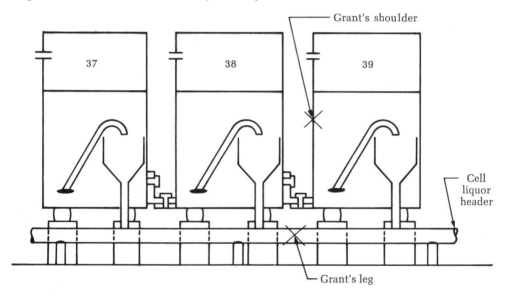

In retrospect, the cause of death was alarmingly simple. Any person with the most fundamental knowledge of electricity should have seen the danger in the equipment design and process layout. The tragic irony was that it was a "miracle" that personnel were not severely injured or killed much earlier since the hazard had existed for 3 years and over 2,000 cells had been renewed during that period. The same renewal procedure was used during the entire period. Grant had been a member of the initial cell repair crew formed at the completion of plant construction and just prior to the start-up. He was considered an experienced, competent cell repairman.

The catastrophe committee was certain to search out other hazards involved in electrolytic cell operation and maintenance now that the consequences were tragically demonstrated. Cardwell reflected with the committee, however, that such dangers should be avoided in future process developments at the Geismar plant by scrutinizing every process and its relationship to the people who operate and maintain these processes. Furthermore, all existing operations were to be reexamined to discover other booby-traps that might exist. In addition, all fail-safes incorporated into job design and work procedures were to be cited, studied, and reemphasized at all work crew monthly safety meetings. This was to be implemented by a series of Job Safety Analyses (J.S.A.'s) prepared for all tasks performed in the plant. J.S.A.'s list each step in a task to pinpoint safety precautions and fail-safes. Each foreman was given a training session on how to develop J.S.A.'s and was then given a deadline for completion of J.S.A.'s for each task performed in his area.

Cardwell also deliberated on how to manage the immediate crisis created by the electrocution. As reported previously, the cell repair crew's attitude was good and the reason for the tragedy was Grant's own negligence or carelessness — "he just wasn't careful." Chaucer (Maintenance Manager) and Buckner (Production Manager) both reported that work was being accomplished in a normal, orderly manner and that fear or panic was almost totally undetected. Cardwell's initial reaction was not to disturb this attitude because a sense of panic would greatly hinder plant operation and might even cause more injuries that stem from emotional, irrational actions by personnel performing delicate duties that require calmness and confidence. In addition, personnel turnover might sharply increase as employees resigned out of fear. It was already reported that a cell operator had resigned and stated that "Grant's death had been the last straw. His nerves were already 'shot' working under such dangerous conditions." This employee had received minor burns from hot, acid brine from a cell eruption two months earlier. At present, this attitude was isolated and there was no indication that anyone else planned to resign.

The recommendations from investigation, however, were certain to include radical and immediate changes in cell process design and work methods. Such changes woud certainly create apprehension among the work force and possibly bring about the consequences stated above. The failure to implement the changes immediately would definitely increase the probability of another serious injury or possibly death. Cardwell knew that he would be grossly negligent if he did not institute the changes. He also knew that it was best not to overreact. How could he achieve a responsible balance?

Discussion Questions

1. What course of action would you recommend to Cardwell?

2. How may radical changes in operating procedures be instituted without causing panic in the plant?

3. What impact does OSHA have on the course of action?

appendix A
All About OSHA

On April 28, 1971, as provided by the act, OSHA became an official part of national labor law. Congress declared the purpose of the act, and hence the Labor Department's and OSHA's mission:

> " . . . to assure so far as possible every working man and woman in the Nation safe and healthful working conditions and to preserve our human resources . . . "

How is OSHA to implement this mandate? Congress was specific:

    a. By encouraging employers and employees to reduce hazards in the workplace, and start or improve existing safety and health programs;

    b. by establishing employer and employee responsibilities;

    c. by authorizing OSHA to set mandatory job safety and health standards;

    d. by providing an effective enforcement program;

    e. by encouraging the states to assume the fullest responsibility for administering and enforcing their own occupational safety and health programs that are to be at least as effective as the federal program;

    f. by providing for reporting procedures on job injuries, illnesses, and fatalities.

The act covers every employer in a business with one or more employees affecting commerce. The act does not affect workplaces covered under other federal laws, such as the Coal Mine Health and Safety Act and the Federal Metal and Nonmetallic Safety Act.

Federal, state, and local government employees are covered under separate provisions in the act for public employment.

The Role of Employers

The act requires each employer to provide a workplace free from safety and health hazards and to comply with the standards. Following is a checklist of employer responsibilities:

1. Be aware of general duty responsibility to provde a place of employment free from recognized hazards and to comply with occupational safety and health standards promulgated under the act.

2. Be familiar with mandatory occupational safety and health standards.

3. Make sure employees know about OSHA.

4. Examine conditions in the workplace to make sure they conform to applicable safety and health standards.

5. Remove or guard hazards.

6. Make sure employees have and use safe tools and equipment, including required personal protective gear, and that they are properly maintained.

7. Use color codes, posters, labels, or signs to warn employees of potential hazards.

Source: United States Department of Labor, OSHA Bulletin 2056.

8. Establish or update operating procedures and communicate them so that employees follow safety and health requirements for their own protection.
9. Provide medical examinations when required by OSHA standards.
10. Keep required OSHA records of work-related injuries and illnesses (if eight or more employees) and post the annual summary during the month of February each year.
11. Report, to the nearest OSHA area office, each injury or health hazard that results in a fatality or hospitalization of five or more employees.
12. Post, in the workplace, the OSHA poster informing employees of their rights and responsibilities.
13. Advise OSHA compliance officers of authorized employee representatives to permit their participation in the inspection walkaround. If there are no such representatives, allow a reasonable number of employees to confer with the compliance officer during the walkaround.
14. NOT discriminate against employees who properly exercise their rights under the act.
15. Post OSHA citations of violations of standards at the worksite involved.
16. Seek advice and consultation as needed by writing, calling, or visiting the nearest OSHA office (OSHA will not inspect just because you call for assistance).
17. Be active in industry association's involvement in job safety and health.

The act also provides specific rights for employers. Following is a checklist:

a. Request and receive proper identification of OSHA personnel prior to inspection of the workplace;
b. be advised by OSHA personnel of the reason for the inspection:
c. participate in the walkaround inspection of the workplace with the compliance officer and in the opening and closing conferences with him;
d. file a notice of contest with the nearest OSHA assistant regional director, within 15 working days of receipt of a citation and notice of penalty, if in disagreement with the citation and/or the penalty proposed;
e. apply to OSHA for a temporary variance from a standard if unable to comply because of the unavailability of materials, equipment, or personnel to make changes within the required time;
f. apply to OSHA for a permanent variance from a standard if it can be proved facilities or method of operation provide protection for employees that is at least as effective as that required by the standard.
g. take an active role in developing job safety and health standards through participation in OSHA Standards Advisory Committees and national consensus standards-setting organizations;
h. be assured of the confidentiality of any trade secrets observed by an OSHA compliance officer during an inspection.

The Role of Employees

The act requires each employee to comply with occupational safety and health standards, as well as with all rules, regulations, and orders issued under the act that apply to his or her own actions and conduct. Following is a checklist of employee responsibilities:

a. Read the OSHA poster at the jobsite;
b. comply with any applicable OSHA standards;
c. follow all of employer's safety and health standards and rules;
d. wear or use prescribed protective equipment;
e. report hazardous conditions to the supervisor;
f. report any job-related injuries or illnesses to employer and seek treatment promptly;
g. cooperate with the OSHA compliance officer conducting an inspection if he inquires about conditions at your jobsite;
h. use rights under the act responsibly.

The Act provides that employees have certain rights. Following is a checklist:

a. Obtain a copy of the OSHA standards and other rules, regulations, and requirements from employer, the nearest OSHA office, or the Government Printing Office;
b. request information from employer on safety and health hazards in a work area, on precautions, on involvement in an accident or exposure to toxic substances;
c. accompany the OSHA compliance officer during the inspection walkaround if designated by your union or employee association;
d. observe monitoring or measuring of hazardous materials, including the right of access to records on those materials, as specified in regulations under the act;
e. submit a written request to the National Institute for Occupational Safety and Health (NIOSH) for information on whether any substance in a workplace has potentially toxic effects in the concentration being used, and have name withheld from employer if so desired;
f. request the OSHA area director, in writing, to conduct an inspection if believed a hazardous condition exists (one should, however, first make a good-faith effort to have employer correct the condition);
g. have name withheld from your employer, upon request to OSHA, if a complaint is filed;
h. be advised of OSHA actions regarding complaint and have an informal review, if requested, of any decision not to make an inspection;
i. file a complaint to OSHA within 30 days if it is discriminated against because assertion of a right under the act and be notified by OSHA of its decision within 90 days of filing;
j. object to the abatement period fixed in the citation issued to employer by appealing to the Occupational Safety and Health Review Commission (it is not possible to do this without having name revealed since the area director must send objection to Review Commission);
k. be notified by employer if he applies for a variance (waiver) from an OSHA standard, testify at a variance hearing, and appeal the final decision;
l. submit information or comment to OSHA on the issuance, modification, or revocation of OSHA standards, and request a public hearing.

How Does OSHA Work?

OSHA adopts standards and, among other methods for accomplishing compliance, conducts inspections of workplaces to determine whether the standards are being met.

Standards

What is a safety or health standard? It is a legally enforceable regulation governing conditions, practices, or operations to assure safe and healthful workplaces.

Compliance with national safety and health standards is what a compliance officer looks for when inspecting a workplace. The officer is concerned with what standards apply there and whether the employer and employees are complying with them.

The standards are published in the **Federal Register.** All amendments, corrections, insertions, or deletions involving standards also are printed in the **Federal Register.**

Compliance and Inspections

Of major interest is the OSHA compliance operation. **The Compliance Operations Manual** is a detailed guide to this function.

Since OSHA began its inspection program, in more than one out of every three workplaces inspected, all the required standards were met, so no citations were issued. That ratio is rising as employers become more familiar with their responsibilities and recognize the positive benefits that accompany compliance with OSHA standards.

Reduced job injury and illness rates, less down time, improved employee morale, and savings in workmen's compensation insurance all demonstrate that "safety pays."

When Will an Inspector Call?

Obviously, not all 5 million workplaces covered can or should be inspected immediately. The worst situations need attention first. So a system of priorities has been established:

1. Catastrophes and other fatal accidents
2. Valid employee complaints
3. Special emphasis programs
    a. TARGET INDUSTRIES
    b. TARGET HEALTH HAZARDS
4. Random selection from all types and sizes of workplaces in all sections of the country

"Special Emphasis Programs" Inspections

There are two areas of program emphasis based on the "worst-first" principle — investigating first those industries or toxic substances that are most hazardous.

1. **The Target Industry Program** is aimed at five industries with injury frequency rates more than double the national average of 15.2 disabling injuries per million employee hours worked:

> a. Longshoring (or Marine Cargo Handling, as it is called) — 69.9 injuries per million employee hours
> b. Meat and Meat Products — 43.1 per million employee hours
> c. Roofing and Sheet Metal — 43.0 per million employee hours
> d. Lumber and Wood Products — 34.1 per million employee hours
> e. Miscellaneous Transportation Equipment (primarily manufacturers of mobile homes, campers, and snowmobiles) — 33.3 per million employee hours

2. **The Target Health Hazards Program** focuses on five of the most commonly used and hazardous of the more than 15,000 toxic substances that have been identified by NIOSH:

> a. Asbestos
> b. Carbon Monoxide
> c. Cotton Dust
> d. Lead
> e. Silica

Who Are the Inspectors?

OSHA calls them Compliance Safety and Health Officers, and Industrial Hygienists. Who are they? They are professionals in the occupational safety and health fields, men and women with years of experience and professional training.

To be sure that they meet OSHA's requirements, each receives a highly specialized training course before moving into the field to make inspections. At least once a year, each compliance officer and industrial hygienist takes a refresher course plus additional training in specialized fields, such as construction or maritime safety. Such training is conducted at OSHA's Training Institute at Rosemont, Illinois, near Chicago.

How Is an Inspection Conducted?

Compliance inspections come under the supervision of the OSHA area director, who assigns compliance officers and industrial hygienists on the basis of the system of priorities listed on page 188.

Before making an inspection, the compliance officer or industrial hygienist learns as many relevant facts as possible about the workplace and determines which OSHA standards are pertinent.

The inspector takes along appropriate special equipment for testing for toxic substances in the air, for noise, etc.

Inspections are conducted during regular working hours of the establishment except in special circumstances. The act and OSHA's regulations prohibit advance notice of inspections except in cases where such notice would make the inspection more effective.

To start the inspection, the compliance officer arrives at the establishment, displays credentials, and asks to meet the appropriate employer representative.

The inspector informs the employer of the reason for the visit and generally outlines the scope of the inspection, including safety and health records to be reviewed, employee interviews, the walkaround, and the closing conference.

The inspector gives the employer copies of applicable laws and safety and health standards and a copy of an employee complaint if one is involved. The employee's name is withheld if requested.

The compliance officer asks the employer to designate a representative for the walkaround.

The employer does not select the employee representative. The employee organization itself does that. If there are no employee groups, the compliance officer discusses conditions with individual employees during the walkaround.

The compliance officer and the employer and employee representatives then proceed through the establishment, and each work area is inspected for compliance with OSHA standards. Neither representative may harass or otherwise obstruct the inspection process.

During the inspection, the compliance officer takes appropriate notes of conditions and discusses them with both representatives. The compliance officer may take photographs of particular situations to record apparent violations or conditions that may change during the inspection or shortly thereafter, and he or she may use other appropriate investigative techniques.

The compliance officer must take special care to protect the privacy of trade secrets or security matters.

He or she also inspects the OSHA records of deaths, injuries and illnesses that employers of eight or more employees are required to keep and determines that the annual summary has been posted.

He or she checks records of employee exposure to toxic substances and harmful physical agents.

The compliance officer may find numerous apparent violations that can be corrected immediately, such as blocked aisles, unsafe floor surfaces, hazardous projections, and unsanitary conditions. The employer representative may, and usually does, direct that they be corrected at once. Such corrections are recorded to help in judging employer good faith in compliance. Even though corrected, the apparent violation may be the basis for a citation and/or proposed penalty.

During the walkaround, any employee may bring to the attention of the compliance officer any condition believed to be a violation.

After the walkaround, the compliance officer discusses with the employer what he or she has seen and reviews probable violations. Also discussed is the time the employer believes will be necessary to abate hazards.

The compliance officer then returns to his or her office, writes the report, and discusses it with the area director. The area director or superiors determine what citations will be issued and what penalties, if any, will be proposed. These are sent to the employer by certified mail with a copy to the complainant, if there is one.

OSHA citations and proposed penalties are similar to traffic violations. If contested, they are subject to final action by a separate authority — in this case, the Occupational Safety and Health Review Commission.

The compliance officer may not, on his or her own, impose or purpose a penalty "on the spot" at an inspection, nor can he or she close down an establishment or process. OSHA can act quickly in the courts to deal with imminent danger situations.

What Are The Possible Results of an Inspection?

The workplace may be found to be in compliance with OSHA standards. In this case, no citations are issued and no penalties are proposed.

Or, violations may be found in the establishment. In that case, citations may be issued, and civil penalties may be proposed.

In order of significance, these are the types of violations of standards normally considered on a first inspection:

1. **De minimis:** A condition that has no direct or immediate relationship to job safety and health (Example: lack of toilet partitions).

2. **Nonserious violation:** A violation that does have a direct relationship to job safety and health but probably would not cause death or serious physical harm (Example: tripping hazard). A proposed penalty of up to $1,000 is optional. A nonserious penalty may be adjusted downward by as much as 50 percent, depending on the severity of the hazard, employer's good faith, history of previous violations, and size of business. This adjusted figure is reduced an additional 50 percent if the employer corrects the violation within the prescribed abatement period.

3. **Serious violation:** A violation where there is substantial probability that death or serious physical harm could result and that the employer knew, or should have known, of the hazard (Example: absence of point-of-operation guards on punch presses or saws). A proposed penalty of up to $1,000 is mandatory. A serious penalty may be adjusted downward by as much as 50 percent, based on the employer's good faith, history of previous violations, and size of business.

4. **Immediate danger:** A condition where there is reasonable certainty that a hazard exists that can be expected to cause death or serious physical harm immediately or before the hazard can be eliminated through regular procedures. If the employer fails to abate such conditions immediately, the compliance officer, through the area director, can go directly to the nearest Federal District Court for legal action as necessary. Citations also may be issued for violations of other OSHA regulations. Examples include:

   a. failure to post citation
   b. failure to post annual summary
   c. failure to post notice
   d. failure to report a catastrophe or fatality
   e. failure to maintain records
   f. advance notice
   g. false information

Follow-up inspections ensure that cited violations have been properly abated.

After Receiving a Citation, What Are an Employer's Review Rights?

Suppose the employer disagrees with the citation and/or proposed penalty. What can he or she do?

First, the employer can request an informal meeting with the area director to discuss the case.

If the employer decides to contest the citation legally, the act contains a specific appeal procedure, guaranteeing full review of the case by an agency separate from the Labor Department. That agency is the independent Occupational Safety and Health Review Commission, which has no connection with the U. S. Department of Labor.

The employer has 15 working days from receipt of the citation and proposed penalty in which to notify the area director, in writing, that he or she intends to contest the citation, abatement date, or proposed penalty to the Review Commission. The area director sends the case to the Review Commission.

The Review Commission cannot act unless the notice of contest was filed in time (the postmark will decide, if the notice is mailed). If the notice is filed in time, the Review Commission assigns the case to an administrative law judge. The judge can investigate and disallow the contest if he or she finds it legally invalid. Or, the judge can schedule a hearing which will be held as close as possible to the employer's workplace. The Review Commission does not require that employers or employees be represented by attorneys.

The employer can accept or object to the judge's findings.

Upon the request of any party, the judge's decision may be reviewed by the Review Commission itself, although it is not required to do so. Any member of the Review Commission can, on his or her own motion, order a review of any contested case. Decisions of the Commission may be appealed to the U. S. Circuit Court of Appeals for the circuit in which the case arose.

If the employer or employee does not contest within 15 days of receipt of the citation, the OSHA action automatically becomes a final order of the Review Commission and is not subject to further appeal or review.

Employees have the right to contest to the Review Commission if they believe the period set by OSHA for abatement of a hazard is unreasonable. After the 15 days, but before the end of the abatement period, an employer may petition the Review Commission (through the area director) for modification of the abatement.

What Records Must Be Kept?

OSHA requires employers of eight or more employees to keep certain records of job-related fatalities, injuries, and illnesses. OSHA requires that only three simple forms be maintained:

1. OSHA 100 — a log on which each reportable case is entered on a single line
2. OSHA 101 — a supplementary record with details on each individual case
3. OSHA 102 — an annual summary compiled from the log (This summary must be posted in the workplace by February 1 each year and kept there one month for employee examination)

If there are no recordable deaths, injuries, or illnesses, there is nothing to fill in.

All employers not exempt (those with eight or more employees) from the record-keeping requirements must have the forms available when an OSHA compliance officer makes an inspection. The forms do not have to be mailed to any OSHA office.

appendix B
Cell Repair
Job Descriptions

The cell repair or maintenance crew consists of approximately 30 workers. Following is a description of the jobs the cell repair crew performs:

Anode Fabrication: The cell anode is comprised of 150 graphite blades approximately 3 ft long, 1 ft wide, and 1 in. thick that are cast into 2 tons of lead. Also cast into the lead are two copper bars (called anode bars), each weighing approximately 400 pounds. The copper bars conduct the current from the adjacent cell through the lead and graphite. The current then passes from the graphite through the brine solution and asbestos diaphragm to the steel/copper cathode and finally to the copper anode bars of the next cell.

The cell repair crew normally assigns five employees each day to build the anodes. The graphite blades are loaded into a jig that properly aligns and spaces the blades. The loaded jig is then placed in a lead mold into which have been placed the two anode bars which have been plated with a special alloy that bonds the bars to the lead. The mold is then filled with molten lead from a furnace. After cooling, the casted lead, graphite, and copper bars are placed in a concrete cell bottom. The anode is sealed in the concrete bottom with a tar compound that protects the lead from the brine in the cell.

Deposition of Diaphragms: The second component of the cell is the cathode, upon which is deposited an asbestos diaphragm. The diaphragm separates the chlorine/ brine from the hydrogen/cell liquor in the cell. The chlorine is formed at the cell anode by decomposition of the brine solution. The brine solution then passes through (percolates) the diaphragm, and the caustic/hydrogen is formed at the cathode.

The diaphragm is deposited on the cathode by creating a vacuum inside the cathode and then dipping the cathode into an asbestos slurry bath. The vacuum pulls the asbestos fibers against the wire screen of the cathode, creating an asbestos coating or diaphragm approximately $1/8$ in. thick. One employee is assigned the task of pulling the diaphragms.

Over time, the diaphragm tends to become plugged with impurities. This condition impedes the brine flow through the cell and hence adversely affects the cell output. When this occurs, the diaphragm is changed. The old diaphragm is removed from the cathode by washing with high pressure water. Typically, one employee is assigned the job of washing cathodes.

Cell Renewal: The balance of the crew is divided into three-man teams to change anodes and diaphragms. The removal task consists of removing one-half the copper intercell connectors from the cell to be renewed to the adjacent cells. The cell can operate on only one-half of the connectors for a short duration if water sprays are used to prevent overheating. The jumper switch arms (2) are connected to the adjacent cells at the terminals vacated by the removed connectors in the previous step. For example, if cell no. 17 is to be renewed, the jumper switch is connected to cell no. 16 and 18. The jumper switch is then closed by the cell operator, which diverts the current from the cell to be renewed through the switch. In the preceding example, cell no. 17 is now out of operation, with the current passing from cell no. 16 through the switch to cell no. 18. An overhead crane may physically remove cell no. 17.

After the cell is "jumped out," it is drained, the top is removed, and the diaphragm and/or anode is replaced. The top is then replaced, and the cell is filled with brine. The jumper switch is then opened, placing the current through the renewed cell. The jumper switch is disconnected, and the intercell connectors previously removed are reconnected for normal cell operation.

Miscellaneous Duties: Miscellaneous duties that the cell repair crew performs include maintenance of the brine, chlorine, hydrogen, and cell liquor headers. The crew also maintains good electrical connections between cells by periodic cleaning, polishing, and silverplating the copper intercell connectors. Finally, the crew is responsible for clean-up and maintenance of equipment used in the cell repair function.

case 44

East Texas
Oil Company

During the week of January 6, 1977, Arthur Kirkland, field supervisor for East Texas Oil Company, listened intently to the seminar lectures on environmental protection sponsored by his employer and attended by managers from several oil and gas production companies throughout the eastern regions of the state. Kirkland was pleased that East Texas Oil had assumed a leadership position in combating problems that had caused extensive and often irreparable harm to streams, lakes, and timberland in the area.

Kirkland vividly recalled the barren acres of land and the waterways devoid of fish life, which resulted from the indifferent and negligent disposal of saltwater over a prolonged period. For decades, saltwater, after being separated from oil and paraffin, was expediently disposed of by channeling it to nearby streams. The royalties paid to land owners from oil production were viewed as being adequate compensation for any loss of timber which might result from such disposal.

Lawsuits for damages, public concern over environmental protection, and legal constraints provided the impetus for action by oil-producing firms. Saltwater disposal wells, high-pressure pumps, and container ponds became commonplace in oilfield operations. Saltwater was transmitted from separators to huge ponds, where it was contained. Periodically, the saltwater was pumped back into the ground via deep disposal wells drilled specifically for that purpose.

Because Kirkland was attending the daily seminars during the second week of January, he had little opportunity to discuss the importance of saltwater disposal with Dennis Zimmerman, a relatively new employee who was substituting for vacationing Harry Hansen. Hansen, a regular pumper for East Texas Oil for six years, routinely performed all maintenance functions associated with his job. Zimmerman, however, spent most of his time keeping the rig motors running in the cold, rainy weather. The inclement weather combined with the poorly tuned engines forced him to neglect the constantly rising water level of the saltwater ponds.

During the early morning hours of January 10, the east Texas area was deluged with a nine-inch rainfall, causing bridges, dams, and firewalls in

194

the oilfields to be washed away. Because of the high water levels in several container ponds, their weakened dams could not withstand the additional weight and pressure of the rainfall.

At 8:00 Friday morning, Zimmerman noticed that three of the company's largest container ponds were empty. A further investigation revealed that their dams had broken, resulting in the dumping of an enormous amount of saltwater into nearby streams.

Discussion Questions

1. How could this incident have been prevented?

2. What policy changes would you recommend to East Texas Oil Company?

case 45

The Saga of
Chrysler's "Clean" Foundry[1]

In 1964, Chrysler Corporation, ignoring the advice of its own engineers and outside consultants, announced plans for the construction of a new foundry within a residential area on the east side of Detroit. The claims were extravagant. The one most frequently heard was that the plant would be pollution-free. It would have to be — rarely had a major foundry been planned so close to private homes.

Some people took the claim at face value. In May, 1967, *Factory Magazine* named it one of its "Top Ten Plants of the Year," citing specifically the lengths management had gone to to protect the environment around the plant.

What the editors of *Factory* overlooked was that less than 30 days after the plant had gone into limited debugging operations in October of 1966, occupants of the small, orderly homes immediately across Huber Avenue, on which the foundry is located, began filing complaints against it.

By the time the awards issue of *Factory* appeared, more than two dozen residents of the Huber community were threatening court action. Today, six years after start-up, Chrysler is still mired in lawsuits over the Huber foundry. Its attorneys like to think the end of litigation will come this fall. But attorneys for the residents like to think they are just getting started.

How did it happen that a so-called "clean" foundry was ever sited next to a residential community? And what ever became of the equipment that was meant to make that foundry "clean"?

The answers are really lessons. Chrysler has learned them at a cost of millions. Others can benefit from Chrysler's bad dream and save themselves the same amount or more.

According to Chrysler's official press release, the Huber Avenue location was selected because the company already owned the land, the site was adjacent to two other Chrysler production facilities, skilled labor was plentiful, and there were excellent rail connections to other Chrysler plants within a 30-mile radius.

---

[1]James Wargo, "The Saga of Chrysler's 'Clean' Foundry." Reprinted from *The MBA*, October 1972, by permission. Copyright by MBA Communications, Inc., 1972.

Deal With Detroit

Jerome Cavanagh, at that time mayor of Detroit, tells it a different way. According to his version, he learned towards the end of his first term that Chrysler was planning to abandon an antiquated foundry on the east side and relocate production in an Ohio suburb.

Cavanagh soon learned that Chrysler's main objection to any site in Michigan was a special state tax on jigs, dies, tools, and fixtures. He felt he had enough political clout with the state legislature to suspend the tax. Would Chrysler, he inquired through channels, build in Detroit if he could get the tax lifted?

No, came the reply, if the tax were removed Chrysler would probably build in nearby Warren, Michigan. Cavanagh applied personal pressure on Chrysler executives, and they relented. The Detroit bloc in the legislature succeeded in getting the tax lifted, and Chrysler soon dropped plans for an Ohio foundry.

Designing a Clean Foundry

Actually Chrysler had reservations about the site other than the taxes. Across the street from what became the main entrance to the foundry was a neighborhood of lower middle-class whites, primarily of central European ethnic origin. While they were good neighbors to a nearby Plymouth assembly plant, was it possible they could get to know and love a foundry as well?

Chrysler engineers said no. Chrysler consultants said no. Common sense said no. But Cavanagh said he had a man, Mort Sterling, in the city's air pollution control bureau who would sit in on planning sessions to guide Chrysler in equipping the foundry with those systems which would best protect the residents. Every pollution control system adopted had Sterling's stamp of approval.

In early spring of 1967, the Huber foundry went to work producing engine blocks, heads, flywheels, brakedisks, and crankshafts. Casting operations were fed by two enclosed, water-cooled cupolas, each 108 inches in diameter and rated at 50 tons per hour, along with five 100-ton holding furnaces.

High-noise areas were protected by extensive sound-deadening devices. An exhaust system, aided by 33 dust collectors, was to have provided a complete in-plant change of air every eight minutes without discharging dust to the neighborhood.

Outwardly Clean

The outside of the plant, fronting Huber Avenue, was designed windowless, but is clean-cut and attractive. To this day it can pass as a long, but not unattractive suburban office structure, set 16 feet in from the sidewalk and fronted with a carefully manicured, treed lawn.

Unfortunately, with the exception of the trees, hardly anything that was designed to make the plant a good neighbor functioned as planned. Chrysler engineers think they know why, and their reason is a good one.

Their theory: the plant was too advanced. Many of the environmental systems were simply not designed to work that close to a residential community. And because environmental concerns were not commanding as much attention in 1964 as they are today, some of the systems purchased were, in effect, ordered out of catalogues — Chrysler was the first to buy them. When these systems malfunctioned, the suppliers were at as much of a loss to explain what was wrong as were Chrysler personnel. As for the neighbors, they really didn't give a damn. They were going to court. At least 328 of them are still there.

Raw Smoke and Dust

The first thing to go wrong were two massive 105-inch fans installed to pull gas through the dust collectors. Within days of their first usage, they began vibrating. Welds at the base of the blades would break, causing noise that was annoying as far as several blocks away. To kill the noise, the fans were shut off. Since Chrysler was depending on the foundry for vital parts, operations continued while raw smoke and dust billowed out to settle over the neighbors.

After each failure there would be a meeting with the supplier, ending with the same conclusion — that the welds had been faulty. In 14 months, five replacement fans were ordered. Soon after installation, the breakdown process would begin again. In addition, the fans were turned on and off so often that the motors wore out. Bigger, more costly motors were ordered.

After the fifth fan failure, it was determined by an outside consultant that the welds had been okay all along — but that the fan housing was poorly designed. It was of such a shape that it compressed the air before releasing it. The constant pulsing set up a rocking motion in the blades, which in turn caused them to wobble and break. More than a year and a half after the first blade broke, a new housing design abetted by tapered blades was put into operation, solving the problem.

But other problems, sometimes more easily solved, continued to plague the pollution control equipment for another two years. Each time one of the failures occurred, antipollution equipment would be shut down and billowing smoke would again blanket the neighborhood. The last cupola breakdown occurred in June, 1970, four years after the plant opened.

The Mysterious Hum

While the worst noise problem was fixed in 1968, grumblings continued about a hum. For months Chrysler officials dismissed these as crank complaints because they could hear nothing. The complaints continued, however, so Chrysler put some engineers on the job of figuring out why. They came back with nothing, yet residents continued to complain of a humming noise.

Eventually Chrysler hired an acoustician, who went from house to house interviewing complainants. An inquisitive man with an open mind, he was willing to consider all factors. After several months, he determined that those complaining found the hum most annoying at night. Checking their bedrooms, he found that most measured 12 feet in width, or close to it. His ruling . . . the sound-deadening chamber above the new fans with their tapered blades was emitting a pure tone with a 12-foot wavelength. Anyone within two miles trying to sleep in a 12-foot-wide bedroom was being slowly driven off the scope.

Thinking the solution was within grasp, Chrysler broke into the sound deadening chamber to install different baffles only to find that the original baffles, glass fiber wrapped with mylar, had deteriorated from the surges of heat experienced with each fan breakdown.

Space-Age Solution

No longer sure that the heat surges were containable, Chrysler searched for a new means of wrapping the baffles. Normal suppliers could offer nothing able to tolerate the 600° F blasts. But an article on space-age technology led Chrysler to DuPont, which had developed a plastic that could take up to 750° F. DuPont was willing to sell Chrysler as much as it wanted, but mentioned as an afterthought that no means of sealing the stuff existed. Chrysler people went into their labs and devised baffles in stainless steel boxes. It worked. Lapsed time: about a year.

Concurrently, other Chrysler engineers were working to correct a flaw in Huber's auxiliary dust-collection system. Originally all 33 collectors were interconnected. When a single one broke down, the option was either to shut down the entire foundry or to keep working while dust poured out into the neighborhood. The obvious solution — and one which could have been avoided in the initial plant design — was to sectionalize the system so that malfunctioning units could be bypassed. In carrying this out, it was discovered that butterfly valves originaly designed to permit manual adjustment of dust flow had worn out because of the frequent adjustments needed.

The butterfly valves were replaced with pinch valves in late 1968. Limited failures of small groups of collectors continue to be experienced, sometimes as frequently as once every six or eight weeks, but they have been mild in comparison with the original ones and Chrysler, although not necessarily the neighbors, regards the problem as solved.

The Rotten Egg Smell

Some 18 months after the plant went into operation, residents began complaining of noxious odors. The rotten egg smell. Like everything else, it got worse. Chrysler checked each venting point under different conditions to trace the source of the foul air. Again a team of consultants was brought in. After several months, they could only reduce the possible source to four auxiliary stacks over the core room.

For a while it was assumed that one of the vegetable by-products used in the core process was the cause, but months of experimentation got them nowhere. Finally, unable to isolate and stop the specific odor, Chrysler gave in and ordered an activated charcoal system for the vents instead. It went into operation in July of this year, with Chrysler officials crossing their fingers. The system, very expensive for a plant the size of the Huber foundry, is even more costly to operate. Moreover, it was ordered without knowing the precise problem it was meant to correct.

The attorney for the majority of the complaining neighbors confided to a reporter that some of his clients admitted the odor problem had abated since the new equipment was installed. But the admission came a week before the activated charcoal system was put into operation!

While Chrysler's engineers and consultants were working to solve each problem that came up, the residents were complaining and suing. Top Chrysler executives were frequently confronted by the residents, by Mort Sterling (who in time was made head of the Wayne county air pollution control office into which his old office was incorporated), city councilmen, and a now-new mayor . . . all wanting to know what Chrysler was doing about the problem at Huber.

With each such visit or contact, Chrysler spokesmen tried to simplify the involved and frustrating work being conducted to resolve each main cause of complaint. The language was so complex, however, that the only thing a complainant would get out of it was, "We're doing everything we can" — an answer that rang increasingly hollow.

Monetary Settlements

When the fan weld problem was at its peak, Chrysler engaged Ottawa Appraisal Services to assess damages on neighborhood cars and houses. Many people were paid for their damages, and a goodly number got sore as hell because they didn't get anything.

It was at this point that the neighbors began pooling their grievances and formulating a class action suit that is still sputtering today. The first person they went to was, of course, Mort Sterling, the people's recourse for air pollution, who understood the complex nature of each breakdown and the long road to each solution. His problem boiled down to one of keeping the citizens happy without unfairly penalizing a company that was doing all it could to solve problems for which it wasn't solely responsible in the first place. After all, Chrysler originally wanted to build in Ohio.

Mort Sterling's Solution

In October of 1971, Sterling found his out. He sued Chrysler under the Michigan Environmental Protection Act, scant hours after the law went into effect. This is a revolutionary law. It permits anyone to sue anyone else they regard as damaging the environment. An almost identical version has been proposed in Washington by Michigan Senator Phillip Hart. Under the Michigan law, only civil action can be brought. You can get a polluter to stop, but you can't get him fined.

Sterling said he sued Chrysler to "get in writing (Chrysler's) oral agreement to shut down whenever equipment breakdown occurred." Chrysler had been doing this for several months prior to Sterling's action. According to others, however, Sterling felt that by using the new Michigan law he could placate those demanding not sympathy but action and at the same time not increase the pressure on an already overburdened Chrysler.

Harried Chrysler officials were reluctant to view Sterling's motives so simply, and company attorneys took great pains in preparing and arguing any agreement they would consent to. They waited too long. According to a member of Sterling's staff, "We were within two paragraphs of an agreement" when the Huber 328 jumped in with both feet, properly entering the case as intervenors.

They had one goal in mind: to force into the court's decree an admission from Chrysler that it had wrongfully polluted the neighborhood. With this admission on the books, it would be child's play to get Chrysler to pay the claimed damages to health and property in a suit the 328 had already filed in another court.

Consent Decree Signed

After intervenors had blocked the signing of the settlement for more than a month, Chrysler attorneys appeared at a hearing and moved that the admittance of the intervenors to the case be reconsidered. Sterling rose and uttered token opposition, following which the judge granted the Chrysler motion and the settlement was signed.

The settlement established a binding policy for cupola shutdown and outlined an extensive maintenance program. Both Sterling and Chrysler attorneys agreed off the record that the entire program was in effect even before Sterling had sued under the environmental protection law.

The settlement was signed in October of last year. The Huber 328 continued their case. In June of this year it went to a jury, which found Chrysler to be culpable for all damages traceable to its plant emissions up to June, 1970.

That would seem to settle the case. Unfortunately, there is a rather large discrepancy between what the plaintiff thinks the jury said and what Chrysler attorneys feel was decided.

The attorney for the plaintiffs thinks the decision included damages to health, and he is prepared to argue each case independently, each one taking a week or more. Over at Chrysler, the jury's ruling is regarded as relating solely to property damages, and they delight in noting that a sizable number of the Huber 328 didn't reside there until after June, 1970.

It's a difference that a court must resolve, and it's one of those things that can drag on and on . . . as the Huber Foundry case has already done for almost eight years.

Racial Overtones

The local press in Detroit, which has never once reported that Chrysler originally opposed building in the city, handles the Huber affair as a straight environmental story. Chrysler has dirtied the air and corroded houses and cars — and the people want payment.

Just as Chrysler's $3 million struggle to make a "clean" plant clean is ignored, so do some nuances in the plaintiffs' motivation go uncommented upon. The residents were assumed to be motivated solely by a desire for a pollution-free neighborhood until the spring of last year, when the Federal Housing Administration announced it would cease guaranteeing loans on homes in the Huber area because of industrial pollution. The ban was subsequently limited to Huber Avenue and the street behind it. Other homes in the area, the revised FHA ruling said, would be eligible for loan guarantee provided the buyer signed a release stating awareness of industrial pollution in the area. With that development, protests against the foundry took on a new stridency.

The FHA release did not specify the foundry. There is ample evidence that other plants in the area contribute substantially to the neighborhood's periodic blanket of dust. Umbrage from the residents, however, was vented solely at the foundry.

The FHA, by its ruling, denied to the residents of the Huber area their one hope of selling their homes for anywhere near the value they themselves put on them. Being in an area long zoned for heavy industry, their homes are now among the least desirable in the eyes of any prospective buyer.

The children of the ethnic groups are moving to the suburbs, leaving only the poor to buy their old places with the aid of federal housing subsidies. Since January of this year, eight welfare recipients buying homes in the Huber area have defaulted and abandoned their homes, leaving them destined for demolition by the government. It is for the old-timers in the Huber area the end of the neighborhood, the end of an era; and, since the foundry was the last thing to arrive on the scene before they noticed the change was irreversible, they are placing the blame solely on Chrysler.

Thus, it is understandable why the counsel for the plaintiffs confides off the record that as soon as he finishes collecting for health damages he intends to launch action to get Chrysler or the government to buy all the homes in the area and then tear them down to create a buffer zone.

How far he gets remains to be seen. He himself admits that several of his clients have lost interest, moved out, and that there is no way for his client base to grow.

One top Chrysler executive, when asked what advice he would give to anyone searching for a site for a foundry, replied, "I'd tell him to get in his car and drive, and drive, and drive."

There is scarcely a city in the United States that is not mourning the fact that business and industry are fleeing to the suburbs. In each one of these cities is a mayor or a chamber of commerce breathing into the ear of the captains of local industry, trying to get them to expand, or at least to remain, in town.

Chrysler bowed to just such pressure in 1964 and has been up to its ears in litigation ever since. There is no doubt a solution to the problems of both the Detroits and the Chryslers. But, as has been learned from the Huber

Avenue experience, these solutions must be proceeded toward very, very carefully.

Discussion Questions

1. What are the issues involved? As a member of Chrysler management, how would you solve each one?

2. Three main groups were involved in this case — Chrysler officials, public officials, and the people living near the foundry. In what ways did each group act responsibly and irresponsibly?

3. To what extent could the problems that Chrysler encountered have been avoided by moving to either of the alternative locations the company originally considered? Explain.

case 46

National Chlor-Alkali:
East St. Louis, Illinois, Plant[1]

In 1970, National Chlor-Alkali, an international producer of chemicals, fertilizers, and dyes, built an $80 million chlorine-caustic soda complex on the east bank of the Mississippi River at East St. Louis, Illinois. The facility was the largest chlorine-caustic soda plant of National Chlor-Alkali and was the fifth largest chlorine-caustic soda plant in the United States. The unit was started up in early 1971 with only minor difficulties. For the most part, output, yields, efficiencies, and product quality met design specifications. Management was generally elated over the apparent success of the new venture.

The Problem

In the spring of 1974, however, a serious problem began to develop. The process sewer system began to collapse.[2] Initial evidence of the sewer system failure was discovered April 14, 1974. The night shift mechanics parked their pick-up truck in front of the control room at approximately 3:00 a.m.[3] The parking area caved in, and the pick-up truck "disappeared." The mechanics were not injured, but the pick-up truck had to be retrieved with a crane. The hole created by the cave-in was approximately 14 ft in diameter and 6 ft deep.

Investigations revealed that almost the entire process sewer system had collapsed and that smaller cave-ins were occurring along the entire sewer line. Moreover, the process waste was channeling into the storm sewer system destroying sections of the terracotta storm sewer piping. (The storm sewer piping is constructed of terracotta or clay, while the process sewer piping is constructed of acid/alkali-resistant resinous materials. The clay piping is eventually destroyed if subjected to strong acids or alkalies.) The consequence was that concrete pads, pipe bridge supports, equipment foun-

---

[1]For previous details, see case 43, "National Chlor-Alkali: Geismar, Louisiana, Plant."

[2]A process sewer conveys chemical or process waste to a disposal system or to a receiving stream, such as the Mississippi River. A storm sewer carries rain water or ground "run-off" to a waterway.

[3]For a plant layout, see Figure 8–4.

204

Figure 8–4   Existing Process Sewers

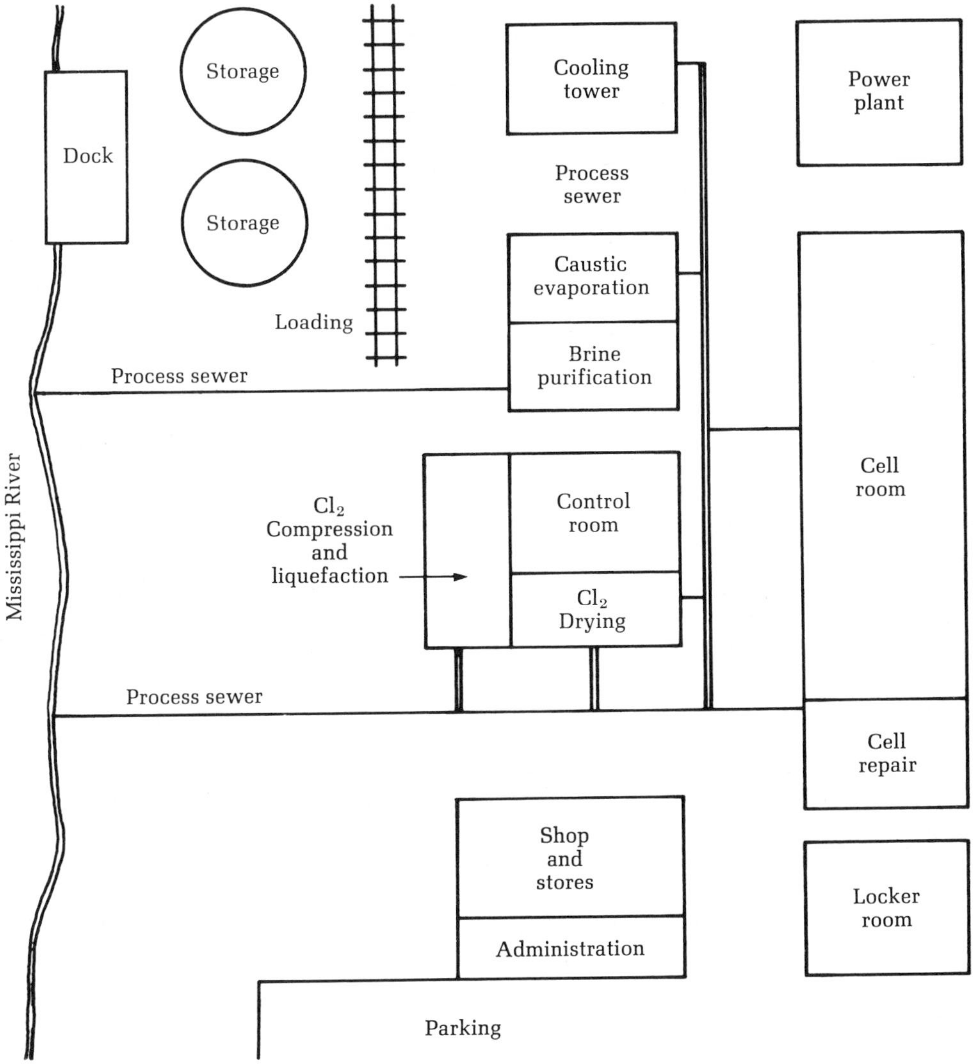

dations, and even road beds were being undermined by the collapsed sewer system.

Large sections of the plant had to be barricaded to prevent personnel injury and equipment damage through ground cave-ins. Even so, the operators as well as vehicles were exposed to chemical attack because of acid and alkali seepage from the ground.[4] This seepage formed numerous puddles in the

---

[4]The acid (sulfuric) is continuously discharged from the chlorine drying area where it scrubs the gaseous chlorine to remove water vapor. The alkali (sodium hydroxide) originates from process spills in the caustic evaporation area; the spills overflow to the process sewer. Both acid and alkali are ultimately discharged to the Mississippi River.

vicinity of the process sewers. Vehicles frequently were driven through the contaminated puddles. Operators and mechanics received minor burns as well as damaged shoes and clothing as they inadvertently waded through the puddles.

The operations department surmised that the process sewer system had failed because of faulty construction planning. They claimed that the sewer system had been installed before the use of heavy construction equipment had ceased. The operation of heavy equipment over the unsettled ground covering the sewers was the alleged reason for the sewer failure. The construction group denied this allegation and claimed that the sewer failed because of abuse sustained during the start-up of the complex. The claim was that huge amounts of acid and alkali were spilled during start-up. The combined streams of acid and alkali underwent a neutralization reaction that produced excessive heat. This heat allegedly caused irreparable damage to the process sewer system and resulted in the ultimate failure.

The Solution

Whatever the reason for failure, it was apparent to all that the problem had to be corrected. The immediate reaction was to replace the collapsed sewer system with piping that was more heat resistant while, at the same time, guarding against the passage of heavy equipment over the new piping until the ground had properly settled. This solution involved the construction of temporary, open trenches to divert the process waste while a new system could be laid parallel to the old one. Then, the process waste could be diverted into the new sewer system during the annual plant turn-around. There was general agreement on the plan among the operations, maintenance, and engineering departments. In fact, planners and schedulers had already begun to contact pipe vendors to select the proper material for construction of the new system. Capital authorization (cost of the new system was estimated to total $140,000) had been given, and work orders had been written to install the new system.

The plan, however, was critically challenged during a routine staff meeting called by the plant manager. At this meeting, the plant manager announced that capital authorization had been received for the new sewer system. The group was startled when the superintendent of environmental protection asked, "Why are we going to spend all that money when process sewers will be obsolete in a few years?" (He knew of the sewer problem but had not been consulted on the resolution.) He then cited provisions of the Federal Water Pollution Control Act Amendments of 1972 (PL 92–500). For a complete description of PL 92–500, see appendix A. The superintendent suggested that the plant revise the scope of its planning from merely replacing a process sewer system to a long-range program of pollution control.

He detailed the need for such a program as follows:

1. The Environmental Protection Agency (EPA) would soon outlaw the direct discharge of cooling water treatment agents (chromates) with

cooling tower blow-down.[5] The treating agents must be removed from the blow-down and recycled back to the tower or disposed in a waste pit.

2. The discharge from the cell rooms had been closely scrutinized for lead content by the EPA. (The graphite anodes used in the cells are cast in lead, which is subject to acid-brine attack. Hence, a small portion of the load is discharged through cell leakage.) The cell room waste must ultimately be treated and the lead removed by filtration before the effluent can be discharged into the Mississippi River.

3. The plant had been put on notice by the EPA that permits for dumping acid, alkalies, and brines into the Mississippi River might be re-called. The new permits would require substantial reduction in such dumping as dictated by the goals of "best practicable" control by 1977 and "best available" control by 1983. Ultimately, the goal of "zero discharge" by 1985 would apply to these pollutants.

Moreover, the superintendent of environmental protection claimed that economic benefits could be forthcoming from a new pollution-control system. He cited that alkalies and brines could be recycled directly to the system to improve yields in these areas. The estimated raw material savings from such a recycle system would total $50,000 per year. He acknowledged that acids could not be recycled and would require neutralization.

The plant manager was impressed by these comments. He instructed the superintendent to work with the operations, maintenance, and engineering departments to incorporate a pollution-control program into the process sewer renewal plan.

On June 4, the department heads, in consultation with the superintendent of environmental protection, presented a plan for process waste disposal (see Figure 8-5). The plan was as follows:

1. Install a cooling water treating agent (chromates) recovery system. Such a system was already being marketed by a firm that specialized in pollution control equipment.
2. Install caustic and brine recovery ponds to collect spills and recycle these streams back to respective processes. (If spills were to exceed pond capacity, operations would have to be temporarily suspended until spills could be contained and recycled.)
3. Install a limestone neutralization pit to neutralize the acid discharge. The pit was to be large enough to allow solar evaporation of the liquid waste.
4. Install a lead treatment pond and filtration system to remove lead from the cell room discharge.

---

[5]Blow-down is the purging of cooling tower water to maintain the dissolved solid coolant at a prescribed level.

This revised system was estimated to cost $750,000. The plant manager and the corporate officers of National Chlor-Alkali reviewed the revised plan.

Figure 8–5   *Process Waste Disposal System*

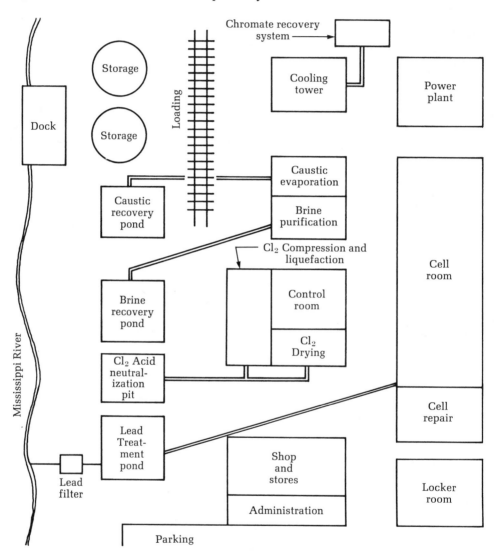

Discussion Questions

1. What are the benefits in installing the pollution-control system prior to an EPA mandate?

2. What are the possible risks in installing the pollution-control system prior to an EPA mandate?

3. What revisions would you recommend in long-range planning for the plant?

appendix A
Federal
Water Pollution Control Act
Amendments of 1972*
(An Analysis of PL 92–500)

Introduction

The Federal Water Pollution Control Act Amendments of 1972 (PL 92–500) represent a fundamental shift in the nation's approach to improving the quality of its rivers, lakes, groundwaters, and territorial waters. This shift in approach is evident in the new legislation's definition of all discharge of pollutants into receiving waters as illegal unless the discharge is made under a permit that specifies the degree of effluent reduction the source must achieve in its discharges. Notable also in the newly legislated approach are the emphases on area-wide planning and management, the authorization of stiff civil and criminal penalties for violation, and the delegation of implementation of these functions to the states under federally developed guidelines.

This complex legislation is the culmination of two years of intensive activity in both houses of Congress. Part of the complexity arises from the provisions required to handle the transition from existing law; more arises from the act's attempt to base effluent limitations on technological capabilities; and still more arises from the need to incorporate public participation in as many phases of implementation as possible.

The basic structure that emerges from PL 92–500 is laid out in Sections 101, 201, 208, 301, and 402. These sections provide:

1. The national goal is to eliminate all discharge of pollutants into receiving waters by 1985 and achieve an interim goal that provides for protection of aquatic life and wildlife and for recreation in and on the water by 1983.
2. Up to $18 billion is authorized for fiscal 1973, 1974, and 1975 for use in an accelerated construction program of publicly owned waste treatment facilities incorporating the best practicable technology. Facilities that integrate treatment of municipal and industrial wastes are to be encouraged. All point and nonpoint sources of pollution are to be identified and a plan developed to bring them all under control.
3. Areas with serious water quality problems are to be identified and attacked first.
4. All point source effluents are to be limited to levels achievable through use of best practicable technology by 1977 and best available technology by 1983.

*Source: David E. Gushee, Analyst in Environmental Policy; Environmental Policy Division; Congressional Research Service; The Library of Congress; published and distributed by Water Pollution Control Federation, Washington, D.C.

5. To insure that point source effluents are limited, each source must obtain a permit that specifies the limitation to be achieved and the measures that must be taken to demonstrate that it is being achieved.

Other major provisions in the legislation provide for federal support of area-wide and state planning for state control activities, for research and development on pollution abatement techniques, for training and monitoring treatment plant operators, for insuring public participation in all nondiscretionary activities from planning through enforcement, for study of the impact of steps taken to reduce pollution on the U.S. position in international trade, for financial aid to small business, and for an environmental financing authority whose purpose is to help provide states with their share of the capital funds necessary for construction of waste treatment facilities.

Restrictions on Point Source Effluents

The national goal of eliminating all discharge of pollutants is to be approached through two interim stages, during which applicable water quality standards, where they now exist, will be continued and, where they do not exist, will be imposed. In addition, effluent limitations will be imposed. Control and enforcement will be based on the effluent limitations rather than on the water quality standards.

The first interim stage, to be achieved by July 1, 1977, will be based on the reduction in discharges of effluents that can be achieved through application of "best practicable" technology and operating practice, taking into account costs of implementation and benefits derived. The second stage, to be achieved by July 1, 1983, is to be based on "best available" technology, again taking into account in defining "best available" the costs of implementation and the benefits to be derived.

The EPA has responsibility for developing and setting forth the effluent limitations. In recognition of the great variability in the nature of effluents, standards of reduction will be set industry by industry, or, if necessary, by process or by product. They will not, however, be set on a plant-by-plant basis.

Publicly owned treatment facilities come under these effluent limitations. Where industrial wastes are processed through these facilities, the wastes will be subject to pretreatment requirements designed to protect the operability of the treatment process and to insure that toxic or other materials that would pass through the treatment process without being removed or made harmless would be removed at the industrial source. Further, whether or not the treatment works processes industrial wastes, its discharges will be limited by July 1, 1977, to a level achievable through application of secondary treatment technology or to the equivalent level through application of alternative approaches.

For areas where effluent limitations are inadequate, as a result perhaps of the concentration of industry along a short stretch of river, to achieve the applicable water quality standards, more stringent effluent limitations (including alternative effluent control strategies) are to be established.

The state is responsible for identifying these areas and establishing maximum daily load limits for pollutants whose presence correlates with water quality criteria. Where limitations required to achieve the desired water quality would be punitively expensive, either economically or socially, the objective of the more stringent limitations is to "contribute to the attainment or maintenance of (the desired) water quality." In cases where such limitations are to be established, the EPA is to hold public hearings to determine "the relationship of the economic and social costs of achieving any such limitation . . . including any economic or social dislocation in the community . . . to the social and economic benefits to be obtained . . ." and to determine whether any proposed limitations are achievable through available technology or combination of technology and alternative control strategies.

Criteria for Establishing Water Quality Standards

The EPA is responsible for developing and publishing the criteria to be used by the states in establishing state water quality standards. The EPA criteria must include information on: (a) the effects of pollutants on aquatic life, shorelines and beaches, aesthetics, and recreation; (b) how pollutants are concentrated or dispersed through naturally occurring biological, chemical, and physical processes; (c) the effects of pollutants on rates of eutrophication and sedimentation; (d) what has to be done to restore and maintain the quality of waters, as a function of the class and category of the water; (e) how to measure and classify water quality; and (f) which pollutants are suitable for maximum daily load measurement correlated with the achievement of water quality objectives.

The EPA has a year to develop these criteria and is to do so "in a fishbowllike atmosphere." They are to be published in the Federal Register in addition to being publicized by other means. They are to be revised whenever new information indicating the need for updating becomes available.

Mechanism for Establishing State Water Quality Standards

States which already have water quality standards — either interstate, intrastate, or both — are to submit them to the EPA for approval if they have not done so previously. The EPA will base its approval of these standards on criteria applicable before passage of this act. If the EPA finds them lacking, it will point out, within 90 days for interstate standards and 120 days for intrastate standards, the changes needed. The states have 90 days to adopt the changes the EPA specifies.

If states do not have water quality standards, they have 180 days from enactment to set them and submit them to the EPA. If any state has not submitted standards within the time required or has not responded to the EPA's specifications of required changes in the time required, the EPA will publish proposed standards for that state and, no more than 180 days later, promulgate the proposed standards as regulations if the state does not act in the interim.

Each state is to hold public hearings at least every three years to determine any need to revise its water quality standards. The revised state standards go through the same process with the EPA for approval, and the EPA has the same authority to take over if the state does not act appropriately.

Establishing Effluent Limitations for 1977

The EPA has a year in which to establish effluent limitations. In doing so for the first interim stage, where "best practicable" technology is to be invoked, it will take into account factors such as the age and size of plants affected, the unit processes involved, and the costs of applying the technology. In some industries, "best practicable" will be based on the average of the best existing performance, whereas, in industries where present practices are uniformly inadequate, it will entail higher levels of control than any in place if, in the EPA's judgment, the technology to do so is available and can be practicably applied.

For waste treatment plants, "best practicable" technology is defined as secondary treatment or its equivalent. The EPA will publish within 60 days information on the extent to which secondary treatment can be expected to reduce the amounts of pollutants in treatment plant effluents. Within nine months, the agency will publish information on alternative waste treatment techniques and systems that are to be considered in lieu of or in addition to secondary treatment.

Establishing Toxic Effluent Standards

Toxic pollutants are subject to individual limitations on the basis of their danger to public health and aquatic life. The EPA will publish, within 90 days of enactment, a list of toxic pollutants or combinations of pollutants for which it plans to establish a specific effluent standard or, if warranted, a prohibition of discharge. Within 180 days, EPA will follow up by publishing its proposed effluent limitations and prohibitions for each toxic material on its list. After public hearings on its proposals, EPA will set the limitations and promulgate them — immediately if the hearings have led to modifications of the original proposed limitations and within six months if there is to be no change from those proposed. The limitations will take effect as specified by the EPA at any time up to one year after promulgation.

The lists and effluent limitations will be reviewed at least every three years.

Establishing Pretreatment Standards

Industries whose wastes are treated in publicly owned treatment works are required to pretreat their wastes to handle materials which interfere with, pass through, or are otherwise incompatible with the treatment processes. The EPA has 180 days to publish its proposed pretreatment standards for these materials and an additional 90 days to hold hearings, if necessary, and promulgate its pretreatment standards.

As technologies change, the EPA will revise these standards as appropriate, again by publishing proposed regulations and holding hearings, if necessary, before issuance of the revised standards.

New sources of wastes discharged to publicly owned treatment plants will be subject to pretreatment requirements also. The EPA will set these at the same time it sets effluent limitations for discharge of the same materials directly to receiving waters.

Establishing Effluent Limitations for 1983

By 1983, effluent limitations are to be set at levels that can only be met by "best available" technology. However, factories, facilities, and process units constructed at any time after "best available" limitations have been established must meet these limitations, even though in operation well before 1983. Existing installations have until 1983 to comply, unless state programs include earlier schedules for those activities able to move more rapidly.

To define the capabilities of "best available" technology, the EPA will proceed in steps. The first step is to identify the categories of sources to be covered. These categories will cover all industries and will follow the general structure of the Standard Industrial Classifications. The EPA has 90 days to generate the list of categories.

The second step is for the EPA to publish proposed regulations establishing federal standards of performance (the greatest degree of effluent reduction achievable through "best available" technology) within each category. The EPA has a year to develop these regulations, consulting with experts, agencies, and industry as necessary. Interested parties have 120 days after publication of the proposed regulations to offer written comments, after which the EPA will issue regulations, adjusted as appropriate on the basis of the comments received.

As with effluent limitations developed under the "best practicable" standard, factors such as cost, benefit, energy consumption, and the like are to be considered in determining the standards to be set.

As technologies and other alternatives develop, the EPA will review and revise these standards, again providing opportunity for interested parties to comment.

Applying and enforcing standards of performance for new sources (except federal facilities) will be delegated to the states upon their demonstration to the EPA that their procedures are adequate.

To provide industry with a consistent basis for planning its pollution control activities and expenditures, any new point source meeting these standards will not be required to meet any standard more stringent than that applicable at start-up for 10 years or the period of depreciation, whichever is shorter.

Monitoring, Control, Permits, and Enforcement

The states retain the primary responsibility and authority to fulfill the requirements of this new law. Where appropriate, states can enter into interstate compacts to enhance their ability to act. If a state program does not operate effectively, the EPA can, after suitable notice, take it over and operate it until the state has met the requirements.

State Control Agencies

Each state vests its monitoring, control, permit and enforcement activities in a state water pollution control agency. The EPA supports the activities of the state control agencies by making grants to them to cover costs of their operations and provides a national standard of effectiveness through its grant requirements. Money for these grants will be allocated to the states on the basis of the extent of their pollution problems. Within 120 days of enactment of this legislation, the state agency must file with the EPA a report on its existing control program, including the criteria by which it establishes priorities among the many wastewater treatment plant construction projects within the state. It must also file with the EPA its plan of action to bring the various effluent sources in the state under control (schedule of compliance).

Beginning in fiscal 1974, the state control agency, to qualify for a grant, will be required to have set up the equipment and procedures by which it can measure water quality throughout the state, and a procedure for an annual updating of these data. By January 1, 1975, and annually thereafter, the agency will file with the EPA a report on actual water quality in the state compared to that set as the objective, an analysis of how the then-existing water quality provides for the protection of aquatic life and for recreation, recommendations for additional actions for continued improvements in water quality, an estimate of costs and benefits of going the rest of the way toward "clean water," and a proposed plan of action to bring nonpoint pollution sources under control.

The state water pollution control agency sets the state's water quality standards, following the criteria outlined earlier. It will hold hearings to review existing standards at least every three years and revise them as appropriate. It will set additional standards as appropriate. All new and revised standards are forwarded to the EPA for approval.

The state agency also identifies those waters where effluent limitations are not stringent enough, by virtue of the concentration of industry, for example, sets priorities for dealing with them, and establishes daily maximum loads of pollutants for those pollutants which the EPA has identified as suitable for such calculation on the basis of their relationship to the water quality criteria involved.

The state control agency is empowered, after EPA approval of its procedures, to apply and enforce standards of performance for new sources of water pollution within its area of jurisdiction (other than those operated federally). The agency also applies and enforces effluent limitations, including those for toxic substances, and pretreatment standards for industrial pollutant sources discharging wastes into publicly owned waste treatment works.

To carry out these monitoring and control functions, the state control agency is also empowered, after EPA approval of its procedures, to require owners and operators of point sources to maintain the necessary records, install monitoring equipment, sample its effluent streams and analyze them, and report the resulting information to it. The agency also has authority to enter the plant site, inspect the monitoring equipment, examine or copy the files, and sample the effluent streams itself. All the data so obtained are to be available to the public, except for those portions related to the owners' need to protect trade secrets.

The Permit Program

Under this legislation, it is unlawful to discharge any pollutant from any point source, including publicly owned waste treatment works, unless the discharger has a permit which certifies that the discharge complies with applicable effluent limitations, water quality standards, and limitations on the basis of toxicity, or he meets pretreatment standards for discharge into publicly owned waste treatment works. The state water pollution control agency administers this permit program once the EPA has issued its guidelines for application forms and minimum procedural requirements (within 60 days of enactment), the state agency has submitted a description of its permit-granting program to the EPA, and the EPA has approved the program.

Until this act was passed, permit-granting activities related to water pollution have been administered under the Refuse Act of 1899 by the Corps of Engineers in cooperation with the EPA. The EPA now takes this activity over until it issues its guidelines to the states and approves the state programs. (On an interim basis, the EPA can authorize a state control agency permit program for up to 150 days after enactment or until it approves the state program formally, whichever comes first. Any permits granted under this interim authority are subject to individual EPA review and possible revision.) Permits granted under the Refuse Act will remain in effect for their term. Applications for permits under the Refuse Act on which decisions have not been reached will become applications for permits under this act.

The state control agency, in operating its permit-granting programs, must notify the public and the EPA of each application and provide opportunity for public hearing before making a ruling. If granting a permit would affect another state downstream from the permitting state, the downstate is notified by the EPA and has an opportunity to express its views.

Each permit granted by a state control agency must have a fixed term and can be for no longer than five years. It must set forth the applicable effluent and other limitations plus the monitoring requirements needed to demonstrate compliance.

The state control agency will notify the EPA of every action it takes on every permit application, including its decision to grant a permit, unless it specifically waives that right at the time it approves the state program.

A permit is also required for the discharge of any pollutant for which there is no established effluent limitation by reason of toxicity. In these cases, the permit certifies that no such limitation exists. If the EPA determines, after public hearing, that a state control agency is not administering its permit-granting program properly, it can withdraw its approval of that program and take over its functions if the state does not correct the problem within 90 days.

Enforcement

State control agencies with approved permit-granting programs have authority to force compliance with the terms under which any permit had been issued as well as to order the cessation of any discharges subject to permit for which permit application has not been made. The state can issue administrative orders requiring compliance or may proceed with civil suits. Willful violation of permit condition, false statements, and tampering with monitoring equipment are subject to criminal penalties.

The EPA will monitor the effectiveness of the state control agencies in enforcing the provisions of their granted permits. It has the authority to intervene in individual cases by either notification that the person or organization is in violation or by issuance of an order for the offender to comply. An order for compliance will specify a time in which compliance must occur.

Should the EPA find that a state's enforcement activities are ineffective, it will so notify the state. If the state does not correct its program within 30 days, the EPA will give public notice of the agency's ineffectiveness and take over its enforcement activities until the state's program is improved to meet the EPA's standards.

Whenever a municipality is a party to a civil action for noncompliance, the state in which the municipality is located is joined as a party. This provision is designed to deal with publicly owned treatment works and other public waste handling facilities.

When a discharge of pollutants in violation of permit provisions is determined to constitute an imminent and substantial endangerment to health or to endanger the ability of persons to earn their living (such as harvesting and marketing shellfish), an approved state control agency, or the EPA if no state agency is approved, can bring suit in the appropriate district court to stop the offending discharge.

case 47

U. S. Plywood
(Part A)

U. S. Plywood is one of the country's leading producers of wood products. One of its plants, located in the southeastern United States, specializes in the production of plywood from southern pines.[1] Throughout the 1970s, the mill, like most other manufacturing firms, has experienced rising production costs caused by abnormally high rates of inflation. The rising costs, in part, stem from increased wages and rising prices of supplies and equipment. The cost of the primary raw material (logs) has remained somewhat constant, however, because of a long-term contract with Crown Zellerbach Corporation, the supplier of the plant's pine logs.

In 1976, the spiraling cost of natural gas was the primary concern of the management of U. S. Plywood. Between 1973 and January, 1976, the mill experienced a fivefold increase in the price of natural gas (from $0.32 per 1,000 cu ft to $1.61 per 1,000 cu ft). The cost of natural gas averages $50,000 per month, but sometimes amounts to nearly $70,000 per month (consumption depends on the volume of production). Moreover, the plant has been put on notice by United Pipeline, the supplier of natural gas, that its consumption may be curtailed to meet residential heating requirements. Price increases and potential curtailments stem from nationwide shortages of natural gas. The mill's use of natural gas for boiler fuel has been given the lowest priority by natural gas suppliers. (The priority rankings are endorsed by the Federal Power Commission.[2]) Consequently, management has been thoroughly reviewing the mill's natural gas consumption.

Natural gas is consumed in several manufacturing operations. First, logs that have been cut into 8-foot blocks are heated to 120° for 24 hours in a steam room. The logs are heated by spraying live steam (generated from a natural gas boiler) into the room. (This process softens the logs to facilitate veneer stripping operations.)

---

[1]For a complete description of the plant and the production process, see case 54, "U. S. Plywood — Part B."

[2]For a complete discussion of this topic, see case 1, "Coastal States Chemicals and Fertilizers."

Another process that requires huge amounts of natural gas is the veneer drying operation. The veneer passes via a belt conveyor through a gas-fired Moore Tube-O-Jet dryer, which is approximately 100 ft long. (The Moore Tube-O-Jet dryer removes moisture from veneer prior to the gluing operation.)

The last process that consumes a great deal of natural gas is the "hot-press" operation. The hot-press consists of a stack of steam-heated, rectangular plates. Each glued plywood sheet is pressed between two steam-heated plates in a "pancake" arrangement. (The hot-press cures the glue that joins the laminated sections.)

Of these operations, the Moore Tube-O-Jet dryer consumes the greatest amount of natural gas. The dryer is relatively inefficient because heat is discharged out the dryer flue stacks. With certain modifications, the dryer can be steam heated to produce more efficient results. Steam heat can be generated by wood-burning boilers, thereby using wood scraps as fuel. Currently, enormous amounts of scraps are passed through a chipper and sold for minor recovery value, or they are incinerated (which causes air pollution).

At present, plans are being made to install a wood-fired boiler to generate steam. The scraps will then be stoked in a "dutch-oven" that has a forced air blower to heat the boiler for the generation of steam. Proper air-fuel ratios together with smokestack arrestors are expected to eliminate air pollution problems from the wood-fired boiler. The steam will be used in the modified Moore Tube-O-Jet dryer to remove moisture from the veneer. The conversion is expected to reduce natural gas consumption significantly.

Discussion Questions

1. Discuss U. S. Plywood's planned conversion of its dryers from natural gas to steam and the implications for other industries.

2. What other courses of action would be open to U. S. Plywood if it converted the dryers from natural gas to steam?

case 48

La Crosse
Furniture Company

The La Crosse Furniture Company of Greensboro, North Carolina, is a relatively small manufacturer of quality furniture which is marketed throughout the Atlantic Coast states. Under the direction of the President and Chief Executive Officer, Frederick Murphy, the firm has enjoyed fifteen consecutive years of profitable operations.

The most serious problem facing the management of La Crosse Furniture Company is turnover of personnel, which, in part, is attributed to unpleasant working conditions. Hazardous tasks and physically demanding jobs cause the relatively poor working environment. In 1969, the firm employed its first safety engineer, Hank Hendershot, to design and implement a safety awareness program to reduce injury-causing accidents and to minimize related costs. The program included proper training of workers, the introduction of protective clothing, the posting of safety notices throughout the plant, and weekly safety meetings. In addition, protective guard rails and screens were installed around hazardous saws and planers; protective goggles became mandatory for workers who performed their tasks in the vicinity of lathes, saws, and planers; and better housekeeping methods were introduced.

Following the passage of the Occupational Safety and Health Act in 1970, additional safety measures were incorporated. Electrical wiring on some machinery was grounded; additional fire prevention measures were introduced; and noise levels were monitored and controlled. Accidents decreased sharply. By 1973, injury-sustaining accidents and resulting man-hours lost were reduced to one-fourth the 1968 level. Even so, many of the tasks associated with the manufacture of furniture remain hazardous. Thus, the nature of the work, coupled with carelessness and/or industrial fatigue of workers, make accidents inevitable.

Hank Hendershot, the company's safety engineer, believes strongly that most accidents are due to carelessness which, to a great extent, is due to industrial fatigue. Consequently, he insists that jobs be redesigned to minimize physical effort and that new machines and tools purchased incorporate energy-saving techniques. Generally, the workers of La Crosse Furniture have readily accepted Hendershot's safety program. Experience has taught them the benefits of goggles, hard hats, and other safety devices. However, there has been considerable resistance to the use of ear plugs.

At present, Hendershot is attempting to reduce the noise level of a planing operation, thereby minimizing the risk of hearing loss. Although the company provides ear plugs for all employees exposed to high noise levels, some workers remove them in defiance of company regulations because they are somewhat uncomfortable. Noise levels associated with the planing operation reach 115 decibels[1]; loss of hearing develops if a worker is exposed to noise levels of 100 decibels over an extended time.

Discussion Questions

1. Suggest methods (other than the use of ear plugs) for reducing noise levels in a manufacturing plant.

2. How should management cope with a worker's refusal to wear ear plugs? What are the risks? The benefits?

3. How would you handle the problem if the noise level of the planing operation cannot be reduced significantly?

---

[1] A decibel is the standard measure of levels of sound. It shows the relationship of specific sound levels to a standard which is defined as the lowest level of audible sound. Typically, pain does not occur until the noise level reaches 130 decibels.

case 49

Dibert, Bancroft, and Ross Foundry

Dibert, Bancroft, and Ross Company (DB&R) was established in New Orleans, Louisiana, in 1895. The firm conducted operations at the New Orleans location for 73 years and then relocated its foundry to Amite, Louisiana, a small town approximately 75 miles north of New Orleans. The Amite facility, which also includes a large machine shop, has more than 300,000 sq ft of floor space.

Dibert, Bancroft, and Ross specializes in producing foundry castings ranging up to 75,000 lb shipping weight. These castings are used in sugar mills, dredge pumps, tire molds, marine fittings, dock fittings, and pile-driving hammers. The castings are produced to the customer's specifications and are sold both domestically and abroad.

The firm also has a large machine fabricating shop, which machines the poured castings to specifications. Equipment includes vertical and horizontal boring mills, which are capable of swinging up to $16^{1}/_{2}$ ft in diameter and of performing to tolerances of less than 0.001 in. Some of the mills are equipped with contour-tracing equipment.

Other machine equipment includes lathes which can turn stock up to 60 in. in diameter and 40 ft in length. Dibert, Bancroft, and Ross has gear cutters which can machine gears up to $13^{1}/_{2}$ ft in diameter with a 20-in. face. Finally, the shop maintains a complete line of welding equipment and hard-surfacing facilities.

The firm points with pride to its pattern shop. In the pattern shop, casting patterns are made of wood or metal to customer drawings and specifications. Craftsmen in this shop maintain excellent dimensional control which results in precise casting dimensions.

Dibert, Bancroft, and Ross maintains excellent quality control in other areas, too. The firm's laboratories perform the following tests: complete chemical analysis and physical testing, microstructure analysis, ultrasonic testing, radiographic testing, magnaflux testing, dye penetrant tests, and hydrostatic testings. Dibert, Bancroft, and Ross can fulfill requests for foundry castings made to A.B.S., A.S.T.M., U.S. Navy, S.A.E., Federal, or Lloyd's specifications.

Scrap iron, steel, and other alloys are raw material supply for the foundry. The primary source of scrap is retired railroad equipment. The scrap metal is melted in the electric furnaces and poured into casting molds. The intense heat required by the furnaces is supplied by an arc from a graphite anode to a cathode.

The Problem

The Environmental Protection Agency (EPA) has claimed that the operation of such furnaces without emission-control devices violates the 1970 Clean Air Act (Public Law 91–604)[1]. This citation was based on the nature of the furnaces used by Dibert, Bancroft, and Ross and not on atmospheric testing at the foundry. In mid-1975, Dibert, Bancroft, and Ross was officially put on notice by the EPA that it was in violation of the 1970 Clean Air Act. Through a series of correspondences, officials from the firm agreed to meet with Region VI EPA officials in Dallas, Texas. According to Dibert, Bancroft, and Ross officials, the EPA attempted to "build a case" against the firm at the beginning of this meeting rather than discussing solutions to the firm's environmental protection problems. This belief was based on the fact that testimony by Dibert, Bancroft, and Ross officials was to be recorded and scrutinized by the EPA legal staff. Dibert, Bancroft, and Ross officials refused to meet under such circumstances, and the EPA then agreed that the discussions would not be recorded.

Finally, on November 3, 1975, Dibert, Bancroft, and Ross officials agreed to install smoke-control equipment on the furnace stacks. The equipment that Dibert, Bancroft, and Ross planned to install on each furnace is a "bag house." (A bag house contains a series of filter bags which remove particles from the furnace smoke.) The cost to purchase and install these devices was estimated to cost between $300,000 and $500,000. Moreover, the firm agreed to have such equipment in operation by May 3, 1978. The EPA set this deadline.

According to Dibert, Bancroft, and Ross officials, this plan did not fully satisfy the EPA. Dibert, Bancroft, and Ross officials claimed that the EPA wanted a signed confession that the foundry was in violation of the 1970 Clean Air Act. Moreover, the EPA established a deadline of November 24, 1975, to receive such a signed confession or the firm would be subject to a $25,000 per day fine for operation after the deadline.

The Shutdown

Rather than admitting to a violation of the 1970 Clean Air Act, officials of Dibert, Bancroft, and Ross closed the foundry on November 24, 1975. Consequently, 350 workers were laid off. Dibert, Bancroft, and Ross officials claimed that the firm could not operate with the possibility of a $25,000 per

---

[1] For a description of PL 91–604, see appendix A.

day fine.[2] The firm took its case to the public and exorted local and state elected officials to pressure the EPA to reverse its insistence on a signed confession of pollution violations. Tremendous pressure was exerted by the 350 employees of the foundry who were facing the holiday season without paychecks.

The Agreement

The Dallas office of the EPA acceded to the pressure and granted Dibert, Bancroft, and Ross a "no-penalty" vulnerability period from December 1, 1975, through December 12, 1975.[3] Dibert, Bancroft, and Ross and the EPA believed a final agreement could be reached within that period. The foundry re-opened on December 1, 1975.

The two parties worked diligently to reach an agreement. A major hang-up, however, was the wording of the section that referred to the furnace emissions. The EPA wanted the furnace emissions to be cited as "in violation of the 1970 Clean Air Act." The firm would not agree to this admission of guilt without an extensive period of atmospheric testing in the vicinity of the foundry. Finally, a compliance agreement was reached on December 15, 1975, after the EPA agreed to refer to the furnace emissions as "alleged" violations of the 1970 Clean Air Act.[4]

Discussion Questions

1. Evaluate the stand the firm took in response to actions by the EPA. Refer to the newspaper accounts of the incident for assistance in your evaluation. (See appendix E.)

2. What effect, if any, did general economic conditions have on the position that the EPA took?

appendix A
1970 Clean Air Act*

Ambient Air Standards

The EPA promulgated national ambient air quality standards for the six major pollutants.

---

[2]For a press release from Dibert, Bancroft, and Ross, see appendix B.

[3]See appendix C.

[4]See appendix D.

Ambient Air Quality Standards

	Primary (enforcement by summer, 1975)	Secondary (no time limit on enforcement)
Particulates		
micrograms/cu m		
annual geometric mean	75	60
max. 24-hr. conc.*	260	150
Sulfur oxides		
micrograms/cu m		
annual arith. average	80 (.03 ppm)	60 (.02 ppm)
max. 24-hr. conc.*	365 (.14 ppm)	260 (.1 ppm)
max. 3-hr. conc.*	—	1,300 (15 ppm)
Carbon monoxide		
milligrams/cu m		
max. 8-hr. conc.*	10 (9 ppm)	10
max. 1-hr. conc.*	40 (35 ppm)	40
Photochemical oxidants		
micrograms/cu m		
1-hr. max.*	160 (.08 ppm)	160
Hydrocarbons		
micrograms/cu m		
max. 3-hr. conc.*		
6–9 am	160 (.24 ppm)	160
Nitrogen oxides		
micrograms/cu m		
annual arith. average	100 (.05 ppm)	100
24-hr. max. average	—	—

*not to be exceeded more than once a year

By August, 1972, every state must enact emission standards so that their air quality falls within the federal guidelines. States must fully enforce the standards by summer, 1975, except for sources with unusual technical problems that may be given up to two years' grace.

The federal government will not tolerate interference with state enforcement plans. The EPA administrator can step in and run an unsatisfactory state program after thirty days' notice. The EPA can also go directly to court using its own lawyers if the Justice Department does not act promptly.

Hazardous Substances

The EPA can set emission standards, even down to zero levels, for hazardous substances. Standards for asbestos, beryllium, and mercury are being set now. Cadmium should be next.

*Chemical Engineering, Deskbook Issue, June 21, 1971, pp. 9–11.

New Sources

The new law requires that new plants or significant additions to old ones have the best available control technology. However, enforcement may be cumbersome since the EPA cannot move to force compliance until after the source begins operations.

Mandatory Licensing

To protect smaller firms, new developments in control technology must be made available if the lack of such technology would cause restraint of trade or violations of standards. The Justice Department will administer this provision.

Penalties

Intentional violations are punishable by fines up to $25,000 and a year in prison. The EPA can ask that offending sources be shut down immediately where clear danger to public health can be proven.

appendix B
Dibert, Bancroft and Ross Co., Ltd.

November 25, 1975

To The News Media:

The Environmental Protection Agency (EPA) shut down the company yesterday under threat of an unbelievable fine of twenty-five thousand ($25,000) dollars per day if we continued to operate.

DB&R employs over 350 people with a payroll of over $3 million. This is in addition to the millions of dollars of services and supplies DB&R buys annually in Louisiana.

The EPA has been after DB&R to install smoke-control equipment. At a meeting with EPA on November 3, DB&R agreed to install the very expensive basic control equipment that EPA wants at DB&R's total expense, which we would be financing through borrowed funds. The cost will be from one-third to one-half million dollars, which we really can't afford because we need all sorts of very expensive production equipment beyond what we can now afford.

Production equipment creates and maintains jobs and improves the company's competitive position. This EPA equipment costs lots of money but does not create any jobs here; it adds to our cost of operating and will never make a cent for the company or anyone working here.

Nevertheless, we have agreed to install the equipment the EPA wants. We have agreed on the timetable for the equipment purchase and installation. We have agreed on this in writing.

The problem is this. Through yesterday the EPA said, in effect, unless we sign a confession of polluting, making us vulnerable to even further harassment, we cannot operate. If we continue to operate, we would be vulnerable to the absurd fine of $25,000 per day. This is a quick way to break a company.

Last night they changed it slightly, saying we don't need to sign it, but the same vulnerability remains.

It appears the EPA's strategy is to get the company to operate while vulnerable to that large fine; then they would have an overwhelming economic weapon which they could use in an attempt to compel us to sign absolutely anything.

DB&R conducts all of its affairs with everyone in a most honorable manner. It would seem we should be able to expect a more ethical conduct from a federal government agency.

The EPA is brutally and arbitrarily playing with what has become an important element in Tangipahoa Parish's economy. DB&R is the largest private employer in the parish, exceeded only by Southeastern Louisiana University, which operates mainly on state tax money.

DB&R was established in New Orleans in 1895 and moved to Tangipahoa Parish in 1967. If Louisiana really cares about preserving existing industry and the jobs it provides and wants to attract new industry to our state, it should not stand by silently and let this unjust thing happen. It ought to at least scream out loud in protest. Please do!

> Sincerely,
>
> DIBERT, BANCROFT & ROSS CO., LTD.
>
> John A. Ross
> President

appendix C
Dibert, Bancroft and Ross Co., Ltd.

November 29, 1975

To The News Media:

Dibert, Bancroft, and Ross Co., Ltd., is pleased to announce that its plant will resume operations on Monday, December 1.

All employees are requested to report to work at their regular scheduled times on Monday.

Today the EPA gave Dibert, Bancroft, and Ross a "no penalty" vulnerability period from December 1 through 12, during which time it is expected a permanent agreement will be reached.

We appreciate the wonderful cooperation of the news media and the general public.

Thank you.

> Sincerely,
>
> DIBERT, BANCROFT & ROSS CO., LTD.
>
> John A. Ross
> President

appendix D
Dibert, Bancroft and Ross Co., Ltd.

December 16, 1975

To The News Media:

Yesterday afternoon an agreement was reached between the EPA in Dallas and DB&R in Amite.

The precise wording was agreed upon over the telephone, and the documents are presently in transit through the mail for signatures. The agreement enables the maintenance of dignity on both sides. It provides us with protection against vulnerability to fines, contains no confessions and not too much intimidation, although the coercive negotiation of the details was humiliating.

The wonderful cooperation and interest of the news media and the general public are greatly appreciated.

Thank you very much.

Sincerely,

DIBERT, BANCROFT & ROSS CO., LTD.

John A. Ross
President

appendix E
Newspaper
Articles

Steel plant closes doors; Blames EPA*

AMITE — Officials of the Dibert, Bancroft and Ross steel plant here are expected to release further information this afternoon on a plant shutdown Monday that idled about 400 employees.

The steel plant blames the shutdown on stringent pollution control guidelines of the Environmental Protection Agency.

The company is expected to release a statement about 1:30 p.m. today, according to Ralph Waits, executive vice-president. Waits told the Daily Star that company president John Ross and other officials met this morning to "work this thing out so it won't be so confusing."

The only explanation Monday came in a printed announcement distributed to employees. The brief letter to the employees said the plant was closing and ex-

---

*Daily Star; Hammond, Louisiana; November 25, 1975. Reproduced with permission of the editor.

plained that the EPA insisted on expensive and stringent smoke control devices at the plant.

The cost of the smoke control devices was estimated as being as much as $500,000, and the company's budget was said to be already strained by the need to install new production equipment.

"Production equipment maintains jobs and improves the company's competitive position. This EPA equipment costs lots of money but does not create any jobs here, adds to our cost of operating and will never make a cent for the company or anyone working here." read the announcement, which was signed "John Ross, President."

"We have agreed to install the equipment that the EPA wants, we have agreed on a timetable for purchase and installation of equipment," it continued.

However, no details of the timetable were included.

The announcement said the company agreed to the EPA's requirements three weeks ago, but it did not say when the discussions with EPA began.

"It will just about paralyze Amite," said an employee at the plant. "The factory has been here about eight years — just long enough for everyone to learn to count on it."

Amite Councilman Vince Labarbera said the shutdown will "definitely have an effect on the city."

Labarbera said the city has never complained of any pollution problems caused by the plant. "The previous Council wrote to the EPA and told them that the smoke from that plant means paychecks on Fridays," Labarbera said.

Labarbera estimated the steel plant has an annual payroll of about $3 million.

EPA denies closing Amite steel plant*

By MARK MATHES
Star Staff Writer

AMITE — An Environmental Protection Agency (EPA) spokesman in Dallas said today that the Dibert, Bancroft & Ross steel mill here can reopen "anytime it wants" without threat of a possible immediate anti-pollution fine.

But DB&R president John Ross said today he has received no communications from EPA on proposed concessions which came to light Tuesday evening. "We want to get back to work," Ross said, "but we can't operate recklessly."

A spokesman for John White, the regional EPA administrator based in Dallas, said that the Monday plant closing has caused concern within the agency. "We don't like to see 350 families out of work, especially if it's so unnecessary," said public affairs director Betty Williamson.

"On Monday Mr. Ross advised Mr. White that he was going to close the plant," said Ms. Williamson. "EPA has never implied or insinuated they would close the plant."

"Mr. Ross can open that plant anytime he wants, as far as Mr. White is concerned," she told The Daily Star.

Ross contends today that the firm faces a $25,000 a day fine if the EPA deems any of his operations in violation of federal pollution regulations.

---

*Daily Star; Hammond, Louisiana; November 26, 1975.

In a prepared statement issued Tuesday, Ross said: "The problem is this. Through yesterday (Monday) the EPA said, in effect, unless we sign a confession of polluting, making us vulnerable to even further harassment, we cannot operate. If we continue to operate, we would be vulnerable to the absurd fine of $25,000 per day. That is a quick way to break a company."

The apparent cause of friction between EPA and DB&R, according to a spokesman for Congressman Henson Moore, has been a proposed letter of agreement.

Press secretary Joe Karpinski told The Daily Star Tuesday that Moore had been working on the problem since last August.

Moore called EPA administrator John White Tuesday on the matter. According to Karpinski:

EPA has agreed not to require a guarantee of equipment.

EPA will require no admission of guilt on the part of DB&R in the agreement.

EPA agreed not to fine the steel plant retroactively for any possible past violations.

"EPA says it will put this guarantee in writing," said Karpinski. "There is really no jeopardy of fines. From where we sit, the problem seems to be solved as far as EPA is concerned," he said. "There was really no reaction from Ross."

Ross said today that the loss of revenue while the plant is closed will be less than the possible $25,000 per day fine.

"We have agreed to install the equipment the EPA wants. We have agreed on the timetable for the equipment purchase and installation. We have agreed on this in writing," said the prepared statement.

Ross said today the equipment, which could cost from one-third to one-half million dollars, has not yet been ordered.

However, the EPA official indicated that DB&R has a total of 30 months to install the equipment and get it operating.

Ms. Williamson said that the steel mill could be granted a further extension in the 30-month time limit if unusual delays or problems occurred. "We understand there are delays in obtaining this equipment and there can be delays in getting it installed," she said.

"We are not in the business of closing down companies by any means," said Ms. Williamson. "We work with companies any way we can."

"In the past year alone. EPA has had over 30 occasions to discuss this matter either by telephone, meetings or correspondence."

The spokesman said the last communication between the EPA administrator and the DB&R president was Tuesday around 12:30 p.m. White attempted to contact Ross again at 1 p.m., said Ms. Williamson, but "he could not be disturbed."

In his statement, Ross said: "At a meeting with EPA on Nov. 3, DB&R agreed to install the very expensive basic control equipment that EPA wants at DB&R's total expense which we would be financing through borrowed funds which . . . we really can't afford because we need all sorts of very expensive production equipment beyond what we now can afford."

"Production equipment creates and maintains jobs and improves the company's competitive position. This EPA equipment costs lots of money but does not create any jobs here," said the statement.

Ross said today that his company has over 350 employees with an annual payroll over $3 million.

The EPA spokesman said that state officials have been working with the company on the matter since 1971.

Ms. Williamson said that EPA attorneys are considering a portion of the proposed consent agreement dealing with possible retroactive fines by EPA for any alleged past pollution violations.

"This consent form is a standard agreement used by every industry in the state and the country that comes under this legislation," said Ms. Williamson. "This is not something we just wrote up for John Ross."

EPA, steel mill seek agreement*

By MARK MATHES
Star Staff Writer

AMITE — The Environmental Protection Agency (EPA) regional director is preparing a telegram today to the Dibert, Bancroft & Ross steel mill here asking the firm to comply with federal and state anti-pollution regulations.

"I'm preparing the telegram today to send this afternoon," said EPA regional director John White in a telephone interview from Dallas. "It will extend the period of no-penalty enforcement to 30 months," he told The Daily Star.

DB&R closed its doors Monday as president John Ross claimed his firm faced a $25,000 a day fine for non-compliance with regulations.

The steel company's executive vice president Ralph Waits said today that his firm is awaiting a statement "in writing" from EPA before they plan to re-open.

"We haven't heard anything from EPA," Waits told The Star. "A verbal communication couldn't hold up."

When the plant closed Monday, about 350 employees were out of work. The firm is considered one of the largest employers in the parish, after Hammond State School and Southeastern Louisiana University.

Earlier in the week, Ross said: "It appears the EPA's strategy is to get the company to operate while vulnerable to that large fine; then they would have an overwhelming economic weapon which they could use in an attempt to compel us to sign absolutely anything."

"The EPA is brutally and arbitrarily playing with what has become an important element in Tangipahoa Parish's economy," said Ross.

The firm was established in New Orleans in 1895 and relocated to Amite in 1967.

The EPA chief said that his communication today with the steel company will not be an agreement requiring a signature by DB&R officials.

"It will be an order telling them that as long as they comply with the order, they will not be penalized," White said.

"All we want them to do is comply with the law," he said. "If he (Ross) decides not to operate, it will not be because of EPA restrictions."

White denied that the EPA ordered the plant to close Monday. "He (Ross) could open today or Monday or whenever he wants," said White.

Tuesday Ross said in a prepared statement: "The Environmental Protection Agency shut down the company yesterday (Monday) under threat of an unbelievable fine of $25,000 dollars per day if we continued to operate."

"We never ordered that he (Ross) close," said White.

---

*Daily Star; Hammond, Louisiana; November 28, 1975

Ross contends that his firm will have to spend from one-third to one-half million dollars on installation of federally-required anti-pollution equipment.

"This EPA equipment costs money but does not create any jobs here," said Ross earlier in the week.

Both Ross and the EPA have estimated that the anti-pollution equipment could take 30 months to install in operating condition. Ross has said that EPA could threaten the firm with possible retroactive fines for any possible alleged past violations.

White said that the EPA has specified to DB&R in the past that no action would be taken on retroactive fines. "He has that statement in writing," said White.

"I frankly don't understand their over-reaction," said White. "We've bent over backwards." "All of this has been on Mr. Ross' violation," said White.

White said the regulations requiring compliance by the steel company are both state and federal laws, based on the federal Clean Air Act of December, 1970.

White said that the firm would apparently be required to install some type of electrostatic precipitator to collect certain particles from exhaust smoke.

EPA Sends Telegram*

Steel mill reopens

AMITE — The Dibert, Bancroft & Ross steel mill, Tangipahoa's third largest employer, re-opened its doors today a week after owners closed down in protest of federal regulations.

About 350 employees returned to work after DB&R president John Ross received a telegram Friday from the Environmental Protection agency (CEPA) in Dallas allowing the firm more time to reach a permanent agreement with EPA.

John C. White, the regional EPA director, sent Ross a telegrom indicating that the company had a 12-day no-penalty period to reach an agreement with EPA on anti-pollution equipment.

In a prepared statement over the weekend Ross said: "Today (Friday) the EPA gave Dibert, Bancroft & Ross a 'no penalty' vulnerability period from December 1st thru 12th during which time it is expected a permanent agreement will be reached. We appreciate the wonderful cooperation of the news media and the general public."

Ross has agreed to install the equipment, which he estimates to cost $350,000-$500,000.

Ross contended last week that EPA was threatening his firm with a $25,000 fine per day for any alleged violations of state and federal anti-pollution laws, particularly the Clean Air Act of 1970.

However, the EPA chief strongly denied that his agency forced DB&R to close last Monday. "He could open today or Monday or any time he wants," White told The Daily star last week. "We never ordered that he close," White said.

The firm will apparently be required to install some type of electrostatic precipitator to remove particles from smoke.

---

*Daily Star; Hammond, Louisiana; December 1, 1975.

Both Ross and White estimate it could take the firm 30 months to install the equipment to operating order.

White said Friday that as long as the company complies with the law, DB&R is not in danger of possible fines. White said further that EPA would not fine the company retroactively for any possible alleged past violations.

EPA, DB&R have come to terms*

AMITE — The Dibert, Bancroft and Ross (DB&R) steel mill has apparently reached a permanent agreement with the Environmental Protection Agency (EPA) on anti-pollution equipment, according to a news release given by a company spokeswoman today.

The release did not give specifics of the agreement, but said the precise wording of the agreement was agreed upon over the telephone and "the documents are presently in transit through the mail for signature."

The news release was signed by company president John Ross.

The EPA had given DB&R a "no penalty" vulnerability period of December 1st through the 12th to reach a permanent agreement on antipollution equipment. Ross has agreed to install the equipment, which he estimates to cost $350,000-$500,000.

The steel mill had closed down the last week of November after Ross charged the EPA was threatening his firm with a $25,000 a day fine for any alleged violations of state and federal anti-pollution laws.

The EPA office in Dallas denied forcing the plant to close.

The steel mill reopened December 1st after the EPA allowed Ross more time to reach a permanent agreement. "The agreement enables the maintenance of dignity on both sides," the news release said. "It provides us with protection against vulnerability to fines, contains no confessions, and not too much intimidation, although the coercive details of the negotiations were humiliating."

Daily Star; Hammond, Louisiana; December 16, 1975.

chapter 9

Integrated Cases in Production/Operations Management

Michigan Alkali
Corporation

Barry Lake, Plant Engineering Superintendent, was summoned to the Plant Manager's office in mid-March, 1973. Upon arrival, he was notified that Bob Starns was being replaced as Manager of Soda Ash Operations. Moreover, the position was offered to Lake. Lake was shocked by the announcement. He inquired into Starns' new assignment. The terse reply was that Starns would be given the opportunity to "resign." The resignation would be accompanied by a two-month notification period and substantial severance pay. Starns would receive full pay for approximately nine months while he searched for new employment.

Lake and Starns

Although the new position represented a prestigious promotion for Lake, he certainly did not relish the offer. First of all, Lake liked and respected Starns. Hence, he viewed Starns' forced resignation as a tragedy.

Starns had been an employee of Michigan Alkali for 21 years. He had graduated in chemical engineering from Michigan State University and was immediately employed as a process engineer by Michigan Alkali. His early performance was outstanding. In fact, Starns was one of the youngest engineers to be promoted to production supervisor. He was always considered to be technically competent and ran efficient units in his earlier supervisory assignments.

When Lake joined Michigan Alkali as a chemical engineer out of the University of Kentucky in January, 1963, he was assigned as a production engineer to one of Starns' units. Lake considered his training under Starns to be invaluable and, in fact, tended to copy Starns' supervisory style when he received his first promotion to production supervisor. This style was characterized by extremely close attention to detail, a hard-nosed attitude in relationships with the local union, strict discipline, and a somewhat uncooperative attitude with those outside his unit whom he viewed as "meddlers." When plant expansion created the opportunity for Lake to advance

233

to a level parallel with Starns, Lake continued to confer and exchange ideas with Starns on problems of mutual interest. In recent years, however, the exchange of ideas between Lake and Starns diminished as their assignments became more divergent with the diversification and growth of the plant. Lake's approach to supervision became more moderate as he came into contact with new employees brought in with plant expansion. Too, Lake received an M.B.A. by attending night classes at a local university. The study of management in the M.B.A. curriculum further moderated Lake's supervisory style.

Starns had been promoted to Manager of Soda Ash Operations in 1969 when plant reorganization resulted in the upgrading of his "superintendent" position to that of "manager." Actually, he had directed the soda ash operations for eight years prior to the reorganization.

Lake was promoted to Plant Engineering Superintendent in 1972 from his previous assignment as chlor/alkali supervisor. He enjoyed working with the engineers assigned to his department because it represented a pleasant diversion from the daily pressures and demands that accompany production supervision. Consequently, Lake did not view the promotion with zest. Moreover, there appeared to be a great deal of controversy prior to the announcement of Starns' forced resignation. Because of Starns' curt and abrupt manner, he had alienated most of the supporting staff departments — maintenance, utilities and services, personnel, traffic, etc. Lake feared that he might become an unwilling party to a plant-wide conspiracy to remove Starns. Lake asked the plant manager whether Starns' removal was contingent upon his (Lake's) acceptance of Starns' position. The plant manager emphatically replied that Starns would be replaced! The plant manager tersely said that the reason for Starns' removal was his growing inability to manage the soda ash operations effectively and efficiently. Lake asked for one week to consider the offer. The plant manager agreed. Two hours later, Starns was summoned to the plant manager's office and his "resignation" was "accepted."

Michigan Alkali Corporation

The soda ash operations is the largest producing unit of Michigan Alkali Corporation's Detroit plant. The plant is Michigan Alkali's largest, with 2,500 employees. It is located in the industrial district of Dearborn, a suburb of Detroit. The site also serves as the R&D/Technical Services Center for Michigan Alkali.

Michigan Alkali was formed just after the turn of the century by a group of investors, primarily from the railroad industry. The initial plant used the ammonia-soda process to produce sodium carbonate or soda ash. (Sodium carbonate is called soda ash because it is the resultant of the exposure of sodium bicarbonate (soda) to intense heat. The sodium bicarbonate (Na

HCO_3) changes to sodium carbonate ($Na_2 CO_3$), carbon dioxide (CO_2), and water (H_2O). This change is called *calcination*. Raw materials for the production of soda ash include limestone and brine. The limestone is burned to produce carbon dioxide gas. The carbon dioxide is reacted with brine ($Na Cl$) which has been saturated with ammonia. This reaction produces soda or sodium bicarbonate. Hence, the soda is heated to form soda ash. The ammonia is recycled in the process.)

Detroit was selected as the site of Michigan Alkali's first plant because of the abundant deposits of the two primary raw materials — limestone and salt domes (for the production of brine) in the immediate area. Other products at the Detroit plant include caustic soda, chlorine, carbon tetrachloride, formaldehyde, bleach, baking soda, and industrial detergents. Moreover, Michigan Alkali has 27 other plants located in 12 states and 5 foreign countries.

Even with diversification, Michigan Alkali's principal product continues to be soda ash. Until the 1960s, soda ash was almost exclusively produced by the ammonia-soda process previously described. Huge deposits of trona or natural soda ash, however, have been recently discovered in Wyoming. Trona ore is mined directly and is purified by dissolving, evaporation, and recrystalization. Production costs for natural soda ash are much lower than synthetic soda ash (production by the ammonia soda process). The synthetic plants remain competitive only by their nearness to markets. Freight rates to ship soda ash from Wyoming to markets served by the synthetic plants tend to offset the lower production costs enjoyed by the mining/purification operations. The principal use for soda ash is for the manufacture of glass. Sand and soda ash are mixed in certain ratios and fused under high temperature to produce glass.

Even with the equalization caused by freight rates, synthetic soda ash producers remain competitive with trona producers only if their plants are operated very efficiently. Synthetic plants consume a great deal of energy in the calcination or heating of the soda to form soda ash. With the soaring cost of energy, this operation must be highly efficient to be profitable. In addition, these plants are maintenance intensive. Equipment tends to be large and costly. If operational control points are not closely followed, this costly equipment is severely damaged, resulting in extremely high maintenance costs as well as a severe loss in productive capacity. Finally, soda ash plants must be well managed because operational upsets are likely to cause environmental protection problems — both water and air pollution. Hence, Michigan Alkali faced serious consequences if Bob Starns failed to manage the soda ash operation effectively. Lake surmised that the consequences must have, in fact, been costly to warrant Starns' removal.

The Condition of the Soda Ash Operation

Even though Lake had worked briefly in one of the subunits of the soda ash operation when he first joined Michigan Alkali, his knowledge of the overall technology was quite limited. He emphasized this drawback to the plant manager when the position of superintendent of Soda Ash Operations was first offered to him. The plant manager replied that Michigan Alkali was one of the leaders in development of the ammonia-soda process and that many engineers would be available to assist in solving technological problems. Moreover, the plant manager said that Bob Starns, ironically, was highly competent in soda ash technology. The soda ash operations needed a leader — a person who could bring together the resources, analyze the problem areas, make the necessary corrections, and maintain standards.

The plant manager reflected that the primary reason that Starns was leaving the company rather than being reassigned was his poor attitude during the past several months. When suggestions were made to improve the soda ash operation, Starns angrily defended his past action and refused to implement any suggestions made outside his own organization. In addition, Starns blamed the recent substandard operation on poor performance by supporting departments. His primary target was the maintenance organization. Starns continuously quipped, "How can we ever successfully operate this plant with such poor maintenance of the equipment?" The maintenance manager would counter with, "The equipment is being destroyed through operational negligence faster than we can make the necessary repairs." Similar conflicts developed between Starns and other departments. For example, Starns blamed the failure to maintain adequate work standards on the fact that the labor relations department was constantly "giving in" to the union.

Lake concluded that everyone seemed to be so opinionated on the plight of the soda ash operations that he must conduct his own investigation to determine the true basis for the problems. He first examined the cost sheets for all of the subunits of the soda ash operation. He discovered that production was 20 percent below standard for 1973 year to date. Moreover, the cost accountants believed that the production reported by the soda ash supervision was inflated. Production reporting was based on the normal capacity and the stream factor for the dryers or calciners which convert the soda into soda ash. (Because of the very large storages (50,000 tons) for the granular product, it is very difficult to measure changes in inventory levels. As the soda ash is discharged by the conveyors into storages, the piles of product assume complex geometric patterns. Hence, the exact weight change in the storage is, at best, roughly estimated. The product is weighed when shipped by hopper railroad car, bulk truck, or when it is put into 100-pound bags. Also, the product is weighed somewhat accurately by drafting techniques when it is shipped in marine vessels. During a period of high shipping rates, the storages are emptied. Then, the book value for "product-in-storage" is adjusted to zero. Subsequent adjustments are then made to reported production rates to reflect the "zeroed" inventory.)

For the most part, Starns was overly optimistic when reporting production. As a consequence, the book values for "product-in-storage" typically indicated 4,000–6,000 tons of product when the storages were, in fact, empty. This required an 8 to 10 percent downward adjustment in reported production per month. A more serious consequence stemmed from the fact that the marketing department based its shipping schedule on book inventory values at its plants. In 1972, a marine vessel arrived at Michigan Alkali's dock on Lake Erie to be loaded with 5,000 tons of soda ash. The book inventory value was 6,000 tons. The storage was almost empty (it contained 200–300 tons). As a result, Michigan Alkali paid a huge freight penalty when the vessel sailed without a cargo of soda ash.

Lake surmised that Starns had been "forced" into such errors by the extreme pressure imposed on him by upper management of Michigan Alkali to increase production rates. The soda ash operation was sold out and enormous profits were lost because of the unfavorable production variance.

Lake also discovered from examination of the cost sheets that raw material consumption variances were unfavorable. Just by walking through the soda ash area, he noted numerous leaks in valves, pumps, pipelines, and heat exchangers that caused loss of raw material/work-in-process liquids to the process sewer or collection basins. Moreover, Lake discovered that liquids flowing into collection basins (installed to recycle such streams back into the process) also discharged to the sewers because the basin pumps were out of order. Lake also noted that important control points (pressure and temperatures) deviated significantly from the process flow charts that established standards for the process operators. Adherence to important control points was essential to achieving good raw material yields and high production rates. The deviation was partially explained by the area foremen, who claimed that the maintenance department was three months behind on cleaning the heat exchangers. (Clean heat exchangers provide adequate process cooling, which is absolutely essential for proper temperature and pressure control.)

With the leakage problems and the delay in heat exchange cleaning, Lake decided to examine the level of maintenance spending. To his astonishment, he found that the soda ash operation overspent its maintenance budget by 50 percent in 1972 and 60 percent for the year to date in 1973. The 1973 budget allowed for 80 maintenance personnel to be assigned daily to the soda ash operation. Lake discovered that 130 to 150 maintenance personnel were actually assigned daily to the soda ash operation. He checked the sampling statistics for the soda ash maintenance crew and found that their three-month moving average P.O.J. was 32 percent. (P.O.J. is "productivity on the job" and is the ratio of the number of "productive observations" to total observations taken by work samplers.) The Detroit plant average was 38 percent; the industry standard was 44 percent. The maintenance supervisor shook his head and told Lake, "P.O.J. isn't the problem here; those knucklehead operators tear equipment up faster than we can repair it; I'll show you an example."

The maintenance supervisor then reviewed the status of the dryer or calciner repairs. He cited that 12 of the 30 dryers were down for repairs. Lake noted that 24 dryers were needed for capacity operation. The maintenance supervisor stated that the primary reason for a dryer being out of operation was a crack in the shell. (A dryer shell has a cylindrical shape that is 80 ft. long and 8 ft. in diameter. The shell wall is one in. thick and is made of carbon steel.) The maintenance supervisor reviewed numerous shell sections in the scrap yard that were overheated and cracked. (When a crack occurs, 10 ft. of the shell on either side of the crack, or a 20-ft. section, is replaced. This normally causes the dryer to be out of operation for at least one month.) The maintenance department had the capacity to overhaul two dryers per month. The maintenance supervisor claimed that the operators had been cracking the dryers at the rate of three per month. He quipped, "It doesn't take a genius to know where that will lead us."

The dryer production foreman philosophically replied, "Sure we are cracking dryers, but we cannot prevent it." Lake asked him to elaborate. The foreman continued, "The poor dryer operator has no temperature controls whatsoever; that is, neither the automatic control or natural gas to the furnace nor the automatic control on the flue gas damper is operational on any dryer. One operator is required to maintain temperature control by 'feel' on one-half of the dryers." (Two dryer operators are assigned to each shift.) Lake noted that little, if any, safety margin was maintained to prevent overheating of the dryers because the dryers that were operational were pushed to capacity and beyond in an attempt to fulfill the ever-increasing demand for improvements in production rate. The dryer foreman further stated that it might have been possible for some of the old-timers to maintain control by "feel," but that it was almost impossible for these "kids" who were new on the job. Lake discovered that many of the older, experienced operators retired recently or had bid into the newer production units built with the recent expansion.

The meter and instrument foreman blamed the poor condition of the dryer temperature controls on the many leaks directly above the dryer instruments. He flatly stated that it was a waste of manpower to work on the instruments as long as they were subjected to leaks.

The maintenance foreman responded, "Yes, we know the leaks are destroying the instruments as well as electric motors and starters, but production supervision tells us that they cannot afford to take the plant outage required to repair most of the leaks." Moreover, the maintenance foreman claimed that the production department set all maintenance priorities and that the maintenance department was guided accordingly.

The area production supervisor countered with the position that the priority list was "meaningless." He claimed that his daily maintenance work schedule included 50 jobs considered to be emergencies because of the adverse impact on production rates. Of these 50 jobs, the production supervisor bemoaned the fact that less than 50 percent were completed each day. Obviously, he pointed to the steadily growing list of emergency jobs.

Lake also examined the disciplinary program to maintain and improve work standards for the process operators. He discovered that the disciplinary program was generally quite strict, but it was inconsistent from shift to shift. The supervision of one shift claimed that they were continuously warning their operators to maintain standards and were holding disciplinary hearings to improve standards. The record of terminations, suspensions, and written warnings confirmed this claim. Another shift had almost no record of disciplinary action. The other two shifts had a record of discipline between the two extremes. (The entire plant is on a four-squad rotating shift schedule.) Lake could find no correlation, however, between the severity of the disciplinary program and the adherence to production standards.

The balance of the performance indicators were in normal ranges. Operating labor cost was below budget because overtime was below budget. Process supply costs were within budget. Tight control was maintained over issuing supplies, such as work gloves.

The Decision

Before Lake reached a decision on whether to accept the Soda Ash Manager position, he conferred with members of soda ash supervision and hourly workers on the subject of Starns' "resignation." A majority of the supervisors and foremen believed that Starns was given a "raw deal" and was made the scapegoat for all the problems. The hourly employees had mixed opinions. A few thought he was the scapegoat, but others thought he deserved the release. The vast majority were mostly indifferent. After the week had passed, Lake notified the plant manager that he would accept the new position.

Discussion Questions

1. Without a detailed technical knowledge of the soda ash operation, outline a program that Lake could institute to turn the soda ash operation around.

2. Discuss the forced "resignation" of an employee who had served the company, apparently with some success, for 21 years.

case 51

Morrison Distributing Company

The Morrison Distributing Company, a franchised wholesale distributor of Schlitz and Old Milwaukee beer and Schlitz Malt Liquor, began operations in Conway, Arkansas, in 1961. The exclusive franchise agreement with the Joseph Schlitz Brewing Company of Milwaukee, Wisconson, permits the Morrison Company to act as sole distributor of its products in a five-county area in central Arkansas (excluding Pulaski County, where the capital city of Little Rock is located). The distributorship has experienced sustained growth since 1961; gross sales amounted to $4 million in 1976, and there were 800 customers.[1]

Personnel and Organization

The Morrison Distributing Company employs twenty-three people, including Mr. Melvin Morrison, the owner and president, James Hinkle, vice-president/ sales manager, two assistant sales managers, two warehousemen, seven truck drivers and their helpers, a bookkeeper, a secretary, and a security guard. Figure 9–1 shows the authority relationships of all positions in the organization.

Each truck driver, in addition to his duties of delivering beer and collecting payments from customers, makes periodic calls on retailers (bars, quick-stop stores, grocery stores, chains, service station, etc.) who do not sell Joseph Schlitz products but who do have licenses to sell low alcoholic beverages. Since all drivers are paid on a salary-plus-commission basis, they are motivated to increase their number of customers. In addition to the commission which results from increased sales, the company gives a bonus (ranging from $20 to $50, depending on the expected volume of sales) for each new account secured by a driver or his helper. Annual salaries for drivers range between $20,000 and $25,000; helpers' earnings average $8,400.

---

[1]Actually, the number of customers varies from week to week due to the awarding of new low alcoholic beverage licenses, suspensions of such licenses, business failures, and so forth.

Figure 9–1

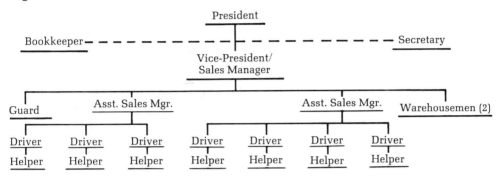

Assistant sales managers supervise drivers and are responsible for getting the company's products to all route customers regularly and for expanding the firm's market share. They record each driver's sales (by customer), contact prospective retailers, and regularly call on existing customers in a customer-relations capacity. Both assistant sales managers are salaried employees.

The vice president/sales manager, James Hinkle, is directly responsible for all marketing activities, including the scheduling of routes, promotional activities, the training of assistant sales managers and drivers, charting and analyzing industry and firm sales (according to different packages, brands, geographic regions, etc.), serving walk-in customers, making special arrangements to serve the needs of special groups (fraternities, for example), and establishing sales goals for each driver and assistant sales manager.

Warehousemen unload and store shipments of beer and malt liquor received by rail from any of the nine breweries of the Joseph Schlitz Brewing Company, load trucks and verify the contents with each driver, and perform routine custodial duties in the warehouse. The security guard aids the warehousemen and provides security for the daily receipts collected by drivers. (All products are sold on a cash-only basis. Consequently, checks and cash on hand total several thousands of dollars each day.) The security guard accompanies the president to the bank each day to make deposits of collections.

Mr. Morrison assumes responsibility for all company operations and directly supervises the bookkeeper, secretary, and vice-president/sales manager. As a specialist in finance and accounting, he performs all financial analyses, including tax requirements. Also, he acts as the public relations officer of the firm and handles all correspondence related to business operations.

Product, Pricing, and Promotion

Melvin Morrison attributes part of his success to his product — a well-known, nationally advertised premium beer. Coupled with the quality product are a good company image and superior service. Morrison Distributing Company has established a reputation of dependable delivery, courteous drivers and salespeople, integrity, and honesty. Excluding keg beer (sold primarily to lounges for on-premise consumption), the firm handles 16 different packages (different brands, various sizes of bottles and cans, different number of items per package, etc.). Pricing is competitive; the gross margin over costs of merchandise averages 18 percent.

The brands which provide the greatest competition in the central Arkansas area are Budweiser (in 12-oz containers) and Miller (in 7-oz bottles), brewed by Anheuser Busch and Miller Brewing Company, respectively. Because of packaging costs, profits on 12-oz and greater quantity packages are higher than on packages of 7-oz bottles. The firm takes advantage of cooperative advertising (which is partially paid for by the Joseph Schlitz Brewing Company) and, in addition, advertises locally via radio and newspaper. The only other promotion is by word-of-mouth and illuminated displays, which are provided free to retailers who request them.

Routing and Delivery

As previously mentioned, the vice-president/sales manager plans all delivery routes, taking into consideration the number of customers, volume of business, and distance between customers. Each driver is able to complete his entire route daily. (Drivers work only four days each week during the winter when beer consumption declines.) Upon completion of the route, the driver and his helper return to the company's warehouse in Conway. Upon arrival, a warehouseman counts the unsold packages remaining on the truck and verifies the data with the driver. Receipts from collections are compared with written order forms, and the receipts are turned in to the vice-president/ sales manager (or president if the sales manager is out). The truck is then loaded by the warehousemen, checked by the driver, filled with gasoline, and parked (and locked) on the company's premises, which are enclosed by a wire fence. Drivers and their helpers typically begin their delivery each morning at 6:30 and return at mid-afternoon.

Inventory

All merchandise is shipped to Morrison's warehouse by rail (the company has its own rail spur adjacent to its storage facility) from one of nine Schlitz breweries located throughout the country. The merchandise is stacked on pallets (according to brand, size of package, etc.) in a manner which facilitates a FIFO (first in–first out) inventory system, and is then tagged to indicate volume and date received.

The company's investment in inventory ranges from $175,000 to $250,000, depending on seasonal variations in demand. This investment represents approximately a three- to four-week supply.

Customer Service

Assistant sales managers and truck drivers make every effort to persuade retailers who hold alcoholic beverage licenses to handle Schlitz products. However, no attempt is made to persuade prospective customers to apply for such licenses. Whenever applications are made (and licenses awarded), the firm is informed through official publications. At that time, each licensee in the area is contacted and offered assistance and advice pertaining to display, pricing, purchasing, and related activities.

All customers, new and old, are treated with courtesy and respect. Complaints are heard and problems are resolved. All severely dented cans are picked up, and the contents are destroyed under state agency supervision. Broken bottles and dented cans are "made good." In general, the company performs any activity which enhances its image and which gives it an advantage over its competitors.

Maintenance and Cost Control

The Morrison Distributing Company owns a small fleet of relatively new delivery trucks and an economy van. New trucks are maintained to enhance the image of the firm, to assure prompt delivery to customers, and to reduce maintenance and repair costs to a minimum. Even so, the trucks sometimes break down, resulting in needed repair. Consequently, Mr. Morrison has an agreement with Ford dealers located in each of the five surrounding counties, under which they agree to provide prompt tow-in and repair service whenever required.

The vice-president/sales manager and the assistant sales manager use their personal automobiles in performing their job duties. Each is reimbursed at the rate of 12 cents per mile. Prior to 1974, company-owned automobiles were provided for these employees, but this practice was considered too expensive and was changed to the present policy. (Insurance rates and rising fuel costs were cited as reasons for the change in policy.)

To reduce costs associated with inventory, the company maintains a small safety stock. (A labor strike or other event outside the control of the firm would cause the inventory to be depleted in less than one month.) Since all sales are cash, the firm does not incur billing expenses or bad debts. Routing is scheduled to minimize time and costs while maximizing customers contacted. A prospective customer is contacted only if the expected revenue will more than offset the estimated costs of serving that customer. In addition, the company takes advantage of all legal tax loopholes. Overall, management's philosophy is one which embraces efficiency, cost reduction, market penetration, and profit maximization.

Discussion Questions

1. Evaluate overall operations of the Morrison Distributing Company.

2. Suggest ways of improving the firm's operations to enhance its profit position.

3. Evaluate the organizational structure and assignment of duties.

H. T. Rosenbloom
Company

H. T. Rosenbloom's, located in Columbia, Tennessee, is one of five branch stores which comprise the Rosenbloom chain of family-owned department stores. Harrison Rosenbloom opened his first store in downtown Nashville in 1965 and thereafter expanded his operations by locating area branch stores in the Rivergate and Hundred Oaks shopping centers. In 1972, a fourth store opened in Clarksville, Tennessee, and the Columbia branch celebrated its grand opening in 1974. Site locations were based on feasibility studies (conducted by a private consulting firm in Nashville) which indicated a need for the existence of a fashion-oriented department store at each location.

Personnel

Whenever the Rosenbloom Company expands its operations into a new location, experienced key personnel from an existing store are temporarily assigned to the new store. Typically, the store manager, buyers, assistant buyers, and department managers are brought in from other branch stores to facilitate the opening of the new branch. Salespeople and other personnel are newly hired from the local community. Whenever a newly hired employee has been adequately trained to make purchasing decisions or manage a department, the experienced buyer or department manager is reassigned to his or her permanent position. Branch store managers typically come up through the ranks of the Rosenbloom organization, and the promotion to store manager represents a significant achievement resulting from the culmination of years of experience, thorough knowledge of all phases of the firm's operations, and hard work.

The training period for department managers and buyers ranges between four weeks and three months, depending upon the job and the trainee's learning ability. All permanent store personnel are employed by the store manager and assigned to the appropriate department. Salespeople are paid on a salary-plus-commission basis; all other personnel, including the department managers, are salaried. Turnover of personnel in the Rosenbloom organization is approximately 50 percent, somewhat lower than the national average for department stores.

Physical Layout and Merchandise

The Columbia, Tennessee, branch store is identical to Rosenbloom's other stores in physical facilities and layout. The store has 30,000 sq ft of floor space, including storage, and houses the following departments: children's department, lingerie, ready-to-wear (dresses, pantsuits, coats), sportswear, bridal department, gift department (including linens, draperies, fabrics, china, small appliances, and home furnishings), cosmetics, men's department, accessory (jewelry, handbags, etc.), and shoe department. With the exception of the shoe department, which is leased to another firm, all departments sell merchandise centrally purchased through the parent store in Nashville. (The parent store purchases for all branch stores to take advantage of quantity discounts. In addition, all marking of merchandise is performed at the central receiving station in Nashville to assure uniform pricing at all stores.)

Company-owned trucks make daily deliveries to all branch stores from the central receiving station in Nashville. Consequently, all merchandise is kept on the floor or in adjacent department storerooms. (Each department has its own small storeroom, which is divided into bins. When merchandise is received at the local store, it is tagged with an appropriate storeroom designation and is assigned to a proper bin by sales personnel.)

Customer Service

All applications for credit are screened at the parent store in Nashville. (The Columbia branch has two direct telephone lines to Nashville to facilitate the handling of credit applications, reporting of daily sales, and so forth.) However, a credit register which lists all credit customers, purchases, and payments is maintained at each branch store. Also, customer billing is done through the parent store. In addition to credit, H. T. Rosenbloom provides free gift wrapping and alterations services for its customers.

The department that Rosenbloom's considers unique is its bridal department. In addition to the bridal gowns, veils, and related assessories sold in each store, a bridal consultant is an integral part of each store's operations. The bridal consultant provides advice and assistance throughout the planning and preparation stages and assists during the wedding ceremony itself. Although the bridal department was deemed questionable when first contemplated, it has proved to be one of the most successful departments in each store.

Control and Security

Two of the greatest problems with which the management of a retail store must deal are theft and bad checks. To minimize the risk of theft, the H. T. Rosenbloom Company has installed a Sensormatic Security system in each of its stores. (Prior to the installation of the security system, shoplifting amounted to 2.9 percent of sales; following the installation of the Sensormatic Security system, the dollar value of shoplifting was reduced to 0.91 percent of gross sales.) The security system incorporates two measures of control:

1. Attached to each item is a security tag which must be removed by a sales clerk following a sale to prevent the ultrasonic alarms located at each exit door from sounding. (A second alarm mechanism is located at each cash register to remind the cashier to remove the tag from the garment to avoid embarrassment to an honest customer who innocently causes the alarm to sound by walking through the exit with the purchased item.)
2. At the close of each business day, another security device is switched on. This sensitive device, which is tied into the local police department, is triggered by the slightest movement in the store. Upon receiving an alarm, the police department dispatches a squad car to the store for investigation and alerts the store manager of a possible attempted robbery.

Each salesperson is authorized to honor checks in payment of merchandise, provided the employee is personally acquainted with the customer. If the salesperson is not personally acquainted with the customer, the department manager approves or rejects the check. In all cases, proper identification, including driver's license, is required. This information is fed to Checks Facts (a private organization which compiles and provides pertinent data to member firms) for analysis. All bad checks (those which do not clear the banks on which they are drawn) are returned to the store manager, who immediately calls the banks to see if the checks will clear at that time. If a check will not clear, the store manager personally contacts the maker and requests payment. (At the Columbia store, an average of five checks per day are returned. Of this number, nearly all are "made good.") Because of the store managers' success in persuading customers to honor their checks, Rosenbloom's does not use a collection agency. In addition to accepting personal checks, Rosenbloom's also honors BankAmericard and Master Charge.

Promotion

The major problem facing H. T. Rosenbloom's Columbia, Tennessee, store is one of promotion. Primarily, the store advertises in a local newspaper, but its entire service area (estimated to be 150,000 people) is not covered. Radio and television advertising has proved to be somewhat ineffective for the Clarksville and Columbia stores. (Both television and newspaper advertising, however, are considered highly effective for the three stores in the Nashville area.) Twice each year, Rosenbloom's, along with other merchants located in Columbia's East Gate Shopping Center, participates in "Midnight Madness" sales. These are the only times during the year when the Columbia store reduces its prices below those of the other branch stores. Essentially, Rosenbloom's competes with other department stores in the area by offering quality merchandise, superior service, and fashion-oriented apparel.

Maintenance

H. T. Rosenbloom's does not have its own maintenance department. Consequently, whenever service is required on a store's air conditioning, lighting, or heating system, the job is contracted to a local service firm. Lighting fixtures are purchased locally too, but store personnel usually install bulbs. All stores are heated electrically. (The company discovered that electricity is less costly than natural gas because store lights produce a tremendous amount of heat in addition to illumination.) Total utility costs, excluding telephone expenses, range from $12,000 to $14,000 annually. Telephone costs, including two direct lines to Nashville ($185 per month each), average $1,000 per month. Thermostats are set at 70 degrees for year-round comfort. Daily cleaning of carpeting and display windows is contracted to local firms.

Discussion Question

1. Evaluate the overall operations of H. T. Rosenbloom's branch store. Suggest measures which management should undertake to improve operations.

Oliver Treated Products
Company

In February, 1977, Oliver Treated Products Company faced its worst economic slump in over twenty-five years. Sales were off 70 percent from two
years earlier; the price of creosote oil had increased from 23 cents per gallon in January, 1974, to 61 cents per gallon; greater amounts of natural gas
were required to heat the furnaces used in the wood-treating processes;
workmen's compensation insurance had skyrocketed; and the costs of cutting and transporting logs to the plant had risen sharply. To make matters
worse, the immediate future looked just as bleak.

Background of the Company

George Oliver started his wood-preservation operations[1] (commonly called
a creosote plant because of the preservative used) in 1939 with one steel
cylinder, a wood-burning furnace, and a single storage tank for the oil preservative.[2] He purchased a special saw for peeling logs, another for cutting
the butts and tips off the peeled logs, and a small planer mill from a sawmill
which had gone out of business a year earlier. Other plant and equipment
included two log trucks, a tramcar, a hydraulic lift for moving the logs to
either the planer mill or peeling station, and a small office building.

During the first years of operations, Mr. Oliver used experimental wood
treatment methods. Adequate treatment was complicated by many factors,
including the species, size, form, condition, and proposed use of the timber,
and the type and amount of preservative injected. Over the years, data produced by technical research and knowledge gained through experience were
incorporated into his operations, enabling his company to provide adequately

---

[1]The Lowry pressure treatment process is used to retard or prevent decay, fungi, and
insect damage to poles, posts, cross ties, pilings, mine and bridge timbers, and lumber
used in buildings where conditions are favorable for decay or insect attack. An explanation of the Lowry and other pressure processes is in appendix A.

[2]For a brief description of various wood preservatives, see appendix B.

treated timbers which could withstand long years of exposure to natural elements.

Between 1955 and 1965, Oliver Treated Products Company added two furnaces (one fueled by natural gas and the other fueled by either gas or wood), two cylinders, which gave the firm a total treating capacity of 186 linear ft, eight log trucks, and a 24,000-lb capacity fork lift. During this time, sales and profit quadrupled; three shifts operated the plant around the clock; and the company began selling to several large-volume customers, including electric companies, oil exploration corporations, and the state and county highway departments. By the mid-1960s, approximately 80 percent of the firm's business was treated poles and pilings with the remainder equally divided among ties, timbers, posts, and lumber.

The Problem

Essentially, the problems Oliver Treated Products faced in 1977 were identical to those confronting most businesses — lagging sales and rising costs. The price of creosote had tripled in two years; labor cost had increased; fuel costs had risen drastically; workmen's compensation insurance had increased; and the costs of maintaining the plant and equipment had surged. Sales were down because Oliver's customers were experiencing similar effects of the economic slump. Too, the elimination of the oil depletion allowance for large oil exploration firms resulted in fewer exploration activities, and hence a lesser need for treated pilings and timbers.

Ironically, whenever sales declined, fuel costs for the company increased. When operating at near-capacity levels, the waste generated from cutting operations provided enough fuel for two furnaces; whenever business declined, costly natural gas had to be used to produce the heat required in the wood-treating processes. Inventory costs were high because the company was required to keep on hand at least two different preservatives — pure creosote (for crossties, utility poles, and pilings exposed to salt water) and an 80 percent creosote–20 percent diesel fuel mixture. Because of the difficulties and problems associated with the delivery of preservatives, the company overstocked in order to handle any large, unexpected orders.

In 1965, the company began cutting its own logs (from standing timber purchased directly from landowners) because subcontracting proved too expensive. In addition, it perfected a waste-disposal system that trapped and separated the excess preservatives from water (after each charge) and channeled the preservatives back into the storage tanks, thereby reducing costs of operations. The company owns its own water well because of the amount of water required in the wood-treatment process. Consequently, the cost of water is negligible. Finally, as a means of minimizing overall production costs, the company eliminated overtime work and quit accepting small orders for treated fence posts (the costs of supplying posts for the typical homeowner exceeded revenue).

Mr. Oliver did not want to close the plant because his employees would possibly go to work elsewhere. Experienced sawyers, in particular, were in short supply. Nevertheless, he knew the business could not continue operating indefinitely at a loss.

Discussion Questions

1. Suggest other cost reduction measures which the Oliver Treated Products Company should explore.

2. What pollution problems would you expect a wood-preservation firm to have? How should they be resolved?

appendix A
Pressure Processes[3]

The most effective method of treating wood with preservatives is by means of pressure. There are a number of pressure processes, all of which employ the same general principle but differ in the details of application. The timber to be treated is loaded on tramcars, which are run into a large steel cylinder. After the cylinder is closed and bolted, preservative is admitted and pressure applied until the required absorption has been obtained. Two principal types of pressure treatment, the full-cell (Bethell) and empty-cell (Lowry and Rueping), are in common use.

Full-Cell Processes

In making treatments with the so-called full-cell, or Bethell, process, a preliminary vacuum is first applied to remove as much air as practicable from the wood cells. The preservative is then admitted into the treating cylinder without admitting air. After the cylinder is filled with preservative, pressure is applied until the required absorption is obtained. A final vacuum is commonly applied immediately after the cylinder has been emptied of preservative to free the charge of dripping preservative.

When the timber is given a preliminary steam-and-vacuum treatment, the preservative is admitted at the end of the vacuum period following steaming. In case the charge has received a preliminary conditioning treatment by the Boulton or boiling-under-vacuum process, the unfilled space at the top of the cylinder is filled with preservative and pressure is applied as soon as this conditioning process has been completed.

It is impossible to remove all air from the wood cells regardless of the method of treatment employed. For this reason, even under the most favorable conditions, there is some unfilled air space in the cell cavities of the treated wood after impregnation by the full-cell process.

---

[3]*Preservative Treatment of Wood by Pressure Methods,* Agriculture Handbook No. 40, U.S. Department of Agriculture, September, 1960, pp. 2-3, 125-26.

When the full-cell process is used for treatment with zinc-chloride solution, it is commonly called the Burnett process.

Empty-Cell Processes

Two empty-cell treatments, the Lowry and the Rueping, are commonly used, both of which depend upon compressed air in the wood to force part of the absorbed preservative out of the cell cavities after preservative pressure has been released.

Lowry Process. In the Lowry process, which is also designated as the "empty-cell process without initial air," the preservative is admitted to the treating cylinder at atmospheric pressure. When the cylinder is filled, pressure is applied and the preservative is forced into the wood against the air originally in the cell cavities. After the required absorption has been obtained, pressure is released, a vacuum is drawn, and the air under pressure in the wood forces out part of the preservative absorbed during the pressure period. This makes it possible, with a limited net retention, to inject a greater amount of preservative into the wood and to obtain deeper penetration than when the same net retention is obtained with the full-cell process. The Lowry process is convenient to use in any pressure-treating plant since no additional equipment is required.

Rueping Process. This process is called "empty-cell process with initial air." The principal difference between the Lowry empty-cell process and the Rueping process is that, in the latter, air is forced into the treating cylinder before the preservative is admitted. The air pressure is then maintained while the cylinder is filled with preservative; thus, the wood cells are left more or less impregnated with air under pressure. In resistant woods this air pressure may penetrate only a short distance from the surface, while in wood that is fairly pervious to the penetration of air and liquids, such as the sapwood of many species, an air pressure is built up in all of the penetrable portion.

In the application of this process, the preservative is often admitted from an equalizing tank (Rueping tank) and the air in the treating cylinder interchanges with the preservative in this tank. In some plants not equipped with a Rueping tank, the preservative is pumped into the treating cylinder against the preliminary air pressure and sufficient air is released during the filling period to keep the pressure constant. Impregnation of the wood is obtained by applying a pressure sufficiently high to force preservative into the timber against the air pressure in the wood cells. Then, upon release of preservative pressure and application of a vacuum, part of the preservative is forced out of the wood by the expanding air. The amount of such recovery will usually be greater with the Rueping than with the Lowry process, under comparable conditions.

There is often considerable misunderstanding regarding the relative merits of the full-cell and the empty-cell methods of treatment. The effectiveness of treatment depends upon the preservative, and the retention and depth of penetration, and not upon the treating process, except as the process used may affect the penetration and the retention specified.

The terms "full-cell" and "empty-cell," as applied to treatment, are very misleading, since the so-called full-cell process does not leave the wood cells completely filled with preservative even when an effort is made to obtain this objective, nor does empty-cell treatment leave the cells empty. The empty-cell process loses much of its value when applied in the treatment of wood that is fairly resistant under normal pressure-treating conditions. The empty-cell treatment is most effective when employed in the treatment of reasonably permeable sapwood, such as that of the pines or the penetrable heartwood of species like the red oaks, black tupelo, or ponderosa pine. In selecting the treating process, the object in all cases should be to obtain the maximum penetration practicable with the absorption specified.

appendix B
Wood Preservatives[4]

Wood preservatives may be grouped into two broad classes: preservative oils and water-borne preservatives. Each of these classes may be further subdivided in various ways. For example, preservative oils include byproduct oils such as coal-tar creosote and other creosotes, solutions of toxic chemicals such as pentachlorophenol or copper naphthenate in selected petroleum oils or other solvents, and various mixtures of these solutions with byproduct oils and mixtures. The water-borne preservatives include solutions of single chemicals such as zinc chloride or sodium fluoride, which are not resistant to leaching, and various formulations of two or more chemicals that react after impregnation and drying to form compounds with limited solubility and sometimes with high resistance to leaching.

Preservatives vary greatly in effectiveness and in suitability for different purposes and use conditions. The effectiveness of any preservative depends not only upon the materials of which it is composed, but also upon the quantity injected into the wood, the depth of penetration, and the conditions to which the treated material is exposed in service.

Coal-Tar Creosote

Coal-tar creosote is defined by the American Wood-Preservers' Association as a preservative oil obtained by the distillation "of coal tar produced by high-temperature carbonization of bituminous coal; it consists principally of liquid and solid aromatic hydrocarbons and contains appreciable quantities of tar acids and tar bases; it is heavier than water; and has a continuous boiling range of at least 125° C. beginning at about 200° C." Coal-tar creosote is highly effective and is the most important and most extensively used wood preservative for general purposes.

Water-Gas Tar and Water-Gas Creosote

Water-gas tar is obtained from petroleum oil as a byproduct in the manufacture of water gas.

Water-gas-tar creosote is produced by distillation from water-gas tar. This creosote is defined as any and all distillate oils from such tars boiling between 200° and 400° C. While water-gas tar and the creosote produced from it are not considered so generally effective as coal-tar creosote, service-test records indicate that they have good preservative properties.

---

[4]*Preservative Treatment of Wood by Pressure Methods*, Agriculture Handbook No. 40, U.S. Department of Agriculture, September, 1960, pp. 3–6.

Wood-Tar Creosote

Wood-tar creosote is obtained from wood tar and distills mostly above 170° C. Since wood-tar creosotes have been produced in comparatively small quantities and have usually sold at higher prices than coal-tar creosote, they have not been extensively used as a wood preservative. Good wood-tar creosotes have demonstrated high effectiveness, but they seem to be somewhat less effective than coal-tar creosote.

Coal Tars

The various coal tars are, in general, unsuitable as wood preservatives when used alone because their relatively high viscosity makes it difficult to obtain satisfactory penetrations. They may not be quite effective as coal-tar creosote, but they possess good preservative properties. Some of them have been used for the purpose and have given excellent results when satisfactory retentions and peneterations were obtained.

Petroleum Oils

Petroleum oils, such as crude petroleum, topped petroleum, fuel oil, and used crank-case oil, as a rule, do not possess toxic properties to make them suitable as wood preservatives when used alone. Although in a few cases good results have apparently been obtained with petroleum oils used alone, in other cases complete failure has resulted. They are used in preservatives merely as solvents of toxic chemicals or diluents of preservative oils.

Creosote, Coal-Tar Solutions

Coal tar is extensively employed in solution with coal-tar creosote for the treatment of ties and, to some extent, other classes of timber. The coal-tar solutions are used principally in the eastern and southern states. Mixtures of coal tar and creosote commonly contain about 20 to 50 percent of tar by volume.

Coal-Tar Creosote and Petroleum Solutions

Mixtures of coal-tar creosote and petroleum are widely used in the western states, principally for the treatment of ties, but also for the treatment of lumber, timber, and land and fresh-water piling. In general, their petroleum content ranges from 30 to 70 percent by volume, but the content is usually about 50 percent.

Since the toxicity of the petroleum mixtures is furnished by the creosote, it is important that the creosote be of high toxicity.

Chemicals Dissolved in Solvents Other Than Water

Preservatives composed of toxic chemicals carried in nonaqueous solvents, such as petroleum-oil distillates, are now being used to an increasing extent. These were originally devised for the purpose of providing a clean treatment without causing swelling of the wood and were originally applied by nonpressure methods.

A shortage of creosote that developed during World War II created an active interest in the use of these preservatives as a possible substitute for creosote, especially in the pressure treatment of poles. Particular attention was directed to the chlorinated phenols, which are known to have a high degree of toxicity. Penta-chlorophenol is the best known and most widely used in this group.

Other preservatives of this type, which in the past have been largely limited to use in surface treatments, are the metallic naphthenates, such as copper naphthenate. The latter has also been used to a limited extent for pressure-treated poles.

Water-Borne Preservatives

A variety of chemicals in water solution are used as wood preservatives. These include zinc chloride, sodium fluoride, arsenic in various forms, copper sulfate, and similar toxic chemicals. Most of these salts are used in combination with one or more other chemicals, frequently including a chromium compound. Chromated zinc chloride, which is composed of a mixture of zinc chloride and sodium dichromate, has come into wide use in recent years. This preservative is now much more extensively used than straight zinc chloride, which was formerly the most widely used water-borne salt.

Sodium fluoride has moderate preservative properties, but it is seldom used alone. It is an important ingredient in several proprietary preservatives, some of which are finding considerable use in the treatment of building lumber and structural timber.

Arsenic compounds have been used as preservatives for many years. They are important ingredients of a number of proprietary preservatives, some of which have demonstrated high effectiveness and are extensively used.

Copper sulfate, although extensively used in Europe for many years and demonstrated to be moderately effective in retarding decay, has found little use for wood preservation in the United States except in certain proprietary preservatives, in which it is combined with other chemicals. Several of these preservatives are of high effectiveness and extensively used. Copper sulfate is corrosive to iron and steel and, therefore, cannot be used alone in ordinary treating equipment.

Proprietary Preservatives

Various patented or proprietary preservatives are sold under trade names for pressure treatment. For the most part, they are composed of various water-borne salts and are injected in water solutions. Others employ a volatile solvent to carry the toxic substance into the wood. Some of the water-borne preservatives contain chemicals that are intended to react after injection into the wood and to form substances that are of low solubility and resistant to leaching.

case 54

U. S. Plywood[1]
(Part B)

U. S. Plywood, a major manufacturer of plywood used in all types of construction, has plants located throughout the United States. One of its production plants, located in the Southeast, is a highly profitable operation and is a "profit center" for the corporation. Its operations are similar to those of other branch plants, but it has the distinct advantage of being one of the newer plants of U. S. Plywood and has enjoyed profitable operations since its opening in 1966.

Logs used in the manufacture of plywood at the regional plant are purchased from Crown Zellerbach, one of the nation's largest producers of paper and paper-based products. The purchase agreement assures the U. S. Plywood plant of a minimum of 32.5 million board ft of logs through 1981. Logs (primarily pine) are cut by Crown Zellerbach and hauled by truck to U. S. Plywood's plant throughout the year. When a load arrives at the plant, it is weighed on U. S. Plywood's scales and unloaded with a Letourneau log loader, and the empty truck is weighed again to determine the net weight of the logs. (The company's conversion chart translates weight into cubic and board ft. Occasionally, however, U. S. Plywood actually scales (measures) the logs to assure accurate weight/board ft conversions.) The operator of the Letourneau log loader, which is used to lift logs from the truck trailers and to stack them in decks, reports the volume of each delivery to his foreman.

In addition to unloading trucks, the log loader operator takes logs from the decks and places them on a conveyor, which supplies logs to a poling machine (a machine which removes the bark from the logs). The poles (logs) are then cut into 8-ft lengths and taken to a steam vat where they are heated for a period of several hours to one day. (The heating process tends to soften the wood in preparation for lathe operations.) Bark is conveyed to a nearby incinerator where it is burned. Butts and tips of the poles are conveyed to a machine where they are chipped for resale to Crown-Zellerbach to be used in making paper. (Attempts to sell the bark for use in flower beds, around shrubbery, etc. have not proved profitable. Presently, the firm is contemplating converting from boilers fueled by natural gas to those which have cap-

---

[1]For additional information, see case 47, "U. S. Plywood — Part A."

abilities of burning wood. If the conversion proves practicable, bark will be burned along with other waste as a source of fuel.[2])

Following the heat treatment process, the 8-ft logs are placed on a conveyor which automatically feeds them into one of two lathes which strips the veneer down to the core. (The stripping process resembles the peeling of an apple as it is turned around a stationary knife.) The thickness of the sheet of wood (veneer) resulting from the stripping process is usually 1/6-, 1/8-, or 1/10-in. Requirements are predetermined, and the machines are set accordingly. When a log is stripped down to its core, the core is released from the lathe and conveyed to a planer where it is planed into a 4" × 4" post and is then cut into two 2" × 4" studs. The studs are sold to a local lumber company, and the chips are air-blown through ducts to railroad cars for shipment to Crown-Zellerbach where they (together with chips from other operations) will be used in the manufacture of paper.

The sheets of veneer pass under a photo-electric scanner which automatically controls the cutting of four-ft-wide sections. Bad sections (those with splits, holes, etc.) are cut into widths of less than four ft and are used for core-filler in the gluing stages of production or are chipped for resale.

The 4 ft × 8 ft sheets are automatically fed into dryers for the removal of moisture. After several minutes of drying, they are checked for moisture content and are either returned to the dryer or accepted for further processing. Those sections which have been sufficiently dried are graded according to quality and stacked according to grade. (Quality determination is a subjective judgment rendered by the production workers. Usually, the sheets are placed into one of seven or eight stacks, each of which represents a different quality. The "best" grades have few knots and a good overall appearance. Lower grades have multiple knots and are easily recognized as being of lower quality.) Some of the sheets are "up-graded" in a process whereby knots are stamped out and replaced with inserts of wood. The "up-graded" sheets, as well as the other graded sheets, are stacked according to quality. From these stacks, they are placed into the gluing and pressing operations, which constitute the heart of plywood manufacturing. (Some of the 4 ft × 8 ft sheets are cut into 4 ft × 4 ft sheets to be used as the core filler.)

The number of "plies" that go into a plywood sheet depends upon the thickness of each individual sheet (1/8-in., 1/10-in., etc.) and the desired thickness of the finished product. (Typically, plywood ranges from 1/4 to 1 in. in thickness.) Filler plies (those plies which constitute the inner core of a plywood sheet) are processed through a gluing machine, which dispenses glue to either side. The grains of each ply are placed in an opposite direction from those of adjacent sheets. When the required number of plies are placed together, they are placed in a dry press and then a hot press which permanently secures the plies together.

---

[2]In 1975, the cost of natural gas for the plant increased by approximately 500 percent, resulting in an average monthly gas bill of $50,000.

Following the pressing operations, the plywood sheets are finished (planed into perfect 4′ × 8′ sheets). The "dry" waste from this planing is chipped and sold to National Gypsum of Mobile, Alabama, and Johns Manville of New Orleans, Louisiana. The final stage of the finishing process takes one of several forms, depending on the desired finish. The most common finish is smooth sanding. However, an Early American Roughtex finish is commonly used on plywood to be used as siding. Both the smooth and Roughtex finishes can be "grooved," giving the plywood a "look" similar to paneling. (The smooth sanded, grooved finish is called Ivy League Decorative.) The dust resulting from the sanding process is trapped in a dust collector for environmental protection.

Plywood of the same size and finish is stacked into bundles which are automatically bound with metal bands. The bundles are loaded onto railway cars with fork lift trucks for shipment.

Although the operations of the plant are highly profitable, problems do exist. Turnover of personnel, rising costs of labor and equipment, increasing fuel costs, and adherence to the Environmental Protection Agency's regulations and to the provisions of the Occupational Safety and Health Act are some of the problems which must be dealt with on a day-to-day basis. In addition, volatile prices of plywood and economic slumps in the construction industry force management to scrutinize constantly all aspects of the operations for cost reduction opportunities and more profitable combinations of output (optimal sizes, finishes, etc.).

Discussion Questions

1. What analytical techniques could be applied to the operations of U. S. Plywood to assure optimal operations? What information would be required?

2. Which aspects of the manufacturing process are closely regulated by the EPA? By OSHA? Which would pose greater control problems for management?

First Central
Bank

The First Central Bank of Hammond, Louisiana, is chartered to conduct banking operations within Tangipahoa Parish.[1] Including the "flagship" branch located in downtown Hammond, First Central is comprised of four branches located throughout the parish. Other branch operations are in Kentwood, Amite (the parish seat), and Ponchatoula.

Other commercial banks which have been chartered to operate in Tangipahoa Parish are Central Community Bank (Amite), Second National Bank (Hammond), and Citizens State Bank (Hammond). Presently, First Central has approximately 53 percent of the total banking market (as measured by total assets which exceed $107 million) in which it competes. Even so, this figure represents a decline in market share, which is attributable to the opening of a new bank (Central Community) in 1967. (Market share of all parish banks from 1962 to 1972, as measured by total assets, is presented in appendix A.) Total deposits of First Central exceeded $104 million in 1975 (representing 52 percent of the parish market); of this amount, almost $59 million were time deposits, and over $45 million were demand deposits.

First Central Bank is a member of the Federal Deposit Insurance Corporation, but it is not a member of the Federal Reserve System. Consequently, it operates with greater flexibility in the management of its resources and has fewer constraints than banks that belong to the Federal Reserve System.[2]

Organization

The organizational structure of First Central Bank is presented in Figure 9–2. As evidenced by the chart, the bank is essentially comprised of two divi-

---

[1] State law prohibits a bank from locating physical facilities outside the parish boundaries in which it is chartered to operate.

[2] All federally chartered banks belong to the Federal Reserve System; state chartered banks may belong. For differences between a federally chartered and a state chartered bank, please see appendix B. *(NATIONAL BANK)*

259

FED ERALLY CHARTERED BANKS HAVE STRICT REGULATIONS.

sions — branch operations and administrative. The administrative division includes Loan Administration, Personnel and Marketing, Operations and Data Processing, and Real Estate. People who manage these administrative departments report to the Vice-President of Administration who, in turn, reports directly to the President of the bank. Reporting also to the President of the bank are branch managers and the manager of the Trust Department.

Figure 9-2   *Organizational Chart of First Central Bank*

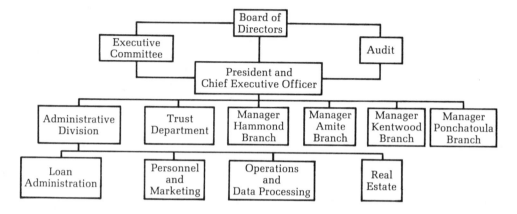

Operations and Administrative Services

Although First Central is a full-service bank, its most profitable operations are in consumer loans. The average daily balance of consumer loans during 1975 exceeded $21 million; the average daily balance of commercial loans varied between $35 million and $37.5 million. Bad debts on consumer loans amount to approximately 1 percent of the face value of such loans.

In 1971, Master Charge was introduced as a part of Central's services. Four years later, BankAmericard was added. (For Master Charge, First Central is a principal bank. It maintains outstandings and sustains all losses. Too, the bank receives all income, interest, and merchant fees associated with the card. First Central is only an agent bank for BankAmericard; Louisiana National Bank is the area principal bank.)

In order to make charge cards a profitable service, the bank actively "markets" the service to area retailers, encouraging retail outlets to honor the cards. The margins within which the bank must operate are quite low; hence, charge cards are not a highly profitable item. Costs associated with Master Charge, for example, include taking and screening applications, preparing cards, billing and other handling expenses, bad debts, and so forth. Income generated from BankAmericard is based on a percentage of the merchant discount. (For example, if a BankAmericard holder charges $100 at a local retailing firm, First Central receives 45 percent of the $3 merchant discount, or $1.35.)

Primarily, the Real Estate Department of First Central Bank acts as a broker in handling long-term mortgages, including home loans. Although the Bank finances a few long-term loans, most are sold to other leading institutions. In addition, the bank accepts and processes applications for FHA (Federal Housing Administration) and VA (Veteran's Administration) loans.

Each branch office has a consumer loans officer who has the authority to make loans up to, but not exceeding, $25,000. Applications for loans over $25,000 are submitted to the bank's Loan Committee for approval or rejection. (The Loan Committee is comprised of board directors and bank officers.) All applications for commercial loans, their screening, and their disposition are handled at the main office in Hammond. Each week, the Loan Committee acts on applications for loans which have been submitted to it during the preceding week and reviews the status of outstanding loans. (Lending restrictions, together with penalties for breaching state laws, are in appendix C.)

The Data Processing division of First Central leases an NCR 200 computer which handles all banking operations. In March, 1976, all branch banks were provided with "on-line" service to the data center, which gave them access to almost instantaneous information regarding customer accounts and pertinent operating and financial data. The storage and retrieval of vital financial information on loans, customers, correspondence banks, and so forth are essential ingredients of the bank's management information system (MIS).[3] Such a system provides management with more detailed and complete information on which decisions are based. As a result of its implementation, management of First Central feels that it makes more profitable decisions with less risk than was possible prior to its use. Excess computer time (that which is not consumed in performing banking operations) is sold to private business firms in the area. This practice enables the bank to recoup a part of its costs while, at the same time, providing a valuable service for the customer (billing, for example).

In addition to the fast retrieval of information at its local data processing center, First Central has immediate access to stored information on Master Charge customers through Southwest Bank Card Center in Dallas, Texas. (Southwest Bank Card Center was formed by First Central and 25 other banks that issue bank credit cards.) By punching in a credit card holder's identification number on an on-line terminal, First Central can obtain instantaneous (eight seconds or less) feedback on the card holder's purchases, payments, balance, line of credit, and so forth.

The Trust Department of First Central was created to provide safe, profitable investments for customers who desire professional expertise in the handling of their funds. Whenever a trust fund is created, officers of the Trust Department provide counseling and advice on investment alternatives which serve the needs of the particular customer. Typically, portfolios in-

---

[3]A management information system provides the communication links among all parts of an organization for purposes of coordination, planning, and control.

clude CD's (certificates of deposit), stocks, bonds, commercial paper, and— to a limited extent—real estate.

Applications for employment are submitted to the Vice-President of Personnel, who reviews the applications, conducts preliminary interviews, and arranges interviews between applicants and branch managers or other bank officers. As a staff officer, the Vice-President of Personnel assists the other bank managers in securing the best qualified personnel available. Final authority to employ or reject an applicant rests with the department or branch manager, however. In addition to the function of recruitment and selection of personnel, the personnel officer and his staff perform all other duties commonly identified with a personnel department. The bank's marketing activity consists of public relations, promotion, advertising, and so forth, together with the marketing of the bank's services to prospective customers.

First Central's security system is designed to prevent losses, thefts, and embezzlements and to minimize related risks. The data center is housed separately from the main office; financial records are audited internally by state agencies and by federal authorities; and the bank employs full-time security guards. In addition, access to the buildings during nonbanking hours is tightly controlled. All measures of security are used to the fullest extent possible.

Recent Growth and Development

In the latter part of 1975, new modern buildings were completed for the Kentwood and Hammond branches. (The ultramodern main office facility was constructed at a cost of $2 million, excluding the cost of land.) In January, 1976, a new data processing center opened, which incorporated a highly refined management information system. Simultaneously, plans were being formulated to construct a new drive-in branch in the Hammond Square Shopping Mall, a new shopping center scheduled to open in mid-1977. First Central has continued to grow and expand its operations, as measured by deposits, assets, and services offered to its customers. In doing so, it has adequately served the needs of the community, thereby fulfilling the purpose for which it exists.

Discussion Question

1. Compare the operations of a bank with those of a manufacturing firm. What are the similarities? The differences?

SIMILARITIES

ORGANIZED THE SAME
MAKING PROFIT
ENGAGE IN COMPETITION
ADVERTISING
FEDERALLY REGULATED
INVENTORY PROBLEMS
SCHEDULING PROBLEMS
FORCASTING PROBLEMS
MAINTENANCE OF SECURITIES

DIFFERENCES

PROFIT IS MADE BY INTEREST RATES BY BANK
SERVICE - BANK   PRODUCT - MAN. FIRM
BANK - ATTRACTS BY INTEREST RATES
BANK - BOOKS CONSTANTLY AUDITED
BANK - STRICT REGULATIONS
BEFORE A BANK STARTS A BUSINESS
THEY MUST GET A CHARTER (THEY
MUST DEMONSTRATE REASON FOR
EXISTANCE) BANKS ARE QUITE REASPONSIB

appendix A
Individual Market Penetrations of Primary Market Area Commercial Banks: As Measured by Total Assets ($000)

Bank	1962	Percent of Market	1967	Percent of Market	1972	Percent of Market	Ability to Maintain Market Share		
							Percent Change 1962–67	Percent Change 1967–72	Percent Change 1962–72
Central Community Bank	$ *	0	$ 3,261	4.8	$ 14,127	10.2	*	112.5	112.5*
Second National Bank	12,851	32.7	21,071	31.0	32,013	23.1	− 5.2	−25.5	−29.4
Citizens State Bank	3,459	8.8	4,988	7.3	16,315	11.8	−18.75	61.6	34.9
First Central Bank	22,899	58.5	38,759	56.9	76,270	54.9	− 2.7	− 3.5	− 6.2
Total	$39,209	100.0	$68,079	100.0	$138,725	100.0			

*Began operations in 1967.

Source: *Polk's Bank Directory*, R. L. Polk and Company, Nashville, Tennessee, (various years).

[Handwritten note: BEFORE BANKS OPEN THEY MUST HAVE A CHARTER WHERE IN A REASON FOR ITS BEING MUST EXIST. BANKS MUST BE RESPONSIBLE TO ITS COMMUNITY AND INTERESTED IN ITS GROWTH. (COMMUNITY IS SOURCE OF INCOME AND REVENUE)]

[Handwritten note: (BANKS NEED GOOD PUBLIC IMAGE) THE COMMUNITY (TOO PROGRESSIVE OR CONSERVATIVE)]

appendix B*

A state bank is organized under a charter granted by one of the States; National banks are organized under charters issued by the Comptroller of the Currency. State banks, like National banks, are organized primarily for conducting a general banking business, and together these institutions constitute the class of banks generally known as commercial banks. Many institutions operating under trust charters, however, have diversified business to include commercial banking and thus have come to be included under the commercial category. In turn, many commercial banks have diversified operations to include trust and savings functions.

State banking laws in the older States antedated the National Bank Act, enacted originally in 1863, and thus served as the model in various respects for the latter. In turn, the National Bank Act influenced State banking legislation subsequently, both in new States and in amendments of the laws of the older States. The "dual" banking system has "competed" to a certain extent in organizational and operating respects, with the State requirements in general less stringent than those for National banks.

Thus:

1. No National bank may be organized with less than $50,000 capital (plus 20 percent paid-in surplus). By contrast, most common minimum capital among the States is $25,000, and a few States permit capital of less than $25,000 in the smaller communities.

2. Legal reserve requirements in some States are much lower than those specified in the Federal Reserve requirements applicable to National banks.

3. Some States permit larger loans to any one borrower than the general 10 percent of capital and surplus limitation on National banks; and are likewise less stringent in restrictions on bank investments.
   Where State banks voluntarily join the Federal Reserve System, they must submit, however, to the same limitations and conditions with respect to the purchase, sale, underwriting and holding of investment securities and stock as are applicable to National banks; and although a State bank upon becoming a member of the Federal Reserve System shall retain its full charter and statutory rights as a State bank or trust company, no Federal Reserve Bank shall be permitted to discount for any State bank or trust company paper of any one borrower who is liable for borrowed money in an amount greater than for a National bank.

4. A condition of membership in the Federal Reserve System, to which National banks must belong, is the acceptance of checks drawn upon them at par. State banks, if not members of the Federal Reserve System, are not required to accept checks at par.

---

*Garcia, F. L., *Encyclopedia of Banking and Finance,* 6th ed., Revised, 1962, pp. 700–701.

appendix C*

No banking association, savings bank, or trust company shall loan to any one borrower more than 20 percent of its capital stock and declared surplus. However, loans secured by pledges of good collateral securities or solvent endorsement shall not be included in the 20 percent limitation. Nor shall any banking association, savings bank, or trust company loan to any one borrower directly or indirectly more than an amount equal to one-half of its capital and declared surplus, either with collateral security or solvent endorsement. However, a banking association, savings bank, or trust company shall loan to one borrower an amount not greater than its capital and declared surplus when such loan is secured by pledge of the obligations of the United States of America, or of Louisiana, or any subdivision thereof, or of readily marketable staples, generally referred to as commodity loans. No banking association, savings bank, or trust company shall make any loans to its president, vice-president, cashier, assistant cashier, or employees, who are in active management, unless these loans are approved by a resolution of the board of directors at a meeting at which the applicant for the loan shall not be present or participate in. Withdrawal of a director, officer, or employee from the meeting shall be done in full compliance with the requirements affecting his nonparticipation and nonpresence. The words "in active management", with reference to employees, mean the employees who have authority to make loans.

Sale of excess reserves by any state banking association to any other bank, on a day-to-day basis, shall be allowed on an unsecured basis, in an amount equal to twice the capital and surplus of the vendor selling bank. Further, the selling to a second or third or more banks, on a similar basis, on any given day, or repeated on successive days, is hereby sanctioned on an unsecured basis, the vendor or selling bank, assuming such risk, or risks, as may be involved in such transaction, or transactions.

Each officer or director who violates this Section shall be fined five hundred dollars or imprisoned for not more than ninety days.

---

*Louisiana State Banking Department, *State of Louisiana — Laws Relating to Banks and Banking*, 1970, pp. 52–53.

case 56

Hammond
Water Works

Hammond, Louisiana, is located in the southeastern region of the state, 40 miles east of the state capital, Baton Rouge, and 60 miles north of New Orleans. The city's strategic location, at the intersection of Interstate Highways 12 and 55, is favorable to rapid growth. The Hammond Chamber of Commerce projects that the Hammond trade area will increase to approximately 125,000 by 1980. As a result of this expected growth, two large shopping centers, the Channel Shopping Center and the Town and Country Plaza, have been built on the west side of the city. An even larger shopping center, Hammond Square, presently under construction south of the city, will encompass a 100,000 sq ft shopping mall. Recently, the city expanded its geographic borders to include two subdivisions, Lakewood and Villa West, whose homeowner associations petitioned the city for incorporation into the city limits.

Coupled with the growth of the city is a substantial increase in the demand for city water and sewage services. The city administration has been rapidly expanding these services to support the phenomenal rate of growth. The municipal water company, in particular, has been sensitive to the growing needs of the community and has strived to meet the increased demands on its operations. The water company doubled its pumping capacity in 1964 and again expanded capacity by 50 percent in 1974. (The superintendent of the water works believes that the existing municipal water system will be adequate through 1982.)

The function of the water company is to supply water of superior quality and of adequate pressure to its residential and commercial users. The water from three 2,500-ft wells is of excellent quality, according to the State Department of Health. In fact, the water is so pure that there is no need for treatment or filtration prior to its use or consumption.[1] The water works conscientiously circulates water in all its tanks to prevent the possibility of

---

[1]The quality of Hammond's city water is comparable to that of Kentwod Spring Water, which is bottled and sold to New Orleans residents who object to the taste and quality of water from the Mississippi River.

"dead" or stagnated water which may taste bad. Problems with water quality arise only when water mains are repaired or when there is abnormal usage (during a fire or periodic flushing of fire mains which are normally "dead spaces" or stagnated lines). Both repair of the water mains and abnormal use cause the water to become cloudy from dislodged mineral suspensions that accumulate in the water tanks and lines. These problems, however, are infrequent and temporary.

The major concern of the Hammond Water Works is providing adequate water pressure to users. The city has two ground-level storage tanks and two 500,000-gallon elevated storage tanks, which are 125 ft high. The elevated tanks develop a pressure of approximately 62 lb per sq in. (psi) at the base of the towers. (Approximately one lb of water pressure is produced for every two ft of tower elevation.) With friction losses through the water mains, valves, and meters, water pressure at residences and business is maintained at approximately 32 lb per sq in.

To maintain this pressure, the water company operates three 2,500-ft wells located in a triangular pattern within the city. Well no. 1, the oldest, is located near the main fire station in the southern sector of the city. This well is 12 in. in diameter and feeds two 1,500 gallon-per-minute (gpm) pumps which discharge into a 250,000-gallon ground-level storage tank. This ground-level storage tank supplies water to the main. Excess supply from the pumps goes to one of the elevated water towers to maintain appropriate pressure. The two 1,500-gpm pumps are spared by a 1,000-gpm pump. Also, a Cummins diesel engine powers a Twin-Disc pump to provide back-up for the electrically operated pumps in the event of a power failure. The diesel pump is set to start when the water pressure drops to 40 lb at the control station. It is operated routinely for 30 minutes each Thursday morning at 10:00 and during severe weather to prevent damage to the electrical pump motors and starters from lightning.

The city firemen monitor the operations of the water system. The system is totally automatic, and alarms trip in the fire station if the pressure drops below 50 lb. There is always someone on duty to respond to an alarm. Moreover, wells no. 2 and 3 are also monitored at the fire station by alarms which are transmitted over telephone lines from the respective well locations.

Well no. 2 is 10 in. in diameter and maintains water pressure in the northern sector of the city. Two 1,500-gpm pumps discharge directly into the main, with excess supply going to the second elevated water tower. This well has a Waukesha engine which powers a Twin-Disc pump to provide an emergency back-up for the electrically operated pumps. The Waukesha engine uses butane for fuel.

The western sector of the city is primarily supplied by Well no. 3, which was drilled in 1974. It is 10 in. in diameter and supplies two 1,500-gpm pumps. One of the pumps operates continuously, discharging into a 250,000-gallon ground-level storage tank, which supplies the water main. The other pump is pressure controlled and cycles on and off to maintain water pressure at 62 lb. These pumps are spared (in emergencies) by a Waukesha diesel engine which powers a Twin-Disc pump.

All three wells have stand-by chlorination stations. Even though the water is almost totally pure, the water company is prepared to inject chlorine into the water immediately if bacteriological count requires such treatment.

Problems that the water company faces include a relatively high turnover of personnel and the maintenance of the water mains. The water company employs nine workers who maintain the water system. Wages of these workers are slightly above minimum. Working conditions are generally unfavorable, because maintenance personnel are often required to work in trenches to repair broken water mains. Consequently, most members of the crew have less than four years of service with the water company.

A continuing problem is maintenance of the water mains. A number of the mains were installed in the 1920s and are subject to leakage. A large percentage of the superintendent's time is devoted to responding to reports of broken water mains. The city has recently received a federal grant of $200,000 to replace leaking water mains. These funds, however, are not expected to solve the problem completely because of the high cost of cast iron used to replace the mains. The price of cast iron ranges from $3.75 per ft for six-in. pipe to $4.84 per ft for eight-in. pipe. (Six-in. and eight-in. pipe are used on most of the city's major water mains. Plastic lines are run from the mains to residences or businesses.)

Discussion Questions

1. Discuss the similarities and differences between the operations of a municipal water company and those of a typical industrial plant.

2. Evaluate the water company's approach to long-range planning.

Louisiana
Department of Highways

The Louisiana Department of Highways, which has its administrative offices in Baton Rouge, is divided into nine field districts. Construction and maintenance operations performed within each district are supervised by a District Engineer, who is aided by two Assistant District Engineers—one for construction and another for maintenance. Figure 9-3, appendix A, shows the organizational structure of the entire department; Figures 9-4 and 9-5 show the authority relationships of the maintenance and construction sections of a district office.

Essentially, each district office performs two major functions—construction and maintenance. The District Engineer, who reports directly to the Chief Construction and Maintenance Engineer, is responsible for the administration of all construction work in his district and for the maintenance of all highways in the state system that are located within the boundaries of his district. He must be thoroughly familiar with the department's regulations and must see that they are adhered to. He makes frequent trips throughout his district to inspect methods used and results attained. Also, he is responsible for the proper expenditure of budgeted funds allocated to his district. Finally, he must see that equipment and personnel assignments do not exceed what is authorized.

The Assistant District Engineer (Maintenance) spends most of his time in the field, checking and directing the work of Engineering Specialists and Maintenance Superintendents. He assists them in planning their work and advises them of approved methods, procedures, and specifications. It is their duty to see that they are provided with all necessary available equipment and materials. In addition, he periodically inspects bridges and roads in the district and makes recommendations to the District Engineer. Also, he prepares all estimates, sketches, etc. which may be required on maintenance projects, reviews time sheets and equipment reports, examines expense accounts, approves overtime, and performs all other maintenance duties assigned by the District Engineer. Reporting directly to the Assistant District Engineer (Maintenance) is an Assistant District Maintenance Engineer who assists him in carrying out his many duties of supervising maintenance activities. (Refer to Figure 9-4.)

The Assistant District Engineer (Construction) supervises the work of the Assistant Construction Engineers and Project Engineers. He makes periodic inspection of all construction projects and reviews the quality of work being performed. Too, he checks the adequacy of plans and specifications as well as the handling of traffic movement on proposed construction projects. He also reviews plan changes and extra work orders and recommends approval to the Headquarters Construction Section of those changes he deems necessary.

In addition to the aforementioned personnel, each district has a Laboratory Engineer who supervises all testing operations. All aggregates, select materials for base courses, concrete cylinders and beams, liquid asphalt samples, bituminous hot mix samples, and soil samples are tested at the district laboratory for construction and maintenance projects. The District Laboratory Engineer is responsible to the District Engineer.

The Awarding and Performance of Construction Contracts

Highway construction is usually performed by private contractors who submit competitive bids on proposed projects. All construction activities, however, are performed under the auspices of the District Office. Personnel who work for the State Highway Department typically perform maintenance of projects.

Whenever the State Department of Highways deems that a construction project is needed in any of the nine districts, an advertisment giving notice of a request for bids is published. The advertisement contains a description of the project; a date for receipt of bids; instructions on access of plans, specifications, and proposals; and the name of the District Engineer. Proposal forms furnished to interested bidders state the description and location of the proposed construction and show the approximate qualities of work to be performed and materials to be furnished, together with a schedule of items for which unit prices are requested. The date, time, and place for opening the proposals are also indicated. The "Notice to Contractors" and "Special Provisions" which are to be included in the contract are attached to the proposal form.

It is the bidder's responsibility to examine the proposal, plans, specifications, special provisions, and contract and bond forms for the work as well as the site of the proposed work. The filing of the bid is presumptive evidence that the bidder has investigated and is satisfied with conditions to be encountered; the quality and quantity of work to be performed; materials to be furnished; requirements of the standard specifications and special provisions; and that he has become familiar with all federal, state, and local laws, ordinances, and regulations which may affect the work. A

Project Engineer or other designated official of the District Engineer answers pertinent questions about the work.

Proposals must be filled in completely and correctly. (A proposal may be rejected if it has an alteration of form or any other irregularity or if it is not accompanied by a proposal guaranty.) Proposals, together with the proposal guaranty, are submitted in a special envelope furnished by the State Department of Highways. Those received after the deadline are returned to the bidder unopened. (A bidder may withdraw a proposal through written request prior to the time set for opening proposals.) All proposals are opened and read publicly at the time and place designated in the notice to contractors.

Prior to submitting a bid, the bidder may be required to file an experience questionnaire and a confidential financial statement which a certified public accountant shall certify. The statement incudes a statement of the bidder's financial status, equipment, past performance record, and personnel. In addition, the bidder may be required to furnish a statement of the origin, composition, and manufacturer of any or all materials to be used in the construction project, together with test samples.

The award of the contract is made only upon the recommendation of the Chief Engineer to the lowest responsible bidder whose proposal complies with all the requirements necessary for a formal proposal. The successful bidder is notified by mail of the acceptance of the proposal. Within 15 days after notification, the bidder must execute the contract. At the time of the execution of the contract, the successful bidder must deposit with the Department of Highways the bond of an acceptable surety company in the amount of the contract. In addition, the contractor is required to submit a progress schedule which shows the proposed order of work and the time required for completion of the major phases of construction. Following the signing of all contractual obligations, a "Notice to Proceed" is given to the contractor.

Whenever construction operations begin, the Project Engineer is in direct charge of all work performed. It is the duty of the Project Engineer and his inspectors to obtain compliance with the specifications and plans approved. He also furnishes necessary engineering data and directs the sequence of work activities. Also, he is responsible for the testing of all materials used in the construction. If a dispute arises between the contractor and the Project Engineer about materials furnished or manner of performance, the Project Engineer has the authority to reject materials or suspend the work until higher authority can resolve the question.

Inspectors employed by the Department are authorized to inspect all work performed and all materials provided. An inspector is stationed at the work site and observes all ongoing activities. If materials or performance do not meet with the inspector's approval, he or she has the authority to suspend construction operations until the matter can be appealed to the Project Engineer.

Whenever the work provided for in the contract has been satisfactorily completed and the final cleaning up performed, the Project Engineer notifies the District Engineer that the work is completed and ready for final inspection. The District Engineer or the District Construction Engineer makes the final inspection. (In the case of major projects, a representative of the Headquarters Construction office is present for final inspection.) If the work complies with the requirements of the plans and specifications, a recommendation for acceptance is transmitted to the Chief Construction and Maintenance Engineer at the Headquarters Office. The Chief Engineer makes the final acceptance.

Discussion Questions

1. Evaluate the procedure of the Louisiana Department of Highways for maintaining quality control.

2. What problems would a public, nonprofit organization encounter in construction activities? How would these problems differ from those of a private, profit-oriented firm?

3. Compare the responsibilities of public administrators with those of business executives.

4. Discuss the procedure of awarding contracts to the lowest acceptable bidder. What are the dangers of this procedure? Would you advocate another procedure?

Figure 9–3   Organization Chart: State of Louisiana Department of Highways

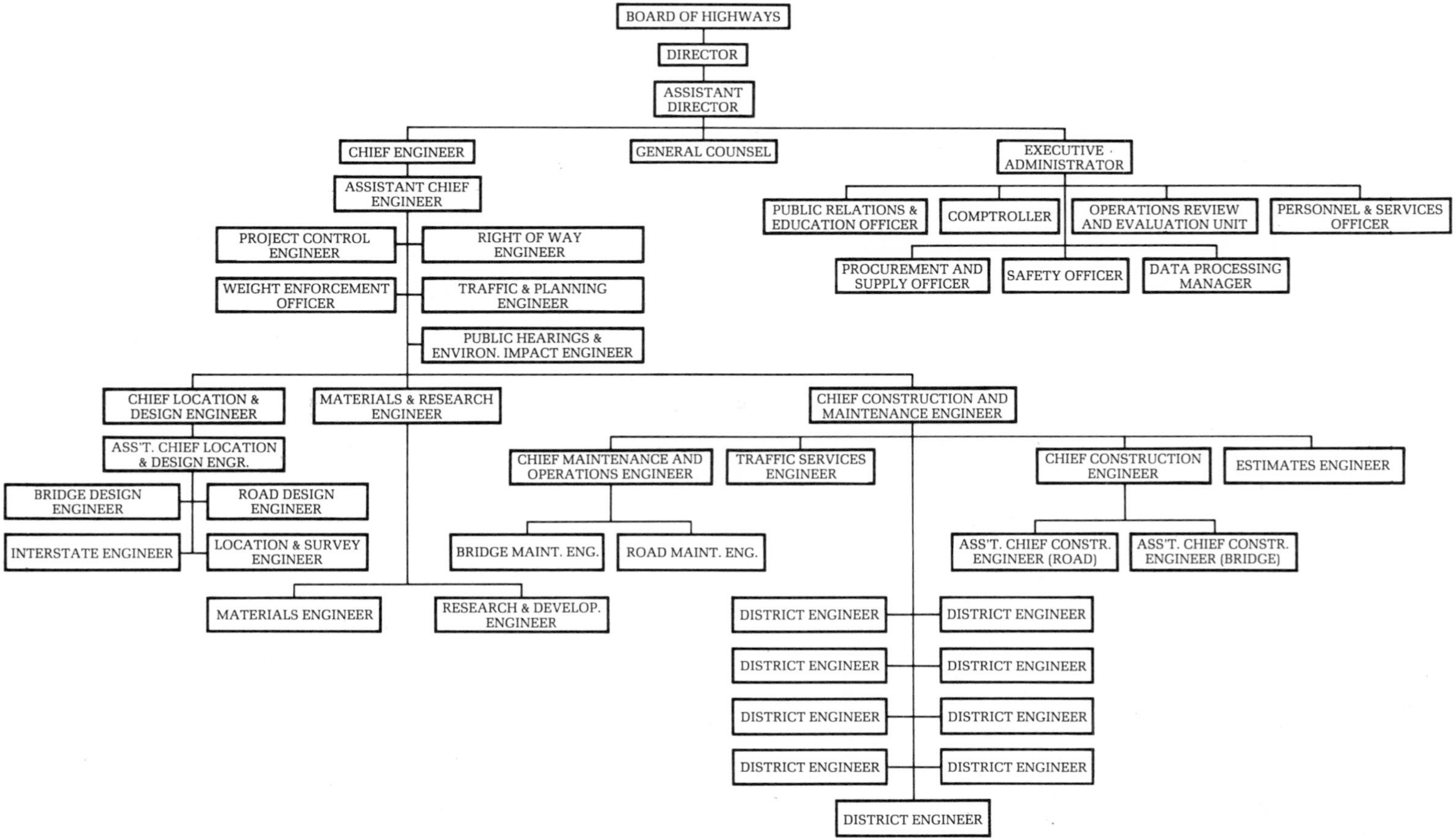

Figure 9-4   *District Maintenance Organization Structure*

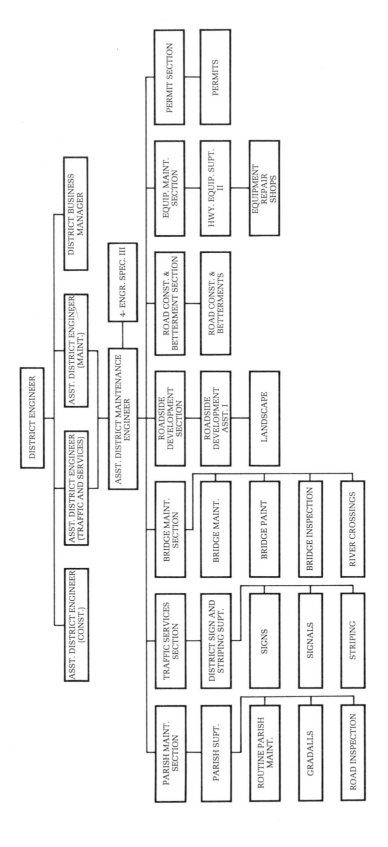

Figure 9–5 Function Chart: Construction Portion of the Construction and Maintenance Section State of Louisiana Department of Highways

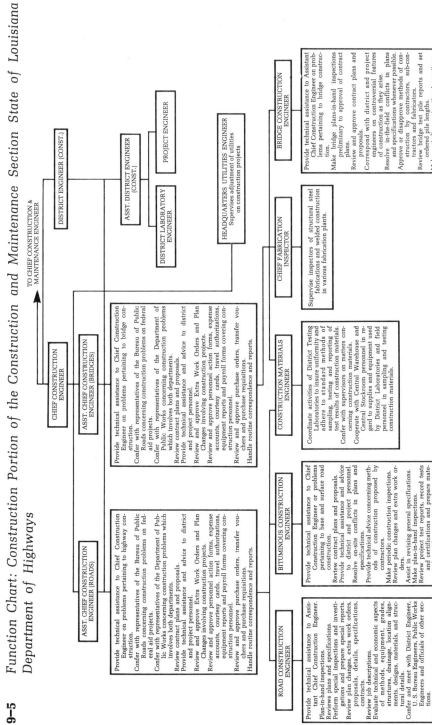